LATINA TEACHERS

Arahi,

So happy to meet you. You are going to make an amazing bilingual elementary school teacher. We need you in Fresno!

Al M—

Latina Teachers

Creating Careers and Guarding Culture

Glenda M. Flores

NEW YORK UNIVERSITY PRESS
New York

NEW YORK UNIVERSITY PRESS
New York
www.nyupress.org

References to Internet websites (URLs) were accurate at the time of writing. Neither the author nor New York University Press is responsible for URLs that may have expired or changed since the manuscript was prepared.

Library of Congress Cataloging-in-Publication Data
Names: Flores, Glenda M.
Title: Latina teachers : creating careers and guarding culture / Glenda M. Flores.
Description: New York : New York University Press, 2017. | "1. From "Americanization" to "Latinization" 2. "I Just Fell into It": Pathways into the Teaching Profession 3. Cultural Guardians: The Professional Missions of Latina Teachers 4. Co-ethnic Cultural Guardianship: Space, Race and Region 5. Bicultural Myths, Rifts and Shifts 6. Standardized Tests and Workplace Tensions." | Includes bibliographical references and index.
Identifiers: LCCN 2016049643| ISBN 978-1-4798-3907-0 (cl : alk. paper) | ISBN 978-1-4798-1353-7 (pb : alk. paper)
Subjects: LCSH: Hispanic Americans—Education (Higher) | Teachers—Training of.
Classification: LCC LC2670.6 .F56 2017 | DDC 378.1208968—dc23
LC record available at https://lccn.loc.gov/2016049643

New York University Press books are printed on acid-free paper, and their binding materials are chosen for strength and durability. We strive to use environmentally responsible suppliers and materials to the greatest extent possible in publishing our books.

Manufactured in the United States of America

10 9 8 7 6 5 4 3 2 1

Also available as an ebook

A mis padres,

con mi más profundo amor y gratitud

CONTENTS

LIST OF TABLES AND FIGURES

ACKNOWLEDGMENTS

This book is a reflection of the inspirational teachers, professors, and organic intellectuals in my life, spanning from elementary school all the way through today. It was truly their belief in me and in my work that gave me the drive to complete it.

First, this research on Latina professionals could not have been completed without the loyal support of my intellectual mentors, Vicki Ruiz and Pierrette Hondagneu-Sotelo. I was trained by two of the leading scholars on women and work that changed their respective fields by bringing the contributions of Latinas to the fore. Both of them have supported me in many ways through my pursuit of the Ph.D., but also in my overall development as a scholar and in my personal growth. I am deeply indebted to both of them as they have groomed me for success. They gave me the tools to study the women who are portrayed in the pages of this book. I am proud to call them my colleagues and friends.

Since joining the faculty at the University of California, Irvine, I have come full circle. I began my academic journey at UCI as a Spanish Language and Culture major. Alejandro Morales exposed me to Chicano/Latino studies through his inspiring course. It was his passion for the subject matter that motivated me to pursue the major wholeheartedly. I poured my heart and soul into Chicano/Latino studies and conducted my first research project on women and work through the Honor's Research Program under the guidance of brilliant anthropologists, Leo Chávez and Michael Montoya. I also became involved in Humanities Out There (HOT), a volunteer program with neighboring Santa Ana schools that eventually gained me entrée and insider access to Latina elementary school teachers in Orange County and opened up the opportunity to examine the lives of Latina teachers in Los Angeles.

At UCI I benefit greatly from the intellectual support of several colleagues, including Belinda Campos, Cynthia Feliciano, Anita Casavantes-Bradford, Louis DeSipio, Ana Rosas, Gil González, Ramón

Muñoz, and Laura Enriquez, who have helped to make the Department of Chicano/Latino Studies a wonderful place for me to cultivate my research interests and bloom in a space that genuinely supports me and my ideas. Professor Raul Fernández read several of my chapters, and he was exceptional at encouraging me in his very humorous way to push myself more. Vicki Ruiz was a wonderful mentor, informing me about institutional resources to support my book. I also benefited greatly from the support from colleagues across disciplinary fields, such as Rubén Rumbaut, David Meyer, Ann Hironaka, María Rendón, Linda Vo, Rodrigo Lazo, Laura Kang, Jennifer Lee, Jacob Avery, Rocío Rosales, and Barbara Sarnecka. Others shared wisdom and tips about the publishing process, including Lisa García Bedolla. My undergraduate students Yoselinda Mendoza, Brianna Ramirez, and Thalia Fabian provided me with helpful research assistance. They exceeded my expectations and I know that they are going to accomplish tremendous feats in the world. I owe a big thank you to Debbie Michel, the department of Chicano/Latino Studies' only office support staff member, for helping me navigate UCI's bureaucracy. I was always amazed at how quickly she could find answers for me.

At New York University Press, Ilene Kalish was thorough and kind in her support of this book, helping me throughout the entire process and offering valuable advice. Caelyn Cobb was exceptional at answering my questions. Kate Epstein and Deirdre Golash offered amazing editorial suggestions. I am also in deep gratitude to Gilda Ochoa and the anonymous reviewers at NYU Press for their thoughtful and critical comments that strengthened the overall theoretical argument of this book. It took me a while to get here, and I could not have done it without their thorough critiques.

When I was at the University of Southern California, I benefited greatly from the guidance of Professors Laura Pulido, Ruth Wilson Gilmore, Amon Emeka, Veronica Terriquez, George Sánchez, and Mike Messner. Tim Biblarz was exceptionally helpful in bringing out my quantitative strengths. Although I am a qualitative sociologist, Tim showed me the value of understanding and knowing both methodological techniques. Jody Agius Vallejo and Leland Saito maintained contact with me and introduced me to the world of book publishing. I am tremendously grateful to these professors, all of whom gave me critical insight on my research at various stages of my academic career. USC provided me with a treasure trove of institutional opportunities, and I am proud to have received my doctoral training there.

The Latina/o Sociology section of the American Sociological Association has also provided me with overwhelming emotional support and an academic family. Zulema Valdez, Silvia Dominguez, Leisy Abrego, Jessica Vázquez, Roberto González, Daisy Verduzco-Reyes, Sylvia Zamora, and Diana Pan have all been extremely supportive in my research endeavors and gave me the opportunity to present my research at various ASA panels. I am also tremendously grateful to the National Center for Faculty Diversity (NCFFD) program. Kerry Ann Rockquemore's inspirational Sunday-night calls got me through the isolating writing periods. I owe much to Coach Mindi and my small group: Aurora Chang, Toyin Babatunde, and Daisy O'Lice. Informal support and motivational comments from Forrest Stuart, Elizabeth Kolkovich, and Victor Quintanilla also helped me to complete the manuscript. The Creative Connections: Writing and Meditation retreat led by Tanya Golash-Boza and Ayu Saraswati provided me with nutritious meals, yoga, and nature walks that helped me complete the revisions phase.

This research could not have been completed without generous support from several internal and external funding agencies. Early support for this research project came from the Department of Sociology at the University of Southern California. A Diversity Enhancement and Placement Assistance Award from the College of Letters, Arts and Sciences and a FIRST Summer Institute Program Grant from the National Science Foundation provided crucial financial support that launched the project in Santa Ana schools. I owe a great deal of gratitude to the Ford Foundation Diversity Fellowship from the National Research Council of the National Academies, the Spencer Foundation Dissertation Fellowship for Research Related to Education (Grant #201200019), and the Myra Sadker Foundation, all of which helped me complete the analysis of racial dynamics in Compton and Rosemead. At UCI, I am immensely grateful that I received funds from the Council on Research, Computing, and Libraries (CORCL) from the School of Social Sciences for research assistance and production costs. This research also received generous support from the UC/All Campus Consortium on Research for Diversity (UC/ACCORD), which helped to support the final writing and editing of the manuscript. Most of the edits for this book project could not have been completed without the help of a subvention for publication grant provided to me by Dean Dave Leinen and Dean Bill Maurer from the School of Social Sciences. A highly coveted Spencer Postdoctoral Fellowship provided me with much-needed time to complete the final stages of writing the manuscript by incorporating reviewers' comments and edits. Joy Bradley and Karen Reiser in the School of Social Sciences were extremely helpful in helping me manage my multiple funding accounts.

I could not have completed this book without the help of many friends who genuinely encouraged me through multiple phases of it. Their friendship and comments on my work have been valuable. My colleagues Emir Estrada, Edward Flores, Lata Murti, Hernán Ramírez, Jazmín Muro, and James McKeever read and commented on numerous analytic memos of the chapters contained here, and I am very grateful for their careful reading and critiques. I also thank Margaret Salazar and Rebecca Romo for their friendship.

Writing this book gave me a greater appreciation for my extended family, friends, and loved ones in my hometown of Santa Ana, California. They have always supported me. I owe much gratitude to my cousins Ana Laura, Miguel Ángel, Liz, "Chachis," Lilis, Melody, and to my *tías* Minda, Laura, and Andrea. I also owe much of my success to Wendy, Sonia, Saida, Mariela, Eddie, and Joevanie, friends whom I have known since I was about eleven years old. I do not think my cousins, aunt, and friends would be upset if I included my dog, Neli, in the same paragraph as them. I think they would know that it means I love them. Neli has been with me for thirteen years now and she found me at the right place and at the right time, right before I began graduate school. I had never really owned a pet before her, let alone a dog. Neli is the epitome of loyalty and unconditional love and was a patient writing buddy.

I always boast that I was blessed with the best siblings and a wonderful mother. My brothers—Ricky and Jorge—have helped me immensely by providing me with healthy and funny distractions away from work. They are the kindest and most generous boys you will ever meet.

This book is dedicated to my father and to my mother, Ricardo and Romelia Flores, to whom I owe much of my success. My mother, Romelia G. Flores, is a sassy woman who knows how to hold her ground.

Perhaps the most important lesson I have learned from watching my mother is that you are responsible for defending yourself. That is one of the reasons why I love her so much. I also thank my loving father, Ricardo T. Flores, who gave me the spiritual motivation to finish the research and writing of this book. My father named me after a favorite teacher he had in Sonora, Mexico, *La Maestra* [the teacher] Glenda. He loved her even though she once smacked him across his knuckles with a ruler for not finishing his homework. His death in 2010 after a long battle with a genetic illness was a grievous loss to us all. Even to the end, his cheerful, positive spirit could have fooled anyone. Even though I wish he were still physically present, I know that he is tenderly singing, "*Mi negra consentida, negra de mi vida, quien te quiere a ti*" to me. I miss him.

Last, I wish to thank the teachers who graciously donated their time to this project, without whom this research would not have been possible. Their work does not end when the bell rings, and they work endlessly to support children and parents in schools.

Introduction

Men make their own history, but they do not make it as they
please; they do not make it under self-selected circumstances,
but under circumstances existing already given and transmitted from the past.
—Karl Marx, 1852[1]

The master's tools will never dismantle the master's house.
They may allow us temporarily to beat him at his own game,
but they will never allow us to bring about genuine change.
—Audre Lorde, 1984[2]

If you ask adults living in the United States, "Who is your favorite elementary school teacher?" they can instantly think of at least one teacher who
inspired them, pushed them, and molded their way of thinking. When
I reminisce about my elementary school days in Santa Ana, California,
during the late 1980s and early 1990s, Mrs. Howell, Dr. Kaiser, and Mrs.
Valentine are the names that instantly pop into my head, all of them
women and all of them white. In writing this book, I often thought about
these college-educated women and how they taught my working-class
colleagues and me how to read, write, and do arithmetic successfully.
With the help of bilingual Latina paraprofessionals, the third-grade
teachers helped us transition to the English language, as the bilingual
program in place at the school at the time required. At such an age, of
course, I never thought about how the political climate within the region
could influence their teaching patterns, and how they perceived us as
students, or our Mexican and Central American immigrant parents.

I began to consider these questions when, enrolled in college in
southern California, I started working in an after-school program as
an instructional assistant provider. Many Latina teachers begin their
careers this way, and I, too, dreamed of becoming a bilingual-education

teacher, preferably in my hometown, in my own elementary school. I even passed several of the teacher certification tests, got a tuberculosis exam and a Live Scan fingerprint background check, and worked as a substitute teacher for a period of time.

Working as a public-education teacher in a Mexican immigrant city in California, I noticed that my colleagues did not perceive Latino cultural resources—my own or my students'—as assets but rather as obstacles to overcome. Drawing on graduate-level sociology courses, I also noticed that my Latina colleagues functioned as what I call "cultural guardians" to Latino students and their immigrant parents.

Before I take up the question of what it means for Latina teachers (I say "Latina" because women continue to dominate the profession at the primary and secondary levels) (Flores and Hondagneu-Sotelo 2014) to be cultural guardians, I want to call the reader's attention to the question of how Latinas find themselves in the profession and their experiences within this formerly white woman's field. These questions bring to the fore the debates between structure and agency, which are a foundational sociological puzzle. I took a different path, but many Latinas do become teachers, especially in schools with many Latino children—which are growing in number throughout the United States (Flores and Hondagneu-Sotelo 2014). As Karl Marx describes, every individual faces choices constrained by societal circumstances. Audre Lorde, on the other hand, would have us believe that any agency exerted within institutional parameters might not suffice to bring about genuine change. Playing by institutional rules, in a sense, will not change the structures of power in place. In this book, I ask how much agency people possess and how much of it they can exert, given social constraints, to bring about change. Indeed, agency can be constrained by the social structure. Latina teachers face larger policies, institutionalized racism, and hegemonic racial ideologies that permeate educational institutions and their work lives, all of which constrain their choices. In this book I strike a balance between the actions of individuals and the constraints and boundaries defined by the educational structures in which they operate because all teachers, not just Latinas, are operating under severe structural constraints in their efforts to reach minority students of color.

Perhaps one of the biggest constraints teachers encounter is that society is set up so that students of middle-class and Anglo backgrounds succeed and experience upward mobility. Yet schools implement a color-blind ideology, the reigning racial ideology of our time (Bonilla-Silva 2003). The idea that actually seeing and talking about race is a problem makes it impossible to address the unequal experiences that students of color face in the classroom and beyond. High-stakes tests complicate this picture, forcing teachers to track students into different academic levels to ensure that they are meeting certain benchmarks. Tracking has long had a profound impact on life-long trajectories (see López 2002; Gándara 1995; Valenzuela 1999). Another form of structural constraints is controlling images, which are larger hegemonic racial ideologies that permeate social institutions and play a tremendous role in race relations between teachers, students, and parents.

Agency, on the other hand, is free will and choice. When Latina teachers manage under a set of conditions they cannot change, they exert agency. However, that agency is always to some extent constrained, and at times the participants in this study face essentially one choice—it may look like a choice, but it is virtually impossible to do otherwise. More often, however, the teachers described in this book, while bound and limited and situated where they find themselves, do make a conscious decision to resist racial hierarchies. Latina teachers remember the racialized penalization they experienced as students and recognize the political, economic, and legal context in which their current Latino students live and learn; they recognize the gaps those students experience because of immigration restrictions—because they have lived them directly or witnessed them in their extended families—and realize that they can be a valuable asset to the Latino community.

The teachers who appear in this book, as cultural guardians, metaphorically resemble lifeguards more than they resemble security guards. A private security guard is in charge of milling around edifices to monitor individuals, enforce rules, and enact punishment if necessary. They surveil the scene and discipline those who step out of line. In Spanish, my mother tongue, the word *guard* has several connotations: *proteger* [to protect], *salvaguardar* [to safeguard or save], and *respaldar* [to support]. In becoming cultural guardians, Latina teachers act to protect, save, and support their students from the waves and rip currents of a dominant culture that threatens to extinguish their language and behavioral codes. They swim in the ocean and bring Latino students to rest on shore. More than driftwood that a desperate swimmer might cling to, they are swimmers who take action, who swim upstream and against the current, or sometimes sideways. Maybe they are also surfers who get on a surfboard and ride the wave to the rescue, risking being knocked into the ocean to return their students safely to shore.

Like the lifeguard at the ocean—but, perhaps, not like a lifeguard at a tranquil swimming pool, whose superior skill ensures her success, assuming she notes the swimmer in distress—Latina teachers face risk in taking on the role of cultural guardians; the ocean is rough and risky for a swimmer who chooses to carry someone else to safety. The massive structural constraints that Latina teachers experience in their work make it risky to become cultural guardians. They know that they themselves almost drowned in the system, yet they choose to enter the waters again to bring to shore as many children as they can.

While I observed that the experiences Latina teachers brought with them to the educational institutions where they work prompted them to become cultural guardians, I do believe that teachers who lack these experiences can do enormous good for Latino students, if they put aside the racism their society instills in them. Moreover, neither are all Latina teachers in racial/ethnic and minority schools uniformly dedicated. Nonetheless, based on my observations, I rejoice that, just as the Latino population in schools throughout the country grows, Latinas are the largest subgroup entering the teaching profession. This book, however, focuses on my observations of Latina teachers at two separate primary schools in California, the vast majority of whom faced the ocean's highest waves and jumped in, swimming with determination to the children and their families and carrying as many as they could.

1

From "Americanization" to "Latinization"

"*Tú vas a hablar el español*" [You are going to speak Spanish], Jacqueline Arenas's grandmother informed her when she began responding to her inquiries in English one day after school. Mrs. Arenas told me about that moment and the fear in her grandmother's eyes to explain why she promulgated native-language retention as an ethnic cultural marker to her students in her classroom daily. She understood how her grandmother feared losing her to a schooling system that promoted English.

Her younger Latina co-workers at Goodwill Elementary[1] in Rosemead, California, consider Jacqueline Arenas[2] as the teacher they aspire to become. At sixty-one years old, Mrs. Arenas is among the oldest of the school's Latina teachers, but she bursts with energy, as I observed one day in October 2009 when she hobbled hurriedly to relieve a fellow educator for yard duty during recess. While I interviewed her, she offered me Twin Dragon almond cookies that one of her Asian students had brought her. We sat by her desk in the room where she teaches a class of mostly rambunctious fourth-grade students, most of them Asian or Latino, after they had left for the day. She was wearing a purple collar shirt, blue jeans, thick black eyeglasses, long blue turquoise earrings, and white *peinetas* (Flamenco hair combs) on each side of her hair—a style she wore daily. I had created a sheet querying teachers about their background, and as she filled it out she talked to me about it, giving me tidbits about her background as the college-educated daughter of two U.S.-born parents who were agricultural workers. Neither of her parents graduated from high school, and they found themselves trapped in low-wage work sectors. The family's hardships worsened when her parents divorced when she was nine and her mother had to pull Jacqueline and her siblings out of school in a *barrio* of La Puente, a city twenty miles east of downtown Los Angeles where Mexican immigrants predominate, to travel to different farms to pick produce to make ends meet. Mrs. Arenas recalled missing the school bus on several occasions from the fourth grade to the seventh grade in the early 1960s. She described hiding behind large trees from other school-aged children because her mother made her wear a "big old hat and long sleeves" to protect herself from the scorching sun in the fields. A Latina professional of Mexican descent,[3] Mrs. Arenas had taken her grandmother's admonishment seriously, and she still spoke Spanish confidently, with no discernible accent. While her schooling was primarily in the English language, her grandmother challenged this traditional mainstream practice by encouraging her to maintain Spanish, something that Mrs. Arenas transmitted to her students' daily despite structural policies that forced her to do otherwise.

While in the twenty-first century it has become more common for Latino children to have a Latina teacher (Flores 2011a), scant scholarship has given voice to the challenges Latina teachers face in teaching Latino families in multiracial schools composed of different racial/ethnic minority groups. Teachers' occupational experiences can be drastically different, influenced by the racial/ethnic dynamics of the schools, institutions, and regions in which they operate. Some, like Mrs. Arenas, have thrived. Many of her colleagues at Goodwill Elementary have as well, but the other school site where I did the research for this book, Compton Elementary, was a more difficult working environment for Latina teachers. School governance structures and colleagues and administration unfriendly to their project as cultural guardians made it a constant struggle to fight off burnout, as this book will describe. To explicate this difference, I examine the pathways into the jobs they have, how structural conditions influenced their agency and directed them to certain districts, and what creates the disparate workplace experiences I observed. The analysis will uncover some of the ways schooling and work and organizations intersect, creating differential race and cultural experiences for both Latina teachers and their families.

Mrs. Arenas's pathway to her job had involved seventeen years at another school, and in the 1980s she was one of a few token Latina teachers. She had been at Goodwill Elementary for only four years[4] and fondly remembered her previous school, which was also in the Garvey District.[5] It had a strong bilingual-education[6] program that catered to Spanish-speaking Latino students, but it was ultimately closed down because of low enrollment, a problem she attributed to misinformation among parents.[7] An avid proponent of bilingual education, she was saddened when California's voters eliminated it. "I don't think people understood the merits of the program," she said.

This book is situated at an important historical moment in California as college-educated Latinas succeed white middle-class women in the teaching profession and the presence of majority–minority schools grows throughout the state. Newly minted college-educated Latinas have been entering this feminized occupational niche in droves, especially in schools in immigrant and racial/ethnic minority communities (Ochoa 2007). While the issue of a lack of minority teachers has typically driven studies on Latina teachers, they are the fastest-growing nonwhite group entering the teaching profession (Feistritzer 2005; Flores and Hondagneu-Sotelo 2014). Women of Latino origin are more than 18 percent of teachers in California, and Latino children, who constitute 20 percent of K–12 schools nationwide, are more than 50 percent of California's student population; thus there is a Latinization of schools and the teaching profession (California Department of Education 2015).[8] These demographic shifts are especially pronounced in Los Angeles, where Latino students now make up nearly two-thirds of the K–12 population and Latinas/os constitute almost 30 percent of teachers (Ed-Data 2015).

Historically, children of Mexican origin experienced "Americanization" programs to hasten assimilation in the United States (González 1997; Ochoa 2007; Urrieta 2010). Remnants of these policies still permeate the organizational culture that Latina teachers encounter daily, but I found that schools where immigrants predominate allow for alternate scenarios. In the schools where they work, Latina teachers are creating apertures and quietly revolutionizing an educational system to bring Latina/o ethnic capital into the classroom, often through practices that challenge norms about culture's place in the teaching profession. I define Latina/o ethnic capital as elements of Latino immigrants' social origins and human capital such as language and behavioral codes. In doing so, they subvert normative rules regarding Latino ethnic culture in their jobs. I show that their efforts meet with varying results in two elementary schools, one predominantly Latino/Black and another predominantly Latino/Asian. Thus, I address the question as to whether Latina teachers' experiences vary according to the racial/ethnic composition of teachers and students at the worksite.

Like the teachers in this study, who found work in the Garvey District in the San Gabriel Valley, most Latina teachers find employment in schools that serve predominantly poor immigrant and minority children and their families.[9] These daughters of immigrants mostly grew up working-class and or poor; most are the first in their family to go to college. My observations suggest these experiences give them a sense of empathy with their lower-income Latino students as they try to find innovative ways to assist these students and their families at home to survive in an often confusing, even antagonistic, educational system. I find ethnic cultural transmission to be one of the most powerful modes of assistance, which Americanization makes vital to the well-being of these children. Whereas such programs were formal up until the middle of the twentieth century and openly degraded Mexican culture to encourage Mexican immigrants and others to shed their ethnic culture and assimilate into a white mainstream (González 1997; Urrieta 2010), children still experience pressure to assimilate and devalue their culture. The idea that Latino culture and foreign-language capabilities were pathological deficiencies and obstacles to schooling success, which schools openly embraced a century ago (Ochoa 2007), persists. And while overt policies encourage multicultural education practices in public schools (Washburn 1996; Delpit 2006; Nieto 2005), a paucity of research investigates how Latina teachers implement Latina/o cultural resources. My own, earlier research shows that when Latina teachers display their culture in schools where the majority of students are Latino, they meet resistance and hostility from white co-workers (Flores 2011a).[10] Similarly, sociologist and educational scholar Angela Valenzuela (1999) suggests that for U.S.–Mexican youth, schools are a "subtractive process" where students of Mexican origin feel that teachers do not care about them or respect Mexican culture and migration experiences. This book outlines the ways in which Latina teachers navigate this subtractive schooling process that has manifested for Mexican children over several decades. These educators have generated a culture of teaching with the ultimate goal of supporting students' long-term educational success. Latina educators now form a part of the middle class, and in their workplaces they see mirror images of their younger selves in their students. They use their own life histories to draw on Latina/o cultural resources and serve as agents of ethnic mobility, actively teaching their students how to navigate American race and class structures while retaining their cultural roots. I contend that Latina teachers serve as cultural guardians because they protect their students' cultural identities and foster their students' learning via their ethnic cultural capital, challenging the traditional Americanization approach that institutions and schools still favor. They are cultural guardians because they guard their students' cultural identities within and beyond the school, but the institutions, standardized testing, and the schools in which they find themselves simultaneously regulate them because they do not follow the Americanization script.

Because all work organizations have "inequality regimes" (Acker 2006)—which serve to maintain class, gender, and racial hierarchies within a particular organization—it is important to take note of where these schools are located in relation to regional racial hierarchies because inequality regimes are fluid and tend to change depending on the organization, its racial/ethnic composition, and racial representation. Teachers who work in urban schools with the children of Latino immigrants may very well have workplace experiences distinct from those who work in suburban or rural locales. Even so, representations of Latina/o teachers in urban schools have captured the hearts and minds of moviegoers, documentarians, and television watchers both in the United States and in Latin America. For example, the movie *Stand and Deliver* (1988) is a classic, portraying the success of Bolivian male mathematics teacher Jaime Escalante at Garfield High School in teaching calculus in East Los Angeles. The documentary *Fear and Learning at Hoover Elementary* (1997), filmed by Laura Simón, a Latina teacher who worked in the Pico-Union neighborhood in Los Angeles, demonstrates the drastic effects of the so-called Save Our State initiative, Proposition 187,[11] on her undocumented students by following the life of Mayra, a Salvadoran student going to school without papers. Simón captures the measure's incitement of racial strife at the school between Arcelia Hernández, an activist Mexican American teacher who fights the measure, and Diane Lee, an Anglo teacher who supports it. Finally, the television series *Carussel* has introduced global audiences to *La Maestra* [the teacher] Jimena, a Mexican teacher who helps her students navigate race and class relations in *La Escuela Mundial* in Mexico, demonstrating that her duties did not stop once the bell rang but extended away from the school and accentuated the reverence shown to all teachers in Latin America. The character is particularly, but not exclusively, famous in Latin America.

The United States does not accord teachers, regardless of racial/ethnic background, the prestige that they receive in Latin America (Hargreaves 1969; Abbott 1988; Gordon 2002)—or, for that matter, in Singapore, Japan, South Korea, Finland, and Canada.[12] Opinion pieces in prestigious publications openly blame teachers for low student achievement and question the professionalization of American education as well as teachers' claim to being skilled workers. One titled "Teachers: Will We Ever Learn?"[13] suggests that teachers are the reason for the "rising tide of mediocrity" of American students because, unlike medicine, law, and architecture, teaching lacks a formal body of knowledge. This environment influences the pathways Latina college graduates take into the teaching profession, as well as their experiences.

Occupational Trends among Latinas

Drawing from demographic statistical data compiled by the Current Population Survey (2007), table 1.1 shows a distribution of the top ten professions/occupations for Latinas who possess a four-year college degree. The "teachers" category includes educators ranging from preschool to high school, ranking as the top occupation among Latina professionals, with three times as many going into teaching than the next most concentrated occupation, nursing.[14] Table 1.1 also shows that Latinas are underrepresented in the better-paying, more prestigious occupations, such as lawyers and doctors, and remain concentrated in a limited set of female-dominated "semi-professions" including education, health care, and social services (Catanzarite and Trimble 2008). While it was common for Latino men to have higher educational levels than Latinas in the late 1960s, today Latinas obtain the education level teaching requires in far greater numbers (López 2002).

U.S. Department of Labor data shows that Latinas represent the fastest-growing nonwhite group entering the teaching occupation, especially in the preschool, elementary, and middle-school sectors, both in the country (2010),[15] and in California specifically (Feistritzer 2005; CDE 2011). At 48 percent, white women still represent a plurality of

TABLE 1.1. Top Ten Professions/Occupations Latinas Enter*

Occupation	Frequency	Percent
Teachers**	225,256	15.3
Registered Nurses	71,384	4.9
Accountants and Auditors	56,658	3.9
Social Work	50,141	3.4
Managers	48,967	3.3
Secretaries/Administrative Assistants	42,598	2.9
Lawyers, Judges, Magistrates, and other judicial workers	19,832	1.4
Nursing, Psychiatric and home health aides	18,396	1.3
Chief Executives	14,133	1.0
Physicians and Surgeons	11,003	0.8

*Findings for first-, second-, and third-generation Latinas were calculated. Regardless of generational level, teaching was the top profession entered by Latinas. The percentage of women in the teaching profession was highest for third-generation Latinas.
**This includes teachers of all grade levels (ranging from preschool to high school).
N=1,471,195

Source: Current Population Survey, November 2007

teachers in California (CDE 2015), but the white teachers as a group are aging. As Mrs. Lomeli, a second-grade teacher and U.S.-born daughter of Mexican immigrants, points out:

> When I started working [as an elementary school teacher] a lot of the staff was Caucasian ladies, which is what you used to think of when you [saw] an elementary school teacher. A lot of them have retired now. As the years [have gone] by you can see [the changes] by the little profile of teachers. The names have started changing, the ages have considerably gone down, and the names have very much been inclining toward the Hispanic. In the first grade [team] we have six teachers: Corrales, Dyer, myself, Villalpando, Pedroza, and Williams. Dyer is married into her last name but she is Hispanic.[16]

In spite of these trends, research has not examined prior to the current project the professional and personal lives of college-educated Latina teachers who share the workplace with a majority of other college-educated, upwardly mobile, Black and Asian women.

The exponential growth of Latinas into the teaching occupation dovetails with structural opportunities that opened up new occupations for educated white women and the graying of the Baby Boom population (Stone 2008; Myers 2007). Affirmative action programs and the passing of California's Proposition 209[17] in 1996 opened up former male-dominated occupations such as medicine and law to white women (Cassell 1998). Although it was widely speculated that racial/ethnic minorities benefited the most from affirmative action programs, in fact, white women were the subgroup that made the most significant gains (Lipsitz 2006). In keeping with this fact, scholarship on women entering the professions in the 1970s examined the ways in which men excluded women in the workplace (Kanter 1977; Lorber 1984). Studies of white women breaking boundaries and entering male-dominated professions such as law, medicine, and managerial occupations focused on the gender hierarchy (Lorber 1984; Kanter 1977; Epstein 1993; Cassell 1998). These studies tended to emphasize gender inequality and undertheorized the salience of the intersection of race, class, and immigration. They also centered on the experiences of white men and women as universals, applicable to all racial/ethnic minorities.

But major inequalities in U.S. society shape where and under what conditions women work, as well as how they see themselves and their options in the workplace (Higginbotham and Romero 1997: xvii). In spite of the remarkable strides made by women and racial/ethnic minorities since the passage of the Civil Rights Act of 1964, what race and work sociologist John Skrentny (2014) calls "racial realism"—the notion that racial difference is a qualification for certain occupations—continues to characterize hiring processes. Thus employers equate employee racial differences, and sometimes immigrant status, with unique abilities or desirable reactions from a population the employer seeks to please. In the case of schools, it is parents. The notion that racial diversity increases workplace potency is also an element of racial realism. The Latina teachers who participated in the study generally believe they have advantages over non-Latinos in the hiring processes for teachers, so my findings support Skrentny's ideas.

The Legacy of Latinas' Occupational Past

Latinas have historically occupied jobs on the bottom rung of the occupational hierarchy because of race and class stratification in the United

States (Barrera 1979; Segura 1989). While some sociologists refer to this phenomenon as double jeopardy, triple oppression, or the simultaneity perspective,[18] others aptly suggest that the intersection of various factors determines women of color and Latinas' experiences in the workplace (Espiritu 2008; Segura 1992a; Collins 2000). Work on Latinas in the workplace has shed light on their economic contributions to their families but has focused mostly on their experiences in informal economy sectors or in low-skill jobs, such as agriculture, domestic employment, canneries, or manufacturing (Ruiz 1998; Zavella 1987; Hondagneu-Sotelo 2001). For example, Patricia Zavella's (1987) case study of cannery workers in the Santa Clara Valley examined the structure of the industry and the social context in which Chicanas decided to *seek* cannery jobs. Historian Vicki Ruiz, studying a similar population in the American Southwest (1998), points out that the majority were "young, unmarried daughters whose wage labor was essential to the economic survival of their families" (63). Looking at Latinas/os in the United States more broadly, Catanzarite (2000) indicates that the population is concentrated in "brown-collar jobs," poorly paid and relatively unregulated fields such as gardening, factory work, and manual labor, and that recently arrived immigrants are particularly concentrated in these fields. Immigrant women are hypersegregated into service and domestic work, and Latinas with a high school diploma are highly concentrated in pink-collar clerical work (Catanzarite and Trimble 2008; López 2002; Smith 2005).

Sociologist Denise Segura drew attention to the large number of Latinas entering clerical jobs in the 1980s, what she called "pink-collar ghettos." These jobs provided an essential source of income and pride for many Chicanas. Secondary schools, Segura found, prepared Chicanas for clerical jobs by curricular placement in "business" classes, as well as youth employment in clerical trainee positions. Chicanas and Mexican immigrant women saw clerical jobs as desirable because they were "clean" and offered a nicer environment than those of farm work and service-sector jobs. But they often described themselves as having to walk on eggshells. They faced racial discrimination and social ostracism based on social class and cultural differences from white co-workers (Segura 1992b).

A good deal of sociology of work and occupations scholarship examining workplace inequalities in the post–civil rights era has focused on women of color from working-class backgrounds who achieved professional careers, most of whom worked in white-majority environments (Higginbotham and Weber 1992; Higginbotham 2001; Chávez 2011; Flores 2011a; García-López 2008). This work describes women of color who acknowledge the sacrifices others made for them and maintain a collective identity and orientation with poorer co-ethnics. For example, research conducted in the 1990s studying African Americans of both sexes shows that they have a linked fate with African Americans across class lines and that they consider giving back financially and socially to the poorer members of their racial group to be essential (Patillo-McCoy 1999; Hochschild 1995; Higginbotham and Weber 1992). Hochschild (1995), in particular, argued that middle-class African Americans maintain a collective identity because of a shared history of racism and exclusion that compelled Blacks to serve their communities. More recently, Vallejo and Lee (2009) built on this work to examine the attitudes of professional Latinas/os. They argue that the immigrant narrative becomes a vehicle to express gratitude toward parents and communities, and that professional Latinas/os give back, even to the point of suffering financial hardship themselves.[19] However, Vallejo (2012) finds that there is a class dimension to giving back, as Latinas/os who grew up in working-class homes are more likely to give back socially and economically than Latinos who grew up solidly middle class.

Beyond pathways into the job and racial dynamics, ethnic culture remains a central determinant of schooling and workplace experiences. Professional racial/ethnic minorities struggle over whether they should hide or express their cultural and ethnic heritage in white spaces (see Chávez 2011; Livers 2006; Dhingra 2007; Feagin and Sikes 1995). Much of this literature began with African American women professionals. Some studies have documented workplace practices like instructing African American women to tie their hair back or not wear attire that looks "ethnic" so as not to cause discomfort for white co-workers, especially when women of color reach management positions (Livers 2006; Feagin and Sikes 1995). Latina business professionals describe feeling that they must navigate two cultural contexts: their own Latina heritage and mainstream white culture (Hite 2007). In some environments Latinas are praised for their bilingual skills (Flores 2011a), but in others they are sanctioned for using their native language (Chávez 2011; Vallejo

2012). These studies emphasize that private corporations and professions require women of color to hide or compromise their ethnic identities. This book will examine such sanctions in educational institutions and how Latina educators incorporate ethnic culture into their jobs when the mission of the school that employs them is to promote students' assimilation to white culture.

Education is a highly specific workplace that differs in many respects from both canneries and offices where women may enter the pink-collar ghetto. Yet all indicators suggest that the ranks of college-educated Latinas who enter teaching will continue to grow in the coming decades. The following sections will illuminate the history of structural and cultural impediments Latinas have faced in U.S. educational institutions, impediments that continue to influence the environment in schools today.[20] In order to understand how Latino ethnic culture is a powerful asset for today's Latina teachers in multiracial environments, it is important to understand the larger macro-structural conditions that subjugated Latino students (and other students of color) in schools over time.

The Era of *De jure* School Segregation

Historically, U.S. schools have been segregated spaces fraught with racialized, political, social, and legal issues (see Fairclough 2007; Valenzuela 1999; Ochoa 2007; González 1990). The 1848 Treaty of Guadalupe Hidalgo[21] stipulated that Mexican families who opted to stay in the newly acquired territories would be granted U.S. citizenship. The treaty promised them the right to maintain the Spanish language and their ethnic culture (Ochoa 2007). However, U.S. policymakers soon used these cultural markers to justify segregationist policies against Mexican children in schools. *De jure* segregation separated children of Mexican descent from children of European descent until *Brown v. Board of Education* (1954). In spite of the common timing of the end of *de jure* segregation, however, the rationale for mandated segregation in schools of Mexican families differed from that of African Americans.[22] Common ways of thinking deemed Black children biologically inferior to white children. Students of Mexican and Latino origin had a racially ambiguous status. Thus court cases would determine if segregation was justifiable based on racial markers usually or ethnic ones.

Some of the earliest court cases concerning school desegregation in U.S. schools involved Latinas/os in the Southwest. In 1925, Adolpho Romo, a Mexican American rancher who lived in an eastern suburb of Phoenix, Arizona, sued the Tempe School District for not allowing his four children to attend school with white students (Muñoz 2001). Mexicans posed a complex educational dilemma as most Mexican Arizonans were U.S. citizens and the state considered them to be white. The judge ruled in Romo's favor because the Spanish-language school did not employ fully credentialed teachers, meaning that students of Mexican origin would not receive an equal education under the law (Muñoz 2006). Another court case, *Roberto Álvarez v. the Board of Trustees of the Lemon Grove School District* (1931), occurred in southern California (Álvarez 1986).[23] Because the decision did not involve a finding of inequality between the segregated schools, it has the distinction of being the first successful desegregation court decision in the history of the United States. In this case, an all-white local school board and teachers in San Diego, California, relegated children of Mexican origin to a separate school known as *la caballeriza* [the stable] in order to undergo "Americanization" before they could integrate with white children (Christopher 1985). Such practices supported perceptions of Mexican children as lazy, backward, and suffering from an infirmity of will; their Spanish-language abilities were perceived as limitations to schooling success (González 1990). The decision in "The Lemon Grove Incident," as it came to be called, established the rights of children of Mexican origin to equal education. The ruling stated that segregation "denie[d] the Mexican children the presence of American children, which is so necessary to learn the English language" (Álvarez 1986: 47). Nonetheless, local, regional, and national sentiment favored segregation and actual deportation of Mexicans, even those who were natural-born U.S. citizens. In the words of Vicki Ruiz, "With the onset of the Great Depression, rhetoric exploded into action. Between 1931 to 1934, an estimated one-third of the Mexican population in the United States (over 500,000 people) were either deported or repatriated to Mexico even though the majority were native U.S. citizens" (Ruiz 2998: 29).

While no state that adjudicated the issue in the American Southwest upheld the segregation of Mexican American children on the basis of race specifically, the practice was rampant and the use of other justifications had legal impact. Efforts at school desegregation cut across class and generational lines within Mexican American communities (Gutierrez 1995). In Texas, more than in the rest of the Southwest, Jim Crow extended into the educational system (Sánchez 1997). As late as the 1940s, some school systems segregated "Mexican" children throughout public schools. As it had been in Lemon Grove, the "language handicap" of bilingual children was used to justify "racial" discrimination against children of Mexican origin (Sánchez 1997). For example, a Texas state court in *Independent School District v. Salvatierra* (1930) upheld the right of the Del Rio school district to separate Tejano (Texans with roots in Mexico) children from Euro-American Texans. Through the League of United Latin American Citizens (LULAC), a largely middle-class Mexican American organization founded in Texas in 1929, Tejano parents had argued against the segregation of children of Mexican descent from children of other white races. The superintendent tried to justify segregation by noting the "decided peculiarities" of Tejano children (Ruiz 2004: 59). The court agreed, saying that segregation of Mexican children— regardless of where they had been born or their language skills—was not racial. LULAC shifted its focus to inequities in school funding (Ruiz 2004). The argument that permitting Mexican children to share their classroom endangered the academic achievement of Euro-American children gained currency (Moore 1970).

The Mexican-origin population of Orange County, California, challenged the logic of separate but equal schools[24] in *Mendez et al. v. Westminster School District of Orange County* (1947). Gonzalo Méndez, a naturalized citizen, and his Puerto Rico–born wife, Felicitas, had attempted to send their three children to the Westminster School, the elementary school Gonzalo had himself attended as a child in the 1920s. The Westminster school district had redrawn boundaries around Mexican neighborhoods in the intervening time. Only the lighter-skinned and less obviously Spanish-surnamed Méndez cousins could stay. Their darker-skinned and Spanish-surnamed Méndez relatives would have to matriculate at the Hoover school. The public schools to which the Méndezes' children and those of three other families that joined the suit had access offered manual and vocational training rather than college preparation, a practice the school district attempted to justify pedagogically (Brilliant 2010; González 1990).[25] The school superintendent in Garden Grove, where one of the families lived, regurgitated tired stereotypes to the *Los Angeles Times*: "Mexicans are inferior in personal hygiene, ability and in their economic outlook . . . [Youngsters] were handicapped in interpreting English words because their cultural background prevented them from learning Mother Goose rhymes."[26] Historian Mark Brilliant (2010) notes, "More than anything else, language—or, more specifically, the school districts' claim that lack of English proficiency was the reason for the segregation they admitted practicing—presented the most salient distinction between segregation of students of Mexican descent in southern California (and elsewhere in the southwest) and African Americans in the South." A year later, the U.S. Court of Appeals for the Ninth Circuit decided that the segregation defined in *Méndez et al.* was not racially based but had been implemented by the school district without being authorized by state law (Ruiz 2004; Strum 2010). The court held that the segregation of Mexican immigrant and U.S.-born Mexican students into separate "Mexican schools" was unconstitutional. This was the first ruling in the United States in favor of desegregation.

Demand for Structural and Cultural Changes

In the 1950s and 1960s, Mexican Americans took part in a national quest for civil rights, staging a series of protests in response to *de facto* segregation—segregation by practice. The Chicano Blowouts, also known as the East L.A. Walkouts, against unequal schooling conditions in Los Angeles Unified School District high schools were among the best-known (González 1990; García and Castro 2011). Sal Castro was one of the few Chicano teachers among the leaders of these protests, although they were largely student-led. Of the protests Castro said,

> These schools were characterized by high dropout rates, a heavily vocational curriculum and a marginalized academic one, low reading scores, few academic counselors, overcrowded conditions, and worst of all, low expectations of the Chicano students by a mostly Anglo or white faculty. Moreover, these schools in no way reflected the ethnic and

cultural background of the kids. These were the conditions we faced in 1968 when the students decided to take things into their own hands and attempt to force changes by resorting to a student strike. (García and Castro 2011)

Castro was arrested in 1968 for participating but was able to resume teaching after his release (García and Castro 2011).[27] The movement demanded more teachers of Latina/o origin, bilingual education, equitable schooling facilities, and culturally relevant curriculum (Chávez 2002). Providing a gendered analysis, Dolores Delgado Bernal (1998) highlights the pivotal role high school–and college-educated Chicanas played as grassroots organizers. Chicanas collected surveys, helped set up campaigns, held office, raised consciousness and awareness, were spokespeople for the movement, and testified before the Los Angeles School Board.

Multicultural pedagogical approaches emerged in the 1970s, responding to some of the demands of the East L.A. Walkouts. However, these efforts concentrated on preparing white teachers to work with and teach students of color (Delpit 2006; Sleeter 2001). In 1974, the U.S. Supreme Court issued its only ruling to date dealing with the language rights of racial/ethnic minority children in *Lau v. Nichols* (Wollenberg 1978).[28] In the case, Chinese American students in San Francisco argued that a lack of linguistically appropriate accommodations effectively denied Chinese students equal educational opportunities on the basis of their ethnicity. The U.S. Supreme Court ruled in favor of families of Chinese origin and expanded the rights of students nationwide with limited English proficiency.[29] However, the 1980s and 1990s saw the re-segregation of Latino children in schools mainly because of residential and linguistic issues, especially in California schools. The English Only movement and the passing of Proposition 227, the English for the Children Initiative, in 1998 drove segregation. Much as Ruiz notes that in the era of the Great Depression "even on the playground, students were punished for conversing in Spanish" (Ruiz 2004: 57), Proposition 227 led to sanctions against teachers who spoke Spanish to children in the classroom, even when failing to do so posed considerable classroom management issues. The model in which Latina/o students must sink or swim in an English-only environment continues in the classrooms I studied.

Throughout this period, class-based divisions characterized Latina/o activism. The words of a school official in San Antonio, Texas, reveal the logic that fueled this dynamic:

> American children and those of the Mexican children who are clean and high-minded do not like to go to school with the dirty "greaser" type of Mexican child. It is not right that . . . [these American and middle-class Mexican children] should have to do so. There is but one choice in the matter of educating these unfortunate Mexican children and that is [to] put the dirty ones into separate schools [and] tell them that they have to learn how to "clean-up." (García 1991: 187)

On the side of middle-class Latinas/os, LULAC gained power representing middle-class Mexican Americans in the Southwest. The group argued that hard work, allegiance to the United States, limited Spanish use, and active assimilation could achieve white acceptance of Latinas/os. As David Gutierrez (1995) notes, LULAC stressed the leadership of an "educated elite" who would lift their less fortunate neighbors by their bootstraps. Racial prejudice, LULAC members assumed, would fade over time. They feared that recent Latino immigrant arrivals would be lumped together with more established, later-generation families, giving the impression that all Latinos were a monolithic group, "un-American" and poor (Gutierrez 1995; García 1991; Ochoa 2004). Moreover, many middle-class Latino elites favored Catholic school education for their own children, believe it would make them *gente decente*," more "civilized" than the Mexican laboring class, whose children were relegated to public-educational facilities that prepared them for vocational jobs (García 1991).

The efforts of groups like LULAC have influenced educational policymakers to direct their attention toward developing effective multicultural education practices and preparing teachers for a racially and linguistically diverse classroom and nation (Sleeter 2001; Ochoa 2007; Ladson-Billings 2005). However, the academic achievement of students of color and English Language Learners continues to decline in U.S. schools and continues to widen (Romo and Falbo 1996; Velez 2008). Current research on multicultural education practices indicates that most schools still stress Anglo conformity. While multicultural education practices have grown, they appear to be poorly integrated in schools, with lessons limited to certain days of the year. Recognitions such as César Chávez Day and Black History Month often fall under the food, fun, faces, and festivities rubric instead of that of serious education (Washburn 1996; Flores 2015a). Education scholar Norma González and colleagues (2005) propose a cultural funds of knowledge frame for integrating multicultural practices in schools. The model suggests that teachers learn and understand the political, historical, and personal situations of their students because the household contains rich cultural and cognitive resources. Montecinos (1996) points out that teachers may not be able to transfer cultural experiences into meaningful pedagogical practices in schools, even if they share their students' cultural backgrounds. The obligation to learn, therefore, may not be confined to non-Latina/o educators. Bernal (2001) anticipates the work of González and colleagues by bringing the *mestiza consciousness*[30] of Chicana students to the forefront to demonstrate the pedagogies of the home they relied upon to supplement their cultural knowledge on their higher-educational journey. While scholarship on Latina teachers is emerging (Arce 2004; Ochoa 2007; Urrieta 2010; Flores 2011a), these studies focus on Latina teachers working with mostly white teachers in schools attended by Latino students and not with another racial/ethnic minority group. Increasing diversity in many regions, communities, and workspaces makes the analysis I offer in this book important.

Interracial Relations and Region

Tomas Almaguer (1994: 206) notes that racial hierarchies are "historically contingent and regionally specific, varying in meaning over time as well as within different regions of the country." For example, in early-nineteenth-century California, racial ethnic groups were racialized in unique ways to keep white racial privilege intact. Almaguer examines that "differential racialization" elevated the status positioning of whites while making distinctions between Mexicans, Asian Americans, African Americans, and Native Americans. While Native Americans were racialized as unassimilable, the Chinese as heathens, and the Japanese as a "Yellow Peril," Mexicans, especially those who were U.S. citizens and of a lighter phenotype, were regarded as almost white. Asian exclusion laws rested on displacing negative controlling images (Collins 2000)—that is, hegemonic racial ideologies—associated with Blacks onto the Chinese. In an attempt to distance themselves from the Chinese, the Black press published anti-Chinese narratives in their newspapers so they could claim moral superiority to Chinese immigrants who were portrayed as alien, unsanitary, and sexually deviant (Jun 2006). The intermediate position of Latinas/os in California one hundred years ago continues to influence their status today.

Differential racialization of Latinas/os operates across the United States. Race relations in the South have largely consisted of Black/white political conflicts for more than a century, but Latino migration has shifted this picture. Laura López-Sanders (2009) and Angela Stuesse (2016) argue that Latina/o migrants are not entering society at the bottom social rungs but rather are inserted into an ambiguous space between Black and white; their positioning in society and in low-wage employment sectors is often shifting and situational. Other scholars, like Helen Marrow (2011), indicate that Blacks are actively excluding newly arrived Mexican immigrants through political ostracism, resulting in a Black/non-Black divide. Paula McClain and colleagues (2006) suggest that Latina/o immigrants hold negative stereotypical views of Blacks and feel more affinity with whites. Daniel Rochmes and Elmer Griffin (2006) argue that tensions between Latinos and Blacks are signs of an emergent white racial formation among Latinos. However, McClain and colleagues (2006) find that whites hold negative views of Latinas/os and that the presence of Latina/os in the South modulates Latinos' negative attitudes toward Blacks. Differential racialization is therefore historically contingent and regional and can produce fluid racial hierarchies (Almaguer 1994). Others have also gone beyond the Black/white dichotomy to look at racialization processes of Latina/o, Black, and Asian populations as well as their conflicts and commonalities in educational spaces (Calderon 1995; Cheng 2014; Ochoa 2014; Saito 1997; Vaca 2004). Alberto Camarillo (2004) and Emily Straus (2009, 2014) examine issues arising in schools in Compton, California, where I did my research. They note that the influx of Latino immigrants has led to increased hostility between Blacks and Latinos as a result of curriculum changes and Blacks' purported unwillingness to share power. Nicholas Vaca (2004) describes this kind of thinking as a "zero-sum" game that deems gains made by one group a direct loss suffered by the other. Addressing the racial triangulation of Asian Americans, Kim (1999) argues that racialization does not occur in a vacuum but is mutually constitutive. Kim describes a hierarchy in which whites have ranked nonwhites along several dimensions. For example, she describes situations in which whites "valorize" Asian Americans to subordinate African Americans on cultural and/or racial grounds or construct Asian Americans as unassimilable through civic ostracism—"forever foreigners"—compared with whites and African Americans. In both cases the objective is to dominate both groups. These processes operate differently in relation to Latinas/os in schools. For example, Ochoa (2014) finds that the achievement gap in Asian and Latino schools leads to a series of negative outcomes for Latino high school students. More recently, Cheng (2014) suggests that in nonwhite multiracial communities, a regional racial formation process occurs, in which a concomitant racialization process of "Asian valorization and Mexican inferiority" emerges. These processes can also be gender-driven (Mindiola et al. 2002).

Undocumented immigration status complicates race relations between people of color (Clark-Ibanez 2015; González 2015; Abrego 2006). Most studies involving the implications of legal status address the ways in which it blocks the progress of the children of immigrants in U.S. schools, including those who have attended schools in America from an early age. While *Plyler v. Doe* (1982) allows undocumented students legal access to K–12 schools, California and Georgia, for example, have drastically different contexts of reception (Portes and Rumbaut 2006) for newer immigrant arrivals. The fact that high-performing Latina/o students cannot attend state college at in-state rates in places like Alabama if they lack documents has enormous ramifications (Abrego 2006).[31] However, research has focused on how legal status plays out in schools where the majority of the student body is white, rather than Black or Asian.

In *Latina Teachers*, I look at how the mechanisms between Latina professionals and their colleagues of various races operate in majority–minority spaces. To do this, I draw on and expand on the rich insights of existing literature to investigate culture and work across two underperforming multiracial schools. I demonstrate how the rise of Chicana/Latina[32] teachers and their use of culture in public schools is challenging the schooling experience of Latino families. A lens that focuses closely on educational and work policies and culture, therefore, reveals a more complete picture of the lives of Latina teachers and their interactions with Latino families. Thus, this book examines schools as workplaces to illuminate how Latina teachers have implemented Latina/o cultural resources and how they have quietly reshaped the way in which schools are run and classrooms are taught. Latina teachers are transforming the ways in which Latino students and their immigrant parents receive, engage with, and become incorporated into American ways of life. Their efforts, however, meet different receptions in different contexts.

The Teachers and Their Narratives

I draw on in-depth interviews with Latina teachers who work in two scholastically underperforming multiracial school districts in the Los Angeles metropolis, Compton Unified School District in Compton and the Garvey Unified District in Rosemead. I call the schools that employ them Compton Elementary (Compton) and Goodwill Elementary (Garvey) to protect the identity of participants. I rely on copious ethnographic fieldnotes as well as tell the nuanced stories of how the intersection of race, gender, class, and immigration shapes their workplace experiences in a feminized white-collar job. Most of these women are first-generation college students. Many are the sole possessor of a four-year college degree from a U.S. institution in their families. The voices of the daughters and granddaughters of immigrants fill the pages of this book. In all, I conducted fifty semi-structured interviews with teachers[33] of various racial/ethnic backgrounds in the two schools, twenty of whom were Latinas. While Latinas' point of view is the focal point of the book, I also include interviews with twenty-five non-Latina/o teachers. The ethnographic data includes observation of teachers of all ethnicities as well as interactions with teachers, students, and parents. This set of data both adds nuance to the portrayal of the organizational culture of these schools and accentuates Latinas' understandings of the racial and cultural dynamics at these schools.

Prior to beginning the interview, each teacher was asked to fill out a demographic questionnaire that queried them about their marital status, their parents' places of birth and occupations, their own place of birth, city of residence, the highest level of schooling obtained, their credentialing institution, and whether they had the training designed to prepare them to teach diverse student populations.[34] Forty-nine of the teachers I interviewed were fully credentialed, meaning they had obtained their bachelors degrees and had completed all of their training at a credentialing institution in California. The single remaining teacher, who works at Compton Elementary, had been teaching for five years and needed to pass one last exam. As the teacher demographics table in appendix A shows, the Latinas I spoke with are a heterogeneous group differentiated by generation and ethnic origins.[35] Three were born in Latin America but migrated before the age of twelve (1.5-generation), eleven are the U.S.-born children of immigrants, four are the grandchildren of immigrants, and two are the great-grandchildren of immigrants. In addition to the thirteen with at least one parent born in Mexico, two had parents born in Central America, one the Caribbean, and two were multiracial (Mexican and white). There were significant differences between the two schools in that teachers who worked at Goodwill Elementary tended to come from families whose immigration occurred further in the past than those who worked at Compton, reflecting patterns of immigration in the two districts. Eighteen had parents who toiled in low-skilled, manual, and manufacturing jobs, typically "brown-collar jobs" (Catanzarite and Trimble 2008) such as welders, seamstresses, domestics, and agricultural workers. The exceptions, a Cuban/Salvadoran teacher and a fourth-generation teacher of Mexican origin, grew up in middle-class homes. The average annual income of the nineteen who supplied their teacher salary was $62,947, much more than what most of their parents earned when they were growing up.

During interviews, some teachers cried. Most expressed zeal for their role as cultural guardians. Others evinced the effects of fighting off disillusionment. Structural changes in the profession and district policies that they believed undermined their classroom autonomy were taking a toll on most participants. Some spoke openly and candidly about their experiences, but others seemed initially afraid of speaking with me, fearing that I was a journalist looking for the latest scoop on teacher improprieties. Teachers in Compton seemed particularly nervous. They often asked me if I had principal approval to speak with them, and my assurances didn't prevent them from lowering their voices when the principal was around. News articles blaming teachers for poor student outcomes and reports of teachers who lost their jobs for implementing particular teaching methods in Los Angeles affected the recruitment process as well as the interviews themselves. However, all ten of the teachers I approached at Goodwill Elementary and eight out of ten of the teachers I approached at Compton seemed eager to participate in a project conducted by a young Latina researcher who focused on their lives as college-educated and "professional" Latinas giving back to the community and Latino families. The two who initially hesitated ultimately agreed to speak with me; I think they were nervous only that I might be there to evaluate their preparedness for high-stakes testing, rather than that they were immune to the inducements that had made their colleagues enthusiastic. The patterns of reticence signaled the structural conditions that teachers face in their jobs and how that affected them at the micro level. The Methodological Appendix provides a complete account of the process I undertook to gain access and entry to the schools.

The schools that I selected are characterized as majority–minority, meaning that teachers, parents, and students are mostly people of color. Both the school districts they belong to are unincorporated,[36] meaning they fall outside of the larger Los Angeles Unified School District. I chose these schools for their specific demographic characteristics—one Latino/Black and one Latino/Asian. The analysis will reveal how local regional racial/ethnic hierarchies have shaped the experiences of study participants and the contrasting ways in which they influenced their workplace dynamics. These patterns reveal their collective understanding and construction of social phenomena, including how they perceive race relations in their own schools. At both schools, I used snowball sampling[37] to recruit participants. The interview instrument included open-ended questions on three broad central domains: pathways into the occupation, the implementation of Latina/o cultural resources in minority schools, and interracial relationships and interactions. Each interview lasted between one to three hours in total, and I met with most participants after school, before school, or during lunchtime. To protect instructed learning time, I sometimes interviewed teachers in intervals of thirty-minute blocks over several days during their lunch breaks. Some preferred to talk about their jobs away from the school.

They invited me into their own private homes or to locations such as coffee shops in their home neighborhoods.

The Districts and Schools

While the interview data provides the bulk of my findings, I supplement the interviews with more than 450 hours of participant observation and focus group data that I gathered between August 2009 and September 2011. I split my time between the two schools over the course of two full academic school years. Site selection for this study was key, intentional, and meaningful to the fields of race/ethnic relations, gender and work, and education. In this book I follow the comparative methods of sociologists such as Christine Williams's (2006) study of race and gender workplace inequalities in two toy stores, one high-end and one big box outlet, and Rachel Sherman's (2007) comparative study of "class acts" at two urban luxury hotels. I purposely and strategically selected two communities in southern California that reflected the demographic breakdown necessary to complete this study: one Latino/Black and one Latino/Asian. I intentionally selected Latina teachers who work in two distinct predominantly immigrant school districts and communities because "more can perhaps be learned about the inter-group relations by studying the minority than by studying the dominant group" (Hughes 1994: 94). I used the California Department of Education's website's data feature to select potential research sites, narrowing down the schools I would visit by the sheer number of Latina, Black, and Asian teachers in each school.[38] This process led me to Compton Elementary and Goodwill Elementary because they offered the most even balance between Latina teachers on the one hand and Black/Asian teachers on the other. As historian Albert Camarillo (2004) writes, "Compton has become a cultural, ethnic, and racial borderland where Latinos and African Americans meet on a daily basis. For the first time in the twentieth century in Los Angeles, Black and brown people are living among one another in large numbers. Their interactions both in public and private spheres are shaping a new frontier in ethnic and race relations in California" (2004: 367). The conditions Camarillo described held true six years later when I began my research. Both Compton and Garvey had experienced considerable growth in their Latina teacher workforce. For example, in

TABLE 1.2. Racial/Ethnic Demographics of Teachers and Students

	Latinas/os	Blacks	Asians	Whites
Compton District				
Teachers	24%	41%	1%	21.2%
Students	77%	19.3%	>1%	>1%
Compton Elementary				
*Teachers**	30%	35%	4%	26%
Students	78%	17%	>1%	0%
Garvey District				
Teachers	28%	3%	44%	23%
Students	41%	>1%	56%	1%
Goodwill Elementary				
*Teachers***	45%	0%	41%	14%
Students	45%	>1%	52.5%	>1%

* *Total: forty-eight teachers*
** *Total: twenty-nine Teachers*

1992, only 3.2 percent of Compton educators were Latina and in 2013 this number rose to 25 percent. Also, in 1992, 17 percent of Garvey teachers were Latina and in 2013 they made up 30.1 percent (Ed-Data, 2015).

Compton Elementary school, a K–5 school, serves close to 900 students. As table 1.2 reflects, in the 2010–11 academic school year, 78 percent of students at Compton Elementary were of Latino origin and 19.3 percent African American (Ed-Data 2015). Teachers at the school often referred to the student ratio as 80:20; a number of them mentioned the only Samoan family with children enrolled in the school. While some Latina teachers referred to the student population as "biracial," others negated the idea that it was diverse because most students were Latino. More than 80 percent of the student body received free and reduced lunch and 85 percent were considered socioeconomically disadvantaged. Nearly three-fourths were considered English Language Learners.[39] The teacher racial/ethnic breakdown in the Compton District was 25 percent Latino, 41 percent Black, and 21.2 percent white (Ed-Data 2015).

Goodwill Elementary, located in Rosemead, serves roughly 600 students ranging from preschool to the sixth grade. Asians and Latinos, who both occupy the perceived racial middle (O'Brien 2008), live side by side in Rosemead, with many Latino families living in apartment complexes. The split between the Asian and Latino origin population hovers around 50:50. When I began my fieldwork, 52.5 percent of the student population was of Asian background and 45 percent were Latino (Ed-Data 2015).[40] The district classified 55 percent of the students as English Language Learners, who speak Spanish, Cantonese, Vietnamese, and Mandarin.[41] The two African American students included a Latina teacher's niece, who was Black and Mexican. The majority of the student body, 85 percent of children in the school, are considered socioeconomically disadvantaged. The distribution of teachers is Asian Americans, 39.5 percent; Latinos, 26.1 percent; African American, 2.9 percent; and whites, 27.2 percent (CDE 2009).[42] Most students who came in with English-language ability had second-generation Mexican parents from working-class backgrounds.

The Data-Gathering Process

I immersed myself in the professional and home lives of the study participants, capturing daily interactions among teachers, students, and parents during school hours, at school events, and at off-campus activities. The data includes observations in a number of contexts, including faculty meetings, the teachers' lounge, the front office, Parent-Teacher Association meetings, the parking lot, and all campus events. From August 2009, when the academic school year officially began, until September 2011, I spent four days a week when school was in session documenting the interactions at both of the research sites. I also at times came to the school grounds on Saturdays, when teachers would hold special fundraisers for their students. I actively volunteered for social events on and off school grounds and served as a translator for teachers during parent–teacher conferences. I completely immersed myself in the social worlds of the teachers at both schools.

I also shadowed four Latina teachers, two at Compton and two at Goodwill Elementary, to document their daily activities and routines. This means that I arrived to their schools at 7:00 in the morning, performed the duties of a teacher aide[43] in their classrooms, and followed them on all of their daily activities on campus until they left the school, which might be 3:00 p.m. or 8:00 p.m., meaning that they served an eleven-hour day. Some teachers allowed me to conduct interviews and observations of their personal lives, away from the workplace and in their homes. A couple of teachers immediately treated me like a friend, inviting me home and trying to set me up on dates with their friends and family members, a point I address in the Methodological Appendix. One respondent invited me to a summer party at her home in an affluent neighborhood of Orange County, and yet another invited me to her *despedida de soltera* [bachelorette party].

Understanding the social worlds of Latinas would not be complete without inclusion of the families they served, day after day. In order to triangulate the data, I conducted a series of focus groups with multiple cohorts of parents in both schools. Recognizing that immigrant Latino parents had distinct experiences in schools from those of U.S.-born Latino families, I determined I would need three focus groups at each site—one in Spanish for immigrant parents, one in English for Latino parents born in the United States, and one in English for non-Latino parents. Across the six groups, twenty-eight parents participated.[44] Although there is a tendency by the U.S. Census Bureau and large-scale quantitative data sets to homogenize the Latino experience and subsume Latinos under one pan-ethnic label (Oboler 1995), the teachers in this study made reference to the distinctions between the daily lived realities of immigrant parents, many of whom were undocumented, and Latino parents who had grown up in the United States and therefore were fluent in English, insights that the focus group data bore out. This aspect of the research helped increase the validity of results by corroborating the Latina teachers' perceptions of racial/ethnic tensions and illuminating the nuances in their points of view.

The schools included in this book are located in southern California, a region that mirrors demographic transformations in many U.S. locales. Both traditional immigrant gateways such as Texas and Arizona and new destinations like Mississippi, Tennessee, and Georgia are increasingly Latino. Thus the lived experiences of Latina teachers who participated in this study may provide valuable insight into emerging regional racial dynamics and their impact in locations where Latino students and their families come into daily contact with one another and with teachers in multiracial communities. In this book, I trace how Latinas "fell into" the profession, explore what happens when they learn that a large number of their students and parents are co-ethnics, and end with an analysis of what will ultimately be the future of the teaching profession in the United States.

Organization of the Book

Latina Teachers is divided into six chapters and a Conclusion. This first chapter has situated the study in the literature from various disciplines, drawing from theories about workplace inequities and educational disenfranchisement. It relies on classical and contemporary educational theories to detail the history of Latino youth in the U.S. educational system and in southern California schools. It connects cultural deficit and "subtractive schooling" theories to argue that these perspectives linger, influencing the measures Latina teachers take once in their workplaces. As I have explained, Latino ethnic culture is a powerful asset that Latina teachers bring to their workplaces, but structural forces work to limit them.

In chapter 2, I explain the forces that channel Latinas into the teaching profession. The changing opportunity structure of the economy, familial social networks, and social structural forces of racial, class, and gender inequalities create a situation in which gender and race refract working-class status, such that primary and secondary teaching has emerged as the top occupation drawing Latina college graduates. Many of these graduates are the first person in their families to graduate from college, and my research suggests a strong obligation on their part to help their families financially. These forces, at work in their families and universities, both constrain and enable their pathways into the teaching and influence the emergence of cultural guardianship once they are in the job. For this reason, I suggest that "class ceilings" help us understand how Latina college graduates navigate their educational and career choices with collectively informed agency and filial obligations to family members.

Chapter 3 elucidates my concept of Latina cultural guardians. I use this term to elucidate the range of sanctioned and unsanctioned strategies Latina teachers consciously deploy in order to protect and help co-ethnic children. Most Latina teachers describe "bumping" into the profession—meaning that they did not intend to pursue this career, and therefore they do not set out to become cultural guardians, but their interactions with poorer co-ethnic students and their families as well as with their colleagues prompt them to adopt the role. Given their own marginalization over the life course, including negative childhood experiences in K–12 schools and beyond, they soon realize how valuable they can be to their working-class Latino students and those students' families. Their educational experiences as Latinas also give them background knowledge that is of value in their role as cultural guardians. At the same time, Latinas who are multiracial (Mexican and white), or who grew up in English-speaking and/or in middle-class families, or are of later generations, can play the role as well as Latinas from working-class backgrounds, especially in multiracial environments, as they all experience exclusion in spaces that privilege whiteness. Cultural guardians therefore include Latinas who do not speak Spanish fluently, or at all.

Chapters 4, 5, and 6 examine Latina teachers' relationships and interactions with students, parents, and teachers of various racial/ethnic backgrounds at the two school sites. Chapter 4 provides a glimpse of how Latina teachers navigate their professional lives with mostly African American and Asian colleagues, students, and parents. The issue of macro-structural racial representations is of central importance to an analysis of race and work in different regions. I find that controlling images, which are hegemonic racial ideologies that permeate social institutions, have been applied to racial/ethnic minority groups and individuals, but much less so to school district space. I argue that controlling images of school district space—in this case the schools these Latina teachers work for—influence racial positioning between Latina teachers and non-Latinos because the context of reception (Portes and Rumbaut 2006) disadvantages Latino students, thus hastening their predisposition toward co-ethnics. Latina teachers working in Compton—a city consisting primarily of Latino immigrants—describe having been encouraged to leave for school districts and workplaces that are not associated with the "Black underclass" when they first took their jobs. Latina teachers in Rosemead, an ethnoburb consisting primarily of Latinos and Asians, on the other hand, enroll their children there and are able to access resources the more socioeconomically heterogeneous Asian population provides. Ultimately, Latina teachers perceive undocumented Latina/o immigrants to be below African Americans and Asian Americans in local racial hierarchies because of the political ostracism of the first group and the valorization of the second group. This process provides the impetus for co-ethnic cultural guardianship to develop. The findings of this chapter also provide an explanation for the absence of guardianship directed toward Black or Asian students, and the racism that Latinos express toward non-Latinos.

Relying on the months of participant observation in the classrooms and parent–teacher meetings as well as through the focus groups, chapter 5 illustrates how Latina teachers are creatively exercising an alternative form of cultural capital I term *Chicana/Latina cultural pedagogies*. This is a central component of cultural guardianship. The focus of this chapter is twofold. First, I define and illustrate how Chicana/Latina cultural pedagogies are different from what we usually associate with Latino cultures, the symbolic forms that appear in schools occasionally. Although Latino culture is not monolithic, Chicana/Latina cultural pedagogies are a set of practices Latina teachers use to subvert normative workplace rules regarding culture in teaching. Chicana/Latina cultural pedagogies comprise immigrant narratives, communication codes, and alternative mathematical problem solving—cultural resources that many lower-status Latino children and their parents possess. Second, I elucidate how Latina cultural guardians faced resistance, especially at Compton Elementary, to their use of Latina/o cultural resources to facilitate Latina/o student progress. While they are informal in practice, I observed that Chicana/Latina cultural pedagogies were at times denigrated or challenged in specific ways by colleagues and administration.

Chapter 6 offers an analysis of how California's structural policies regarding high-stakes testing and the academic labels applied to language-minority children fuel interracial conflicts between Latina teachers and their African American and Asian American co-workers. Chapter 6 demonstrates how cultural guardianships extend outside of the classroom as well. As cultural guardians within the classroom and beyond the school gates who rely on ethnic cultural resources to facilitate their students' educational success, Latina teachers resist structural inequality. This includes biased standardized testing that racializes their students and drastically affects their students' well-being in the long term. Thus, chapter 6 explains the workplace tensions that high-stakes state testing creates for Latina teachers and the ways in which they shield co-ethnic children from inequitable racialization processes. This process, however, comes at a cost to African American teachers and students.

The Conclusion ends the main part of the book by summarizing its main contributions. It describes whether Chicana/Latina cultural pedagogies can be learned and implemented by non-Latina teachers and ends with a discussion of the possible negative repercussions of Chicana/Latina cultural pedagogies in multiethnic metropolitan regions across the nation as Latino families settle in new immigrant gateways. It also provides policy implications for educational reform for students who attend schools in multiracial spaces.

This book is for anyone interested in how the U.S. school system might serve its burgeoning Latino population and for anyone interested in promoting teaching strategies that support the educational achievement of immigrant populations. It has particular insight for readers interested in the obstacles that Latina/os encounter in professional occupations in general and in occupations that serve Latinos, as the teachers in this study serve students and their families, in particular. It is also for those who already feel that they are a cultural guardian in their jobs as I believe it will help such readers make sense of their experiences—including the obstacles they face and the triumphs they celebrate.

2

"I Just Fell into It"

Pathways into the Teaching Profession

In August 2009, Mrs. Franco[1] was packing up her classroom, placing her chapter books and number lines[2] into a big brown box, sealing the flaps with a tape dispenser, and labeling it "Bungalow 9" with a black Sharpie pen. Holding the pen in her right hand, she got up from her kneeling position and said, "I never thought I was going to be a teacher. . . . You aren't going to hear an uplifting, inspirational story from me." She put more of her materials into a foldable teacher's cart. Mrs. Franco is a thirty-year-old Latina who had been working as a fourth-grade teacher in Rosemead, California, for nine years. She has spent four of those years in her current teaching job at Goodwill Elementary, a predominantly Asian and Latino school located in the larger San Gabriel Valley. Mrs. Franco described growing up in a much different Rosemead, one in which the majority of residents in her vicinity were of Mexican origin and many of her neighbors were her extended kin. Her grandmother lived across the street from her parents' small house. Her mother was an undocumented immigrant from Guadalajara but was eventually able to secure a job as a teacher's aide in an elementary school. Her father, on the other hand, was born to Mexican immigrants in California and worked as a plumber. Neither of her parents had navigated the rigors of college life or knew how to guide their daughter through college and into a white-collar job. When she was about to embark on her collegiate studies, her parents were unable to fund any part of her schooling, even though, according to her, her family had "never [been] without."

In the twenty-first century, teaching has become the top occupation for college-educated Latinas (Current Population Survey 2007; Flores and Hondagneu-Sotelo 2014). When I asked Latina teachers why this might be, some of them described teaching as the professional version of child care, as this has become a gendered occupational niche for immigrant Latinas. Work and gender scholar Pierrette Hondagneu-Sotelo (2001) notes the racialized, gendered, and classed aspects of labor in the United States, focusing on domestic work. While historically Latinas did not hold these jobs,[3] many affluent white families in the United States today prefer to hire Latina immigrants.[4] Similarly, while it was common to see white women standing at the front of the class in the 1960s, or African American women in the South teaching a class of their own in race-segregated schools from emancipation in 1863 to integration almost a hundred years later (Fairclough 2007), these demographics are changing as college-educated Latinas enter the teaching profession in droves—slowly transforming an occupational niche that was until recently primarily the province of white women. Because of these changes, some scholars now refer to teaching as a "semi-profession" in the United States (Abbott 1988; Williams 1992), a sentiment that was duly noted by Mrs. Bianca Franco.

This chapter discusses the pathways that college-educated Latinas took to get to their teaching jobs, suggesting that *class ceilings* and filial obligations to their financially struggling family members lured them into the profession. In contrast to previous studies arguing that Latina teachers enter because of "a calling" (see Suárez 2002) they recognized at a young age, I find that the structural context of their families drive Latina teachers' entry into the occupation. I underscore the important role of working-class constraints, as reflected through family, Latina/o ethnicity, gender, and regional demographic change, in shaping occupational outcomes. A central component of the class ceiling is the collectively informed agency that Latina teachers exhibit. Because of their structural position in society and class ceilings other family members experience, Latinas carry invisible burdens that white middle-class women do not (Stone 2007), in the form of obligations to help their parents and extended kin (Vallejo 2012).

What factors shape Latina pathways into the teaching profession? When I interviewed these women, the majority said they had not planned on a career in teaching. When sociologists attempt to explain the persistence of occupational sex segregation—that is, men and women working in different fields—they examine it in two primary ways, vertically (within occupations) and horizontally (across occupations) (Gottfried 2006; Reskin and Roos 1990). Similarly, feminist scholars analyzing gender and race inequality within work organizations have coined terms such as the *glass ceiling* (see López 2002) and *glass barriers* (Wingfield 2009) to document the experiences of white women and people of color in occupations where white men experience greater opportunity for advancement. Sociologist Nancy López (2002) documents the colored and gendered glass ceiling that West Indian and Caribbean, such as young, second-generation Dominican women, experience in the workplace in New York City. Feminist scholar Christine Williams uses the term *glass escalator* to capture the idea that men who work in culturally feminized occupations such as teaching and social work advance to management far more consistently than their female counterparts. Offering an alternative account focused on nurses, Adia Wingfield (2009) proposes that the glass escalator is a racialized and gendered concept that does not capture the glass barriers Black men experience.

These race and gender theories are crucial to our understanding of workplace inequities for women of color, but they address privilege or discrimination within feminized jobs only once women have entered the occupation or try to climb up in the work hierarchy. The unbreakable link of race, gender, and class for women of color, however, was forged even earlier in the process for Latinas, channeling them away from the occupations they once hoped to enter and into the teaching profession. I find that the structural context of the family channels many college-educated Latinas into teaching. This previously ignored dynamic precedes the encounter with the glass ceiling but nevertheless matters greatly for Latina integration and mobility.

This was especially the case for Mrs. Franco. The day of our interview in September 2009, Mrs. Franco wore a purple sweater, a white t-shirt with birds and hearts, blue jeans, and matching purple Vans shoes. Mrs. Franco was of light phenotype and her hair was dyed a very bright yellow, almost peroxide yellow. Her hair was tied back in a ponytail and she wore a purple headband. Her brown roots were slowly coming in. The pink hue on her lips matched the bright pink rouge on her cheeks. She was standing on top of a table, stapling her classroom rules to the bare walls. She hopped down from the chair she had been standing on and sat in her comfy black teacher chair as I squatted down somewhat uncomfortably in a small blue student chair. She offered me a bigger chair, but I said I was fine. Before we began the interview I handed her a demographic questionnaire sheet to fill. One question queried her about bilingual ability. A little embarrassed, she said, "My Spanish isn't that great. Should I write that down?" Mrs. Franco, who was born in the United States, indicated that she had retained some Spanish because her grandmother took care of her when she returned home from school while her parents worked. Her ability to speak Spanish had been a significant factor in her landing a teaching job quickly despite her having only a CLAD teaching credential instead of a BCLAD credential,[5] the latter of which signifies bilingual authorization.

Although she had attended an elite four-year college, UCLA, for her bachelors degree in sociology, Mrs. Franco was ashamed to reveal where she received her teaching credential, because although the program was costly, it was not at a similarly prestigious institution. As she scribbled "University of Phoenix" in purple ink, she said, "This one is really embarrassing! You just give them a lot of money, and you get what you want. It's kind of like a drive-thru university," she chuckled. She was adamant that she initially did not want to be a teacher but said she developed a passion for the job once she saw what a valuable resource she was for Latino families who were having trouble navigating institutional bureaucracies and finding support for their children, whom they wanted to succeed in America.

Throughout the interview Mrs. Franco compared teaching with more lucrative careers such as law and medicine and her teacher's salary with the income that lawyers and doctors make yearly. "I never wanted to be a teacher, I never wanted to go into education. . . . I didn't really know the salary of a teacher, but I remember hearing as a child that a garbage man makes more money than a teacher and I was like, 'I don't want to be that.'" Instead, she aspired to enter the medical field, where she would be able to make enough money to provide for herself and help her family financially. She said:

> I wanted a profession that would give me a lot of money because I could see my parents struggle and I didn't want to have to do that, to struggle. I wanted to be able to give something back to my parents. As far as [my] going into teaching [is concerned], it wasn't something that I planned to do, but something that motivated [me] to stay in the profession was

what I [would] see. I would see [Hispanic parents] kind of lost. They didn't know how to help their kids. I saw that I could do something to help. Not that I leave my Asian students out, because I don't, but it is kind of like I can "give back" to my community as far as Hispanics or Latinos go because I can help them and I can relate to them. Unfortunately I try, but I can't probably do the same [for] my Asian community of children, because I don't speak the language[s] and I am not part of their culture so it is a little different, but that doesn't mean that I don't go above and beyond for them, because obviously all of my students, I see them all in the same likeness.

Mrs. Franco's social pathways into the teaching profession are not uncommon. While a few of the Latina teachers who appear in the pages of this book said that they had always aspired to become teachers, the vast majority reported that they became teachers "by accident." They explained their pathways into the teaching profession as happenstance, a serendipitous fluke of fate. They said, "It's not like I grew up thinking I was gonna be a teacher" or "I just bumped into it." Rather than chance events, however, interviews with Latina teachers at Compton Elementary and Goodwill Elementary suggest that a series of patterned social factors led to a concentration of Latina college graduates in the teaching field. Mrs. Franco's narrative is an example of the thwarting of other occupational aspirations held by Latina college graduates as a result of family financial constraints and a lack of understanding of the higher-educational system. We also see in Mrs. Franco's words how the seeds of cultural guardianship were planted once she was in the profession: She explained that she was motivated to stay in the profession because of the Latino population that was struggling to integrate. The experience of Latina teachers demonstrates ethnic succession into a professional occupational niche for Latina college graduates. In the following sections I detail how structural factors, such as the opportunity structure of the economy, familial social networks, and intersections of race, gender, and class, worked on the social level to channel Latinas into teaching.

Opportunity Structure of the Economy

Supply Meets Growing Demand

The growth of the Latino immigrant population in the last two decades of the twentieth century, particularly in southern California, fueled a skyrocketing demand for bilingual and bicultural teachers in public schools, immigrant communities, and at Compton and Goodwill Elementary. Resulting changes in the opportunity structure of the economy and more Latino students in schools in conjunction with smaller class sizes allowed Latinas to enter the teaching profession.

The 1996 Class Size Reduction Program[6] called for a 20:1 ratio in classrooms and also for emergency credential programs, opening a door for college-educated Latinas. A growing demand for teachers, especially for bilingual and minority teachers, in the 1990s was fueled by increases in the Latino student population and in bilingual education programs (Ryan and Cooper 2010; Hart and Burr 1996). Many of these demands came from immigrant and racial/ethnic minority communities, which seemed to change demographic characteristics overnight. During this period, California schools "were hiring teachers like crazy," said one Latina teacher. While the recent financial crisis (2008–11) resulted in layoffs and contractions, the number of classroom teachers in elementary and secondary schools is today projected to increase until 2018, primarily because of teacher retirements, and student enrollments are also projected to increase (Ryan and Cooper 2010; Hussar, Bailey, and National Center for Education Statistics 2009). Most of the teachers retiring are white; as their positions are filled by Latinas, the face of the profession is rapidly changing. This is consistent with other demographic changes, as more professions (such as law and medicine) continue to open up for white women, drawing them out of the lower-status professions that were previously dominated by women. In effect, it is primarily second-generation, working-class, college-educated Latinas who are now filling the teaching jobs, especially in California.

Increased immigration from Latin America and Asian countries in the 1980s and 1990s fueled demand for bilingual educators to provide services that monolingual, white middle-class teachers could not (Su 1996). This sort of thinking was institutionalized through legislation. For instance, the Bilingual Education Act of 1968 provided federal funds to aid language-minority students in the acquisition of the English language, and the Class Size Reduction program resulted in more job openings in kindergarten through third-grade classes. Bilingual educators were in high demand because many students spoke a foreign language.

To meet rapidly growing demand for teachers, emergency credential programs started as early as 1989, and by 1994–95 the number of teachers in California working with emergency credentials or waivers grew to 50 percent of all teachers (Hart and Burr 1996). During this particular period, most emergency-credentialed teachers were hired in southern California, 60 percent of the statewide total in Los Angeles County alone. In 1991, the most dire need was in bilingual education, which then accounted for 72 percent of Los Angeles Unified School District's emergency teachers (Ed-Data 2009; Hart and Burr 1996). Districts sought teachers who would be able to communicate with Spanish-speaking Latino parents and children and recruited bilingual Spanish-speaking teachers. As the Latina teachers explained, teaching credentials were not obligatory at the time because the "[school districts] were just getting anybody" who had a B.A. in any subject and had passed the CBEST exam. Notably, financial aid was also available:

> When I first started working here they had incentives for [your] being bilingual. When I started working here we had the bilingual program here. We don't have it any more, but during that time we had the bilingual program, so to be bilingual and have all that was just a plus. After I got my B.A., they gave us an emergency credential, which means you can teach but you have to go back to school and get your credential. So that is how Compton worked. You were actually working. They were taking anybody, in any subject. They needed teachers that badly. (Mrs. Rivas, Compton)

The passage of Proposition 227, known as the English for the Children Initiative, in 1998 ultimately dismantled most bilingual-education programs in the state of California. But until that happened, jobs were plentiful. As Mrs. Arenas (Goodwill) recalled, "At the time, the population here in this district was maybe 60/70 percent Hispanic and they had the Title 1 program which is the bilingual program. . . . Being bilingual and being Hispanic [was] an advantage."

There are few professions where college-educated Latinas have an advantage or an "in," even if they speak Spanish, but teaching became an exception. The teachers still marveled at this because speaking Spanish has historically been met with hostility, or at least ambivalence, in the United States (González 1997). But in the 1990s, Spanish–English bilingualism was perceived as an asset, and these Latina college graduates were placed higher in the job queue than were monolingual teachers (Reskin and Roos 1992). Mrs. Madrigal said, "It seemed like one door opened another door. . . . I was just in the right place at the right time when it opened up." Class-size reduction under state Senate Bill 1777 opened more doors for Latina teachers, and many of them then took advantage of the credential programs, which they perceived as quick and easy. As Mrs. Estrada said, "[The credential] seemed like the most appealing and fast." There were multiple ways to obtain a credential, and many of them did not require Latina teachers to "pay a dime." Some reported obtaining their credential online.

Most of the Latina teachers started teaching with an emergency credential. Half of the Latina teachers who worked in Compton Elementary described taking advantage of the District Alternative Credential Program (DACP), a program that was specifically designed to recruit teachers into schools that were suffering from high teacher turnover rates. The program took effect after the district made the decision to stop relying on Teach for America[7] students or teachers from abroad. Latina teachers working for Compton Unified, which underwent a massive teacher shortage in the mid-1990s and early 2000s, noted that they had taken advantage of the DACP, which was advertised in the newspaper at the time. This program helped them pay for school with many of them being "hired on the spot." Mrs. Becerra, one of those who took advantage of the program, said, "Compton was offering at that time a program were you can be working as a teacher with help and getting your degree and school in [the] afternoon, so I said, 'Perfect!' I get the morning [to get my children ready for school], a salary at the same time that I was working to get my degree, so that was perfect for me at that time. . . . The District Alternative Program was just ideal for me. It was the scheduling [and] the distance." Other Latina teachers were directly recruited into the teaching profession. This was especially common at Compton Unified. There is a long history of direct labor recruitment for

Mexican immigrant men, through *enganchadas* [hooks] and the contracts of the Bracero Program (Martinez 1996). These direct recruitment strategies are also used by military recruiters, who specifically target urban and low-income schools (Mariscal 2003). Here we see something similar, but within the context of college settings and college-educated Latinas working for disadvantaged schools. The Latina teachers reported encountering recruiters at their college campuses, sometimes holding "Teacher Fairs" where they were eagerly sought out and encouraged to interview and apply right on the spot. Mrs. Estrada said, "I went to a job fair, it was a teacher job fair and there was somebody there from Compton, and I didn't have my credential then and he was like 'Try the internship program at Compton.'" Mrs. Díaz, a Cuban/Salvadoran teacher, had just finished speaking with an academic counselor about her difficulty passing her courses as a biological science major when she encountered a recruiter by chance as she exited the office. As she recalled, "I just happened to meet a Compton recruiter at Cal Poly Pomona one day who told me about their district intern program and how you can pursue your credential through their program and work at the same time. . . . It almost was 100% that you would get employment through Compton. . . . Work always comes first, so to work and go to school at the same time was the incentive." She changed her major to liberal studies that day.

Working and studying at the same time was an attractive option for these working-class students. Many Latinas took advantage of district programs, which would help them pay for their credential and guaranteed them employment if they remained with the district. Beyond their college campuses, some Latina teachers said that former teachers and administrators had encouraged them to get into teaching.

Teaching Requirements and Advantages

Compared with law or medicine, the teaching profession requires a relatively short course of study, usually four years of college with an extra year to obtain a credential (State of California Commission on Teacher Credentialing 2010). In California, there are various ways to obtain a teaching credential after completing a bachelors degree. One way is through independent credentialing via online courses, like the one Mrs. Franco took. Another way is to enroll in a credential program (in conjunction with a masters degree) at a college institution while teaching part-time. Last, some teachers enter through emergency credentials. Because entry requirements are less stringent than those of other professions, teaching is relatively accessible and offers secure prospects. Notably, it is often possible to work in a teaching capacity while still in college (e.g., as a substitute teacher or instructional aide). Teaching-credential programs are also perceived as easier than other degree programs. While a high GPA, attendance at an elite college, and stratospheric board scores may be necessary to attain entry to many professional and graduate programs, a schoolteacher in California must obtain a B.A./B.S. in any subject, successfully complete three tests,[8] and obtain a multiple-subject teaching credential. Latina teachers indicated that they entered the profession because it required a shorter period of educational preparation, it allowed them to work while finishing school, and there was a degree of certainty that a job would be readily available, especially in immigrant communities.

However, it was social class and limited cultural capital that channeled working-class students, many of them the daughters of working-class Mexican immigrants, into teaching. As Bourdieu (1973) has indicated, class social reproduction hinges on cultural capital, or accumulated knowledge and attitudes that allow for the accumulation of status, education, and power. These Latina college graduates were upwardly mobile, but their mostly working-class parents had not passed on to them the kinds of informal know-how and information that upper- and professional-class parents are able to impart to their children, and hence these women were restricted in navigating the higher echelons of education and the professions on their own. Most parental support throughout collegiate attendance for first-generation Latino college students takes the form of verbal support and encouragement (Gándara 1995). Children in working-class immigrant families are unlikely to have been concertedly cultivated with professional-class privileges, resources, and expectations, and they are also less likely to have connections with elites (Lareau 2003). Even Latina teachers like Mrs. Claudette Díaz, who grew up in middle-class families, explained that their parents did not have elite connections in the United States and were unable to help them pursue higher-status occupations. Mrs. Díaz explained that, while her father was a bank executive and her mother a licensed vocation nurse (LVN), neither of them had elite social connections in the medical world. She said, "It takes a lot of resources to be a doctor. A lot of kids will say 'I want to be a doctor.' I said that, for crying out loud. But did I have the right tools to get there? No! And I considered myself pretty affluent." Mrs. Díaz's occupational dream of becoming a doctor had been stymied by several circumstances. A college professor had dissuaded her from pursuing medicine, telling her, "You are never going to get into medical school." She also had difficulty passing "weeder" courses such as chemistry in her biology program, and she failed out of the program within the first two years of college.

Although all the teachers I interviewed disliked that society perceived elementary teaching to be easier than other professions, they said they did not pursue other careers because they worried whether it was possible for them to succeed and secure employment. Several Latina teachers seemed to doubt their capabilities in their original intended fields, shortchanging themselves in a way and second-guessing their abilities. These doubts were a direct result of the fact that they did not see anyone who held their social background characteristics in higher-status jobs, a situation that they perceived to be a result of gender or racial discrimination. Mrs. Irene Robles, a fourth-generation Latina teacher of a darker phenotype with curly hair, who studied health science, said she saw too much competition in health science and worried whether it would be possible to get a job in the medical field. "I saw a lot more competition in the health field. . . . [I]t seemed like it was hard to get in." Others were wary of entering elite, white-dominated professions where they feared that they would not be selected by potential employers. To Latina teachers, teaching seemed like a fairer profession where jobs were allocated more democratically. They saw teaching as unlike business or other fields in that elitism and racism would not be decisive factors in the allocation of jobs. Latina teachers noted that when they pursued other fields they could tell "who was going to get the job because of their looks and who wasn't." For instance, Mrs. Madrigal contemplated becoming a police officer but ultimately did not because of perceived racism and gender discrimination. Teaching, according to her, was the "fairest" of all jobs because it did not matter whether applicants had attended a private elite university or the California state system. Mrs. Guadalupe Becerra did not pursue a medical career, as she had originally planned, because she was worried about her ability to pronounce medical terminology properly: "When I lived in Mexico I thought I was going to be a doctor. That was my goal. Then I come here. The other reason why I did not pursue the doctor career, medical career, was because of the language, you know, the terminology is very difficult to pronounce." Instead, she studied finance and was contemplating moving up in the marketing world, but self-consciousness about her accent led her to renounce that aim as well; in the end, she obtained an emergency credential and entered teaching, where she had the impression that Latinas were the "preferred" labor pool in immigrant enclaves and communities.

Family Social Networks

Latinas often find employment at schools in their neighborhoods as lunch ladies, yard duty supervisors, secretaries, teacher's aides, or administrative staff. These Latina school employees help carve a pathway to teaching for their college-educated daughters and nieces by passing on information about job openings and providing personal references.

Most Americans are familiar with the axiom "It's not what you know, but whom you know" that determines where you get a job, as many job seekers rely on social networks to secure employment. This principle holds among Mexican migrant agricultural workers, domestic workers, and factory workers (Massey et al. 1987; Waldinger and Lichter 2003), as well as among professionals seeking highly coveted positions (Lin 1999; Lin et al. 1981). For Latina teachers, social ties—especially to family members—served as important channels of information about job opportunities in schools. In her influential study, sociologist Silvia Dominguez (2010) examines the social support networks of immigrant women living in high-poverty neighborhoods and their patterns of positive and negative social mobility. She finds that the most successful women are those embedded in reciprocal social networks who thus have greater access to resources such as encouragement and emotional support. While the majority of teachers I interviewed came from working-class families where the parents held jobs in factories, construction, and services, nearly half of them reported having family members—typically cousins, sisters, and aunts—who worked in schools. These family ties helped draw them into teaching jobs.

Most of Ms. Ana Gutierrez's siblings had been able to secure jobs in the white-collar world. When she was figuring out what path she was going to take in the late 1990s to early 2000s, she never envisioned teaching. Out of the six brothers in her family, three were service engineers. All of them attended Wiley Engineering later on in life in the early 1990s and received the appropriate licenses and certifications to do their work through this vocational school. Her oldest brother was a technical engineer, another one was a refrigeration engineer, and the pride of the family worked as a NASA engineer. She emphasized that her parents did not want the men in her family to enter teaching because they could make a lot more money in the engineering fields. The women in her family, on the other hand, were working in feminized occupations such as clerical work.[9] One of her sisters worked as a clerical assistant for the human resources department at Los Angeles Airport, and the other worked as a secretary for Hawthorne District. While one sister tried to dissuade her from entering teaching because of the pay, her sister-in-law, who worked as a teacher for Compton Unified, urged her to apply so they could work together.

As noted earlier, most of these women reported initial ambivalence about going into teaching. Yet family members with ties to the teaching profession or to other jobs in the schools had provided important job leads at a time when they had been uncertain about other job aspirations. For example, when Ms. Arlene Dávila finished her B.A. in theater arts, she had no job offer and had had no luck in drama-related fields or with a record company. She was close friends with the Latina principal at Goodwill Elementary. She reported:

> I needed to make money to pay rent, so I started as a substitute teacher, and I was really good at it. The principal [her friend] wanted me to apply for the position and encouraged me to apply. So I did and I liked it. . . . I realized I could incorporate some drama into it. . . . I need[ed] to be employable immediately and the principal just said, "I can give you some part-time work in the school doing some drama, and while you're doing that you should go back to school and finish your credential." That's how it happened.

Here, thick, localized neighborhood networks included the friend who was a principal. Not everyone could cite teachers or principals who had drawn them back to the schools, but family connections were common. Ms. Sánchez, a third-generation Mexican American teacher, reported a similar path, with family members drawing her into teaching. Her sister, she said, was instrumental in helping her find a teaching job: "I went into [studying] computers but didn't find a job in computers. And so then I managed to come across—actually my sister told me about a program about getting credentials, it was a masters and a credential. So that's actually how I really got into it." Neither of these women had aspired to go into teaching—Ms. Dávila had a B.A. in theater arts, and Ms. Sánchez had studied computer technology—but they were all facing urgent financial difficulties and uncertain career paths. With family and community social networks linking them to the schools, they were pulled onto the inside track for teaching jobs.

Family members, more than friends, were critical in drawing Latinas into teaching. This speaks to the strength of family relations in Mexican and Chicano families (Zinn 1979). Half of the twenty Latina teachers interviewed reported having cousins or other family members who worked as teachers. Family was defined expansively, beyond the nuclear family to include cousins, aunts, and uncles. For instance, Mrs. Yolanda Ybarra and Mrs. Melody Godínez, fraternal twin sisters born to Mexican immigrants, were both hired at Compton Elementary at the same time. They also went through most of their schooling together in order to provide social support for each other. Mrs. Godínez heard about the job openings at a teacher fair, and she informed Mrs. Ybarra about them. Mrs. Godínez said, "[Mrs. Ybarra] is my twin sister. We went through school together. We both had the same undergrad majors. We both graduated the same year from our credential program. She stopped at the credential. We both got hired [at Compton] at the same time."

Mrs. Franco cited several family members who drew her into teaching: "My mom worked in education [as a teacher's aide], my *nina* [godmother] worked in education, and then my brother. . . . [H]e started teaching and it seemed like he liked it. So it was kind of like I just fell into it because it was around, and I didn't really know what else to do, and it was something familiar." Indeed, Mrs. Franco alludes to the notion that that teaching sounded like a familiar career choice within her Latino family. In his seminal book *Schoolteacher*, sociologist Dan Lortie (2002) notes that teaching draws many college students who begin their studies with other career ambitions, especially students with limited financial resources. Although the majority of the teachers included in his book were white, I encountered many Latina teachers who had initially aspired to become lawyers, doctors, or professors and had never imagined entering teaching. In the end, teaching seemed a more financially feasible, less competitive, and more certain option. A combination of self-doubt, lack of money, the urgency of the need to begin earning a regular salary soon after college, and, notably, the desire to seek an occupational space where they would be protected from overt racism and elitism directed college-educated Latinas toward teaching. Having internalized the inequalities around them, some Latina teachers felt that this was their "proper" place, but also a place where they found job satisfaction.

Ms. Sánchez voiced these sentiments: "It's not like I grew up thinking I was gonna be a teacher. . . . My sister works for the district. . . . And my nephews used to come here, and my niece. So I knew about the teachers because my sister and I talked. . . . My sister told me about a program about the teacher and getting credentials." Mrs. Robles, for example, explained how she began working as an instructional aide at the school where she later became a teacher: "One of my aunts was an office manager at a school, and I was going to college at Cal State L.A., and she asked me if I was interested in trying to work at the school and I said, yeah, I would give it a try." And Mrs. Romero, whose mother worked as a teacher's aide and whose father worked at a car wash and as an electrician, found herself ultimately persuaded by her father's exhortations to try substitute teaching (open to all college graduates) at her mother's school: "That was him telling me, 'Start subbing, start subbing at your mom's school. You're gonna like it, you're gonna like it.' I was like, 'Dad, I don't want to work there, I don't want to be a teacher, I don't want to be that.' And he was like, 'No, no, no, just try it. It's good income.' And then I started liking it, and he was like, 'See, I told you so.'"

In his classic article on the importance of weak social ties, Mark Granovetter (1983) showed the important role that even relatively fleeting and weak social networks can play in job recruitment. But here we see something different: the importance of strong family ties operating within the context of Latino/Chicano familism. This Latino/Chicano familism involves expectations of mutual support and assistance, regular socializing with kin, and often selection of *compadres* [godparents] from kin (Keefe and Padilla 1987; Álvarez 1994). These strong ties in large extended families and regular contact with many cousins, aunts, and uncles, together with expectations of mutual aid, create a dense web of social networks that translates into job contacts. Moreover, as we have seen, for some of the Latina teachers, especially at Goodwill Elementary, there are strong patterns of residential neighborhood stability, and public schools in Latino neighborhoods serve as hubs of employment for Latinas. All of the Latina teachers included in this book went to college locally, in southern California, and many returned to work in their neighborhood schools, or in schools located just a few miles from where they grew up, as was the case for Mrs. Franco. This results in a type of cumulative causation, as the new recruits help to expand and reproduce the social network that drew them into the schools. Latina teachers, as well as teacher's aides and other school support staff, establish a foothold in schools in Latino neighborhoods and they recruit their female kin into the profession.

Intersections of Race, Class, and Gender

Familial Educational Encouragement and Scarce Resources

Across the city, roughly twenty miles away from Goodwill Elementary, Mrs. Maribel Madrigal, a 1.5-generation Latina teacher, invited me into her home in Paramount, California. Mrs. Madrigal, a fourth-grade teacher for the Compton Unified School District, wanted to meet at her home to avoid school politics and because she had trouble finding an affordable babysitter. When I walked to her home, I opened the chain-linked gate and watched my step, jumping over exposed tubing. Her husband, a Compton police officer, was working on the pipes in their newly purchased home. The front yard had been excavated, exposing the plumbing. "Sorry for the mess. A pipe burst. Watch your step. *No se caiga* [Don't fall]," Mrs. Madrigal said to my mother, who was accompanying me to monitor and supervise Mrs. Madrigal's three elementary school–aged children—Rosy, Kevin, and Michael—to whom she had given Anglicized names so they would not be teased in school.

Similarly to Mrs. Franco, and just about all of the Latina teachers in this book, Mrs. Madrigal did not originally intend to enter the teaching profession and just "fell into it." Mrs. Madrigal emphasized her family's dire financial predicament and her duty to help them financially at a very young age because her father did not make enough in his less than $9.00 an hour backbreaking job as a welder and her mother was a home-maker. She also alluded to gendered expectations within her family to contribute to household chores as the eldest daughter. To make ends meet, Mrs. Madrigal worked in several jobs. As a result she was trapped in the community college system for "over ten years" until she finally garnered enough credits to transfer to California State University (CSU), Los Angeles. As she explained,

> My focus has always been helping my mom, with bills and just helping out emotionally and with other aspects I had to do in the house. . . . So when I got to Cal State and I heard [teaching] was not so long [years], I jumped on it. . . . It's just my responsibility. . . . I guess when I was little it's because I was the [eldest girl]. I felt obligated to help. So then as I grew older, got married, financial stability is there so now it's more of a, more of a responsibility. . . . I am going to do that until, you know, until they're not here. . . . You have to give priority to your family first.

The vast majority of the Latina teachers at Compton and Goodwill Elementary indicated that witnessing their parents' toil in arduous and taxing blue-collar jobs pushed them to get professional jobs. The "immigrant narrative" (Vallejo and Lee 2009) or "immigrant bargain" (Smith 2006) is common among Mexican immigrant parents, who invoke stories of their hard work and sacrifice to induce their children to study and get good jobs. Most of the Latina teachers said this dynamic had been important in their upbringing. These women painted vivid portraits of the workplace struggles their parents had encountered in the United States as gardeners, janitors, or domestics, and they described how their parents used their own low levels of education and wearisome manual jobs as sources of motivation to push their daughters toward higher education and upward mobility. As Ms. Lizet Tiscareño, whose father worked as a custodian, said:

My parents came from Mexico as immigrants, and every single year that I can remember, they instilled in me a need to always succeed in education . . . They wanted to make sure that I got the opportunities that they felt they didn't [get] because they didn't have the opportunity to get educated in Mexico. They had to work rather than go to school. They had to make sure that I knew how important an education was because they didn't want to see me with any of the stereotypes that we as Hispanics face. They would mention to me, "Please don't end up as a worker in a cook line," and they would tell me also, "I'd rather have you choose your profession rather than it being chosen for you."

Mrs. Romero, a kindergarten teacher at Compton Elementary, and the daughter of a mother who worked as a teacher's aide and a father who worked in a car wash, explained: "[My dad] would say simple things, like he came to this country when he was like 18, right? And he told me that he was working his first job at a car wash in Chicago in the winter, below freezing. . . . It was like 'You are here, I came to this country to give you a chance, you have no excuses.'" The Latina teachers credited their parents' immigrant backgrounds with giving them an inner drive and a fervor to succeed in school, but at the same time they said that their parents had been unable to help fund their college educations. The vast majority received little or no parental financial support for college. Like Ms. Ana Gutierrez, they turned to scholarships, loans, part-time jobs, and other sources of support. Another teacher, Mrs. Cynthia Rivas, explained how a Cal Grant she qualified for because of her underprivileged background had paid for her B.A.s in psychology and Chicano/Latino studies and her emergency teaching credential.[10] She credited this grant with helping her complete her studies to become an elementary school teacher:

My mom was a single parent so she worked all of the time. She couldn't really take care of me [financially]. During that time [getting my B.A.] I was working. I was working as a TA [teacher's aide]. [For my] B.A. I was lucky enough to get *una beca*. A scholarship. I was really lucky that they paid for everything. . . . I was Hispanic from a single parent and we didn't have a house so they pretty much paid for everything. I didn't have to worry about that.

The overwhelming majority of these women had fathers who worked in blue-collar occupations as welders, construction workers, plumbers, and janitors, and in warehouses as stockers. A quarter of their mothers were homemakers, while others worked in factories, as domestics, in agricultural fields, or in education (as aides, preschool, teachers). As Vallejo and Lee (2009) show, many Latinas/os from working-class backgrounds who experience upward social mobility wish to "give back" financially and socially to their families and communities. This social dynamic was important for the Latina teachers, as they cited "giving back" as both an expectation on the part of their families and as a personal motivation for starting their post-college earning careers sooner rather than later. Teaching, which requires a shorter period of schooling than most other professions, offered them the opportunity to do so.

This relatively short period of educational preparation was important, as these daughters of Latino immigrants wanted to help their parents financially. The desire to help their families both economically and emotionally, they said, began when they were children and adolescents. As youth, many of them had accompanied their parents to work and had also worked jobs in high school to help supplement the family's income. Most of the Latina teachers recalled being aware of their family's precarious economic status and felt a responsibility to ensure their families' well-being before their own. For this reason, most of them worked while in college.

Latina teachers also explained that going to school not only was a financial sacrifice but also added to the "emotional work" they expended within their families, who often made them feel that time devoted to school infringed on their ability to help the family financially. Mrs. Elisa Estrada, for example, described how she had felt torn by the strain of simultaneously studying and trying to help out her family monetarily and socially. Mrs. Estrada wanted to be interviewed in her quiet home in Torrance. When she opened the door, she gave her infant boy to the Latina nanny. The day of our interview, she was casually dressed, wearing black sandals, exposing the blue nail polish on her toes, a black tank top, long earrings, and khaki capris. I sat down at her kitchen table and settled in, noticing the new Ford F-150 pickup truck in her driveway, a nicely manicured lawn, and a large Diego Rivera painting in her living room, mounted above her large television. Throughout the interview

Mrs. Estrada was very animated and laughed a lot, providing many insights into her life and her assessment of Mexican and American family values and how they affected her own college experiences. She described this as the differences between American family values, which mandate "do for yourself first and then the family," and Mexican family values, which require "you'll do for the family before you do for yourself."

> I think the Latino community sees [it] more like let's help the family and then do the self. I think the American culture is the opposite; it's like "Let me do for me, and then if I have anything left, then I will do for everybody else." An "American" family would be more "Okay, he is going to college, you are studying, you are doing this." The Mexican family would be more like, "Help me with this. I need help with this or help with that." Like I'm telling you, I would be sitting there [at home] and they would be telling me to wash the dishes and mop and clean and then I can do my work. Or "Go and help Lali [older sister], she needs babysitting." And my mom would babysit my nephews, and she would leave me there with them. It was like "Here, watch them, watch them, I have to do this." . . . I think the Latino family is more "Help us, help each other," and it's not in a bad way. We don't mean it in a bad way. But let's help each other— grandma needs help, or this person needs help, or this uncle needs help, and then you could do something for you. It would be okay if your family wasn't in a financial crisis and you decide to go to college instead of help out, wouldn't they be looking at you, kind of like, they would be kind of like, "Oh, you are so selfish." Anytime you are doing something for you, it's like you are selfish.

As soon as Mrs. Estrada finished saying this, the nanny came back in with her wailing baby. "Come here, *papis*," she said as she cooed at him and gave him his bottle. She continued, "It comes with guilt. . . . You are going to school and you feel the guilt. Or you are reading a book and you are feeling the guilt, so it is really hard" (laughs).

Some of the Latina teachers, like Mrs. Estrada, felt guilty for pursuing their own education while family financial urgencies remained. As a consequence, many of them reported that obligations to help their families had required them to forgo professional careers with longer courses of study, in favor of teaching. For example, Ms. Tiscareño recalled that her parents "could not help [her] pay for school," but she knew they were counting on her, and she could not disappoint their hopes for future stability. With aspirations to become a doctor, Ms. Tiscareño spoke of the message reverberating through her mind in college, getting "paid well" so that she could help her parents financially and socially:

> They are the ones that I help financially. They are the ones, because of all the support they have given me. I feel that they have sacrificed so much for me, that it's out of love and respect that I provide for them what I can. I could help with their car insurance payment or their house payment or whatever utilities I can, I take care of that for them. I pick up my mom on a daily basis from my sister's house and take her to Long Beach, you know, to our house.

The responsibility to "give back" and take care of parents was echoed by other Latina teachers. Mrs. Franco, who was introduced at the beginning of this chapter, said she had initially wanted to become a doctor and had not planned on becoming a teacher, but she did so in order to give back: "I could see my parents struggle and I didn't want to have to do that. . . . I wanted to be able to give something back to my parents. . . . I always wanted something better . . . I wanted to give my parents something better. . . . I thought if I had a job like that, then I could kind of like repay them for what they did, even just make a better life for myself."

Latina teachers wanted the ability to provide financially for themselves and their nuclear and extended families. This cultural tradition from their working-class Latino background propelled them to think about their family's well-being and directed them to select careers as teachers.

Economic Feasibility

Growing up in a very crowded household, from which her father was largely absent, Ms. Ana Gutierrez, mentioned earlier in connection with the family ties that brought her into teaching, began strategizing early on how to make money. She did not want her Mexican immigrant mother to have to spend any of her few dollars on her. "I always gave her some money," she said. Ms. Gutierrez was the eleventh of twelve children:

She had six brothers and five sisters. As a teenager, she worked a series of insecure jobs and sought several licenses, none of which ultimately led to long-term, financially stable employment. Her first job, at the age of fifteen, was at an indoor swapmeet, where she was paid under the table by her Asian boss. When she qualified for a work permit at the of age sixteen, she landed a retail job where she worked up to forty hours per week while going to high school full-time. "I've always had a full-time job and full-time school," she said one hot July day during her lunch break from teaching summer session. She signed up to teach during the summer vacation to supplement her income. She continued, "I started working at a really young age, so I tried different fields." She had worked as a receptionist for a construction company and at Broadway (now Macy's). Through her tenure at these jobs, she also obtained a license in insurance policies and a certificate in retail management, prompting her to study business administration for one semester when she initially enrolled at West Los Angeles College after graduation from high school. Because of her heavy work schedule, it took Ms. Gutierrez ten years to complete her course of study at West L.A. College and transfer to Cal State L.A., where she obtained her B.A. in liberal studies. Her schooling was tough for her because she worked in a child development center full-time for about eleven years while completing her B.A., but she described teaching as a "natural progression" from that.

Some scholars have suggested that teaching is a sex-segregated and feminized occupation because it is "caring" work for children (Padavic and Reskin 2002). Jobs in care work with children and the elderly are usually devalued and underpaid. This is why some scholars refer to teaching as a "semi-profession" in the United States (Abbott 1988). In fact, when Latina teachers were asked about why they thought so many other Latinas were entering the occupation, they described teaching as the professional version of babysitting. At the same time, they downplayed the stereotype that Latinas were naturally more "nurturing" and caring by highlighting larger economic and structural inequalities. Mrs. Franco said:

> It is a stereotype that [Latinas] are very nurturing or caring and I think to be a teacher you need to be that. . . . I mean I said it is very stereotypical but that could be very generalized as all females. It just seems that more

in the Latina culture . . . they are very nurturing because I just think of my grandma, like seven kids; very mothering and very nurturing. And then like a lot of [Latinas] if they don't have their papers, like a lot of them are caretakers, they babysit, so it's like almost the professional version of babysitting is teaching. It's an added—because you have the education where I am actually teaching them something. . . . That's not to say that people who don't have their papers are not educated; it's just that they don't have their papers and they cannot utilize their education. So they may still be educated women; it's just that they don't have the paperwork that is needed to obtain a professional job to earn a living.

Mrs. Franco makes a striking point. Latinas in the United States have traditionally been "hypersegregated" in low-wage service or pink-collar work, such as domestic, day care work (Catanzarite and Trimble 2008; Hondagneu-Sotelo 2001), and clerical work (Segura 1992b). Some suggest that teaching meshes with feminine gender ideals, arguing that, like nursing and social work, teaching is perceived as a feminine "helping" profession, one associated with motherhood, nurturance, social reproduction, and caring for others (Etzioni 1969; Acker 1989). Correspondingly, teachers' hours of work duty are also seen as compatible with the social organization of motherhood and family obligations, offering holidays, summer vacations, and a work day that presumably ends at 3:00 p.m. These are powerful forces for Latinas, who are traditionally dedicated to motherhood and caring for extended kin (Segura 1992a; Zinn 1979). Unlike the legal profession, from which many women ultimately depart because of work–family life tension and their perceptions of their limited opportunities for promotion and career advancement (Walsh 2012), teaching is often seen as congruous with domestic activities. However, while middle-class white women's family needs are generally oriented toward their children (Stone 2007), Latinas carry additional felt obligations to help their parents, family of origin, and extended kin (Vallejo and Lee 2009; Hite 2007; Alvarez 1994; Segura and Pierce 1993). There is a long sociological tradition of seeing Mexican and Latino families as "familistic": ruled by family solidarity, values, and actions that seek to preserve the family over the individual (Moore and Pachon 1985; Keefe and Padilla 1987). At times, this tradition has been viewed as a Latino cultural pathology—as an instance of the family holding back the individual. I do not subscribe to the pathology view (see Zinn 1994; Zavella 1987), but I emphasize the gendered nature of these practices: The burden of maintaining Latino family solidarity often falls on the shoulders of Latino mothers and daughters. This burden has consequences for mobility. As Vallejo and Lee (2009) underscore, the upwardly mobile daughters of poorer Latino immigrants must often delay attending college, buying a home, or childbearing because of obligations to their families of origin. In Mexican and Latino immigrant working-class families, this more expansive view of family obligations plays an important part in channeling Latina college graduates into teaching.

Ultimately Ms. Gutierrez "bumped" into teaching in the early 2000s at the age of thirty-one: The child development center where she had worked for more than a decade was willing to train her, and she was able to pay for an online teacher-credential program offered through CalStateTEACH. The program was short and fast, and it allowed her to work while completing it. Her classmates in the program were twenty-eight other Latinas, one white woman, and one African American woman. It took her about a year and half to get her teaching credential. As she explained:

> [Teaching] was the shortest and fastest way to get a job. . . . It was one of the jobs that I didn't need very much because they didn't really require very much. . . . I did my credential online with CalStateTEACH. I had a mentor even though it was online. When I had to do the hours, how do you call that, the internship, I got hired after the first semester. So that was good because otherwise it would have been impossible for me to do the internship by not having any income. . . . I've always been very open to learning so I knew I needed training and the company was willing to train me.

It is less expensive to acquire the credentials to enter the teaching profession than it is to acquire the credentials to enter the professions of medicine or law. Additionally, students from working-class backgrounds incur more debt than those from affluent families because they cannot rely on accumulated wealth and family support. The median amount of debt reported by medical school graduates varies from none at all to more than $350,000 (Jolly 2005). The median debt at graduation for a Latino medical student is just shy of $95,000, compared with $85,000 for a white student and $75,000 for an Asian student (ibid.). And, compared with all medical school graduates of 2012, Asian graduates were less likely to report having education debt (Jolly 2005; Youngclaus and Fresne 2012). Taking on a school loan of more than $100,000 did not seem feasible to these Latinas. Of course, doctors and lawyers are expected to make up that money and be able to pay off their loans after securing employment, but the Latina teachers in this book were less sanguine about being able to pay off student loans quickly. The daunting prospect of such debts, combined with the greater flexibility of teaching, which allowed Latinas like Mrs. Gutierrez to help their families while simultaneously navigating their work/school schedules, contributed to their choice of teaching as a career.

Financing Their Education and Training

Exerting what I call *collectively informed agency*, Latina teachers were savvy about finding financial support, seeking part-time jobs, or accessing programs that would help them pay for their schooling. While agency is usually defined as the property of individuals, I define it as collectively informed rather than exclusively individual to help us understand how Latinas are both self-propelled and channeled into teaching. William Sewell (1992: 21) remarks that "the agency exercised by individual persons depends profoundly on their positions in collective organizations." If we replace the word *positions* with *obligations* in this phrase, we then have a very accurate understanding of Latina pathways into the teaching profession as Latinas sought loans, scholarships, financial aid, and, often, part-time jobs to finish college and help their families. More than half worked while in college. They worked at indoor swap-meets, shopping malls, offices, and chain stores, and as tutors. As Mrs. Quiroz explained, "Luckily I was able to obtain a lot of financial aid, but then I had to pay for my books and things like that. I just did part-time jobs, just to do that." After obtaining their college degrees, Latina teachers also found financial support for their credential programs. Some were also linked with disadvantaged school districts that offered enticing financial-aid programs to pay college costs for graduates willing to work in those districts for a certain number of years.

Latina teachers also defrayed expenses by attending colleges that were in close proximity to their homes and workplaces. All of the interviewees in this study attended colleges located minutes from their homes. They all attended college in California; eighteen graduated from the CSU system. Among the most affordable higher-education systems in the nation, CSU is also the biggest producer of California teachers. As Ms. Maciel said of her collegiate experience at CSU Los Angeles: "It worked out perfectly that it was really close. I wasn't even driving . . . [laughs]. I would take the bus, and it was just—it was just very convenient." Some Latina teachers explained that they were admitted to other colleges for which they would have had to move away, but they opted for CSU because they were attempting to save money and limit reliance on loans. This finding resonates with Zarate and Pachon's (2006) study, which indicates that Latino working-class families hesitate to take out educational loans and to incur vast debt. Affordability and proximity to home were important considerations in choosing a college and course of study. As Ms. Dávila, a third-generation multiracial Latina/white teacher, recalled:

> It was really close to work. . . . It was just kind of on the way home and you just go from work, you stop at school, you go there for a couple of hours, and you head home and it was affordable. I could pay for it without having to take out a loan and a lot of other teachers [at the school] had done their credentials there, so they were familiar, and I knew that I could call them if I needed help with anything, and that was it, basically just convenience and price.

As Lortie (2002: 48) claims, state colleges that specialize in teacher training can become "more than an institution of socialization—[these institutions] also recruit [sic]. One finds a kind of 'entrapment' as such colleges draw in students of limited opportunity whose initial interest in teaching is low." This limited opportunity is especially significant for working-class Latina teachers because, in addition to the financial constraints they faced, Latina teachers were also eager to avoid college loans and to find occupations in which they could succeed, rather than be overtly rejected because of race, class origins, or lack of elite connections.

Although Latina teachers did not cite giving back to the Latino community as a motivation for entering the profession, upon setting foot in their own classrooms, and as they worked in a teacher capacity once in the occupation, their observations of the needs of Latino families in schools sparked a desire to serve them. As they gained experience within teaching, they became what I will call "cultural guardians," acquiring an enthusiasm for teaching that approached a sense of social responsibility to teach.

Conclusions

Few studies have looked at the dynamics of occupational segregation among college-educated Latinas, some of whom have made inroads into gendered professional niches. Previous explanations for Latina pathways into the teaching profession have focused on racial–ethnic community empowerment, gender ideals, and family socialization. Those are important factors, but the interviews with Latina teachers underscore the importance of *class ceilings*—working-class constraints, as reflected through the family, Latina/o ethnicity, gender, and regional demographic change—in shaping occupational outcomes. This book shows that these Latina college graduates were channeled into teaching by social structural forces of racial, class, and gender inequalities. These forces were acutely felt in their families and universities, both constraining their choices and enabling their pathways into the teaching profession. Many of them were the first in their families to graduate from college, and they also expressed strong obligations to help their families financially. For this reason, I suggest that the notion of class ceilings helps us understand how Latina college graduates navigate their educational and career choices with collectively informed agency and filial obligations to family members.

As we saw from their stories, family is important for these Latina teachers, but only a few reported that their parents had steered them in the direction of teaching. Their immigrant parents had exhorted them to study and stake out a profession, but they chose teaching because it would enable them to begin earning post-graduate income in order to help their families financially. Nearly all of these Latina teachers came from working-class immigrant families with precarious finances, and they wanted to help relieve this stress on their families. These dutiful working-class daughters were eager to find a profession that would provide them with a steady income. Unlike careers in medicine and law, teaching offered them the ability to give back financially during college, and to give more soon after graduation.

These Latinas were also drawn to teaching because it seemed feasible both to afford the training and to succeed in the competition for seats in professional school and for later employment. As working-class students, they knew there would be no family safety net to support their higher education. They often combined different strategies of self-funding, such as attending community colleges and state colleges near home, working part-time while studying, and living at home while in college. Unlike the longer and more onerous pathways to becoming a doctor, dentist, lawyer, business executive, or professor, the road to teaching seemed short and accessible, and the profession was open to all who completed the basic requirements. Attending a CSU might not gain them admission to a competitive professional school, but it provided a nearly seamless feeder into teaching. College-educated Latinas also had the sense that, in teaching, potential employers would not undervalue their collegiate educations, institutions, or credentials, and overt racism would be less of a factor in their gaining employment.

Finally, strong Latina/Chicana familial ties with aunts, sisters, and female cousins, embedded in neighborhoods, pulled these Latina college graduates into teaching. Strikingly, it was not friends but family members and relatives who told them about openings for teaching positions. With a growing proportion of school staff constituted by Latinas working in jobs as yard duty supervisors, lunch ladies, teacher aides, and secretaries, these young Latinas were drawn into the teaching jobs, many of them into schools that they themselves had attended as children. Because schools are a locus of blue-collar entry-level jobs that employ people without much formal education, less-educated Latinas/os in these jobs can pave the way for college-educated Latinas in their family or social network to become teachers. There is evidence that the same may be true in other industries, such as suburban maintenance gardening (see Ramírez 2009, 2011), a gendered occupational niche for

Mexican immigrant men. Men in these jobs have created jobs and hired newer arrivals, and some have created their own landscaping companies that their U.S.-born children now run. As a result of such processes, there are now a number of occupations to which Latinas/os have laid a special claim.

It is important to note here that the Latina teachers from working-class immigrant families described in this book are exceptional in their levels of educational attainment. Individuals with their level of education are a highly educated numerical minority within their racial/ethnic minority group. Today, only 30 percent of the U.S. population holds a four-year-college degree, and, alarmingly, only 9.6 percent of Latinos attain such a degree (U.S. Census Bureau 2010). Clearly, these Latinas are the success stories in their families and communities. These women followed the rules set out by the promise of meritocracy and the American dream of higher education—that is, the idea that studying, working hard, and graduating from college will lead to a panoply of career choices.

Intersecting relations of class, Latina immigrant ethnicity, gender and place were crucial in channeling them into the teaching profession. As these women gain experience with teaching, they report high job satisfaction, even an enthusiasm for their work that approaches a sense of social responsibility to co-ethnics. They cite their ability to serve Latino families socially and financially as a major motivation for staying in their jobs. But during the social process of securing a career, individual agency and choice were less operative for Latina teachers than were the collectively informed agency that constrained and enabled them toward teaching and the strong social channeling of class constraints, as refracted through gender, ethnicity, and family and contextualized through demographic transformations and structural employment demands.

In the next chapter, I give the reader an insider's view of how Latina teachers become cultural guardians once in their jobs and provide a closer examination of the school districts and communities these Latina teachers serve. As cultural guardians, Latina teachers guard and protect their co-ethnic students but are simultaneously regulated by school rules that pervade their work. As first-generation college students and the few in their social circles to obtain jobs in white-collar fields, Latina teachers were highly aware of the institutional barricades that Latino students and their families face. Although all of the Latina teachers in the pages of this book serve Latino families socially in multiple ways, their experiences once in their respective school districts were vastly different, as we shall see in the next chapter.

3

Cultural Guardians

The Professional Missions of Latina Teachers

I figured out it's not that they [Latino students] don't want to go [to college]. . . . I felt, "Well, if I can't go to medical school, at least I can help someone get there."
—Mrs. Díaz, third-grade teacher

I argue that middle-class Latina teachers, most of them also from working-class origins, adopt the role of *cultural guardians* in their work with low-income co-ethnic students and their families. I use this term to describe upwardly mobile[1] Latina teachers who are in direct daily contact with underprivileged students and who consciously deploy a range of sanctioned and unsanctioned strategies in order to protect and help children they see as sharing their cultural roots.

Latina cultural guardians typically do not come to the teaching profession with a sense of social responsibility to Latino children: They develop it after they begin teaching. Once they enter the profession, Latina teachers explain, they notice the scarcity of professional Latina role models who share the immigrant and Latino ethnic origins of the students they serve. Given their own marginalization over the life course, including negative childhood experiences in school arising from their own social locations, they soon realize how valuable they can be to their working-class Latino students and those students' families. Their social location as the college-educated daughters of Latino families and their experiences of discrimination in school increase their desire to help their own students to succeed. Because of their educational experiences as Latinas, these cultural guardians have valuable background knowledge that they can use to help co-ethnics. Cultural guardianship is not exclusive to Latinas who grew up in working-class homes with immigrant parents: Latinas who grew up in English-speaking or in middle-class families, are multiracial (Mexican and white), or of later generations have also experienced exclusion in spaces that privilege whiteness. Thus, even Latinas who do not speak Spanish exhibit forms of cultural guardianship of Latino students, especially in multiracial environments.

As cultural guardians, Latina teachers address the hostile contexts of reception that Latino immigrant families are exposed to by making educational spaces less antagonistic for their children. On the other hand, Latina teachers are also regulated by the institutions, faculty, and the schools in which they find themselves. Because of the unique structural constraints that Latino children and their families face in schools, Latina teachers often find it necessary to stretch and bend school rules, state and district policies, and other structures of administrative oversight that pervade their work in order to serve as *agents of ethnic mobility*— highly educated minority professionals who guide minorities through bureaucratic institutions—for students and to give back socially by providing more-than-routine service (Moody and Musheno 2003; Dodson 2009) to Latino children to ensure their integration. Latina teachers are cultural guardians, not in the sense that they are traditionalists but in the sense that they draw on carefully selected elements of both American and Latino cultures to help their co-ethnic students and families thrive in what is often a hostile environment.

Within the classroom, Latina teachers protect their students to facilitate their educational incorporation and success via ethnic-based strategies, such as transmission of ethnic capital. Cultural guardians are different from cultural brokers (Vallejo 2012), who use bilingual skills to mediate interactions between immigrant parents and those in positions of authority, in that they draw on Latino immigrants' social origins and human capital and integrate them into their work lives to make educational spaces more welcoming for their lower-status students and their parents. These teachers can also be guardians of their students' extended families and friends. Beyond the classroom, the Latina teachers' role as cultural guardians allows them to attempt to transcend or challenge structural inequalities within the larger community. They may help students incorporate, combat racial/inequality or challenge the racial hierarchy, or resist biased standardized testing that forces them to racialize students, as I will show in later chapters.

The Latina teachers self-identified in various ways, such as Mexican, Guatemalan, Mexican American, or multiracial, as the detailed demographics table in appendix A shows. Notably, Central American teachers and later-generation Latina teachers, as well as the daughters of Mexican immigrants, also exhibited cultural guardianship, noting similarities in elements of Latino cultures, such as the Spanish language, and indicating that the majority of the students they helped were of Mexican origin. Their own generational level in the United States also served to help them understand Latino families' experiences.

Cultural guardianship is not always limited to Latino students. But in multiracial schools, Latina teachers become cultural guardians of co-ethnic students. While Latina teachers maintain that they teach and try to reach all of their students in similar ways, larger patterns of racial inequality and stereotypes applied to students in schools affect their relationships with non-Latino students. In the sections that follow, I explicate the ways in which cultural guardianship arises and works in practice by first drawing on the life experiences of Mrs. Claudette Díaz, a thirty-three-year-old Latina teacher, whose words are quoted in the epigraph that opens this chapter.

Mrs. Díaz, who was briefly introduced in the previous chapter, explains her struggles in navigating the higher echelons of educational institutions as the American-born daughter of immigrants. Although her parents were born in El Salvador and Cuba and had retained their Spanish-language skills, Mrs. Díaz had difficulty expressing herself well in the language. However, her concerns about the educational experiences of Latino students and their families in the United States show that she feels a strong sense of social responsibility that inspires her to help students who share her ethnic and cultural background to succeed academically, and especially to guide them toward lucrative professional careers.

Like Mrs. Díaz, many Latina teachers develop a quotidian capability for guiding their Latino students through the daunting labyrinth of the educational system. They become fierce advocates for their underprivileged Latino students because of the limits they have faced as a result of poverty and other institutional barriers. These experiences affect the way they see their role as teachers: Like Mrs. Díaz, they are determined to prevent other children from being blocked from reaching their full potential.

As cultural guardians, Latina educators adopt many of the functions of "street level bureaucrats" (Maynard-Moody and Musheno 2003) in finding creative ways to meet the needs of the children of Latino immigrants they encounter in their classrooms. While Latina educators are not actually bureaucrats, they are necessarily highly aware of policies, rules, and administrative mandates and regularly make judgment calls about how to work with (or around) the people they encounter in a highly regulated workplace. Moreover, they exercise substantial discretion in selectively choosing to ignore directives or to challenge their supervisors and agencies in order to help needy clients—in this case their students and families—or to punish those they judge to be unworthy of assistance, even while remaining highly aware of and adept at negotiating their way around state policies and school district rules that prohibit certain modes of intervention in students' lives (Lipsky 1980; Maynard-Moody and Musheno 2003; Marrow 2011; Dodson 2009).[2]

Like Mrs. Díaz, the vast majority of these Latina teachers develop a heightened sense of social responsibility to Latino students and their families *after* beginning to work as educators. As discussed in the following paragraphs, this sense of guardianship emerges as a result of direct daily contact with poorer children in the classroom and in their homes, where Latina teachers witness first-hand the dire needs of children and their families.[3] As first-generation college graduates who are among the select few from their communities to obtain white-collar jobs, Latina teachers often personally identify with the experiences of lower-income co-ethnic children and are highly aware of the institutional barriers to academic success, many of them ethnically based, that Latino students and their families face daily. At the same time, Latina cultural guardians rely on their own childhood recollections of bicultural conflicts in schools and gendered expectations within their families to deflect racism and level the playing field for their Latina/o students. As highly educated professional women, one of the ways Latina professionals do this is by addressing intergenerational dynamics and disrupting gendered expectations within Latino families. Thus they rely on both conforming and divergent means to advance their goals as guardians.

Mrs. Díaz's Development of Cultural Guardianship

On a warm Orange County summer night, at an end-of-year pool party thrown by a Latina first-grade teacher for her colleagues, Mrs. Díaz asked me a series of questions, many of which centered on gendered expectations within Latino families and higher education. "Are you married? Do you have a boyfriend?" she asked. "No," I replied. "Why don't you?" she probed further. "My grad program takes a lot of time," I said. "You should come to my class and give my kids a speech about college," she replied. "I always tell them about college, but they probably need to see somebody in the flesh, especially the girls."

We made plans to meet a couple of days later, and Mrs. Díaz drove up in her silver Toyota Prius hybrid to a Starbucks coffee shop in the city of Santa Ana. I offered to buy her a drink, but she turned down my offer and came back with her own coffee cup, ready to share her story.

The youngest of three children, Mrs. Díaz grew up in Chino Hills, a middle-class suburb that shares borders with Los Angeles, Orange, and Riverside counties. With a population of less than 100,000, Chino Hills has been noted as one of the safest cities in the United States by the FBI. While Mrs. Díaz was growing up in the 1980s, however, Chino Hills was almost completely Anglo. Mrs. Díaz saw her eldest brother go off to medical school, but he eventually dropped out. Her older sister subsequently attended St. Mary's College, a private institution in Moraga, California, a small suburban community near San Francisco. Because her father had been a professional in Cuba, Mrs. Díaz and her siblings were expected to obtain a higher education, but her parents did not deliberately cultivate her academic development (Lareau 2003) or instruct her about the rigors of college life, instead pushing her to rely on high school counselors. This was in part because her father had not attended schools in the United States, and her mother, a Salvadoran immigrant, did not speak English. "They talked to me about 'Oh, you need to take your SAT, you need to apply to college,' but they never sat down and looked at colleges with me," Mrs. Díaz said as she sipped from her drink, wiping the froth away from her upper lip with her hand.

In her junior year of high school in the early 1990s, her parents revealed that they did not have any more money to cover her schooling and that she had to select a state school—an immediate "downgrade" in her eyes. Although she had excelled in high school, her parents were not fully aware of scholarships and were reluctant to co-sign for a student loan. Despondent, Mrs. Díaz said, "I felt cheated. . . . My high school counselor told me, 'You should just go to community college.' Even though I was a 4.2 GPA, Honors, Advanced Placement, to go to a community college. Absolutely no ambition for me whatsoever, and I couldn't understand why."

This lack of support followed her to Cal State L.A., where her professors did not encourage her ambitions. She transferred to Cal Poly Pomona, which she thought would be a better environment for her and where she expected to get more help with her studies. While she was initially doing very well at Cal Poly, her new professors similarly told her that her grades were not good enough for medical school, and that she would never be a doctor. "A lot of doors closed on me and I got frustrated," she explained. Increasingly discouraged by the lack of support, she eventually decided to switch her major. "The professors did not want to help me. They would get frustrated at the fact that I would come to their office [during office hours] and ask them questions. Not all of them, but more than enough, especially in science courses." She had a very difficult time passing her required general education chemistry and physics courses: "It gets to the point where you can't have too many B's and you can't have C's in that kind of stuff for med school. At least that was the message I was getting. I didn't know any better because I don't know any doctors. . . . It just became a task I didn't think I could handle."

Mrs. Díaz's experiences in the U.S. educational system underscore the weight of culture, class, and institutionalized discrimination in Latino students' educational lives. As a woman of color with limited financial resources, she experienced sociostructural disadvantage early on— whether intentional or unintentional—at the hands of many individuals whom she came across at various institutional levels and in a curriculum for which her high school courses had left her woefully underprepared. Disappointed and frustrated, she elaborated:

I felt like, why is it so difficult for me to get information on how to be a better student? Why aren't people willing to help me? I would go to tutoring sessions and office hours but it was a chore to get help for myself. My parents are both college-educated but they didn't know how to show me the way to go about college.[4] They didn't tell me what courses to take, how I needed to be successful, how long it should take going to grad school. It felt like I had a serious disadvantage. I was smart, driven, there were obstacles but I just thought, "Why couldn't I be like my friends from high school who went to Berkeley and UCLA, who went four years and then they were done?"

Despite Mrs. Díaz's impressive drive to succeed in college, and even though she took many proactive measures to "make it" in her intended field of study, she ultimately decided to give up her plans of becoming a doctor. Thus, as described in chapter 2, her subsequent decision to pursue a career in education was, if not accidental, at least initially a compromise. However, after she became a teacher, Mrs. Díaz's desire to help Latino children, and especially girls, to succeed quickly developed into a professional and personal mission:

If I have it this hard and I came from a middle-class family, imagine what these [Latino] kids, what obstacles they are going to face. *Who the hell is going to point them in the right direction?* . . . I saw that they were bright, but there were issues with language, there were issues with what I felt was institutionalized racism in the schools. No one is helping these kids. Who is talking to them about college? If their parents are like my brown mother, who doesn't speak English, how are they going to get there? It takes a lot of resources to be a doctor. A lot of kids will say "I want to be a doctor." *I* said that, for crying out loud. But did I have the right tools to get there? No, I didn't, and I considered myself pretty affluent. I saw them [Latino students] on a daily basis, and they would ask me about college, and I really enjoyed talking to them about it and thinking "God, I hope you really make it."

Many Latina teachers similarly describe entering teaching as a serendipitous fluke of fate, and it is once in the profession that many of them develop their occupational identities as cultural guardians. Having suffered from a lack of guidance themselves, both in K–12 and in higher-educational contexts, these teachers are deeply motivated to provide extra support to their working-class Latino students.[5] But how do they do this? And what does it look like when they do it in non-institutionalized ways?

In the paragraphs that follow I examine how other Latina teachers, informed by their childhood recollections, develop a passionate devotion to the educational futures of their co-ethnic students, a commitment that drives them to provide Latino youth with "more-than-routine" service as teachers. I argue that these cultural guardians should not be understood as traditionalists; instead, they choose with care which elements of American and Latino cultures to use in promoting the well-being and socioeconomic mobility of their Latino students and their families. They thus draw upon and selectively deploy a range of cultural goods for the benefit of co-ethnic students.

Marginalization over the Life Course: Childhood Recollections

Various scholars have documented the obstacles to learning that children of Latino immigrants to the United States face in a new land (Taningco et al. 2008; Gándara 2006; Suárez-Orozco et al. 2008; Ochoa 2007). For example, in *Learning from Latino Teachers*, sociologist and Chicano/Latino studies scholar Gilda Ochoa (2007) unravels the unequal schooling experiences for Latina/o teachers in Los Angeles schools. Many of these teachers, who came from working-class and immigrant families, were tracked into inferior schools, were pulled out of the class, segregated from their peers to receive additional instruction in English as a second-language strategy, and were encouraged to enter vocational tracks that did not require a college education. Similar school experiences left lasting psychological scars on the Latina teachers examined here as well, but they drew on their own struggles for the motivation and knowledge they needed to provide nontraditional support and assistance to co-ethnic children. Many of the Latina teachers mentioned that their siblings and cousins, especially the men, had not fared well in school. In one way, the context for these women changed over time: In the early 1960s, men were more likely to obtain a higher education (Gándara 1995), and since then that trend has changed (López 2002). As some of the few Latinas to overcome these institutionalized blockades, they picked up a number of ways to help a new generation of students.

Much like Mrs. Díaz, many Latina teachers recount their own negative schooling experiences. These experiences ran from the moment they stepped into the kindergarten classroom at the tender age of five all the way to college and, for many, motivated them to "stay in teaching" and help Latino families. They recount vivid examples of their own hardships in schools as the daughters of immigrant and/or working-class parents and are adamant that they do not want their own Latino students and their families to encounter the same obstacles. As Mrs. Estrada, a self-identified Mexican American teacher who attended elementary school in the 1980s, explains:

> In kindergarten the teacher only spoke English, and I was just [thrown] to the side. I remember she asked, "Do you want to replace your folder?" I'm seeing everyone else say "yes" and I'm like, "no." She said, "Okay! Well then go sit down!" I ask my cousin, because she was in the same class with me, "*Qué dijo*?" [what did she say?] and she said, "You were supposed to say 'yes.'" So I get up in the middle of class, I think [the teacher] was reading a book, and I say, "Yes." She's like, "Nope, time's up." I think the teacher thought, "She is not going to succeed, amount to anything. She's Latina. She's going to be doing this, doing that." I see, now, teachers thinking, "Oh, these kids are not going to succeed," and they just throw you to the side; kind of given to the aide. I was just always lost.

Mrs. Estrada's parents were Mexican immigrants of working-class origins, and she explained that she was always lost in class because she could not comprehend her monolingual English-speaking teacher's directives. Mrs. Estrada also vividly recalls "peeing" herself in elementary school because she did not know how to ask her teacher to be excused to go to the restroom. Having attended schools in Fullerton, California, located in northern Orange County, she discussed seeing similar treatment of Latino children by some of her monolingual English-speaking colleagues. These experiences allow Latina teachers to develop an affinity for the plight of Latino children and families in schools.

Mrs. Carla Quiroz, the daughter of Central American immigrants from Guatemala, also elaborated on the struggles she experienced in school over her Spanish-speaking abilities. Spanish was the primary language spoken with her Guatemalan immigrant parents at home; she was

enrolled in a bilingual public school before they moved her into a parochial school that was English-only in the 1980s. She said, "I was a student
who spoke two languages. At times I struggled a little bit with developing English, so I thought definitely, learning how to teach [Latino] kids
that do struggle with the language. [I wanted to be] in a place where I
would be working with kids with that status." Mrs. Quiroz explained
that her own struggles would give her "a better basis" for gauging how
to help children learn another language. Mrs. Godínez, a self-identified
Mexican teacher, noted that she thought her struggles with language
throughout elementary school in the late 1970s and early 1980s had set
her back. In comparison, her fraternal twin sister, Mrs. Ybarra, caught
on to the English language much faster, leaving Mrs. Godínez to feel insecure and inferior in school. Her difficulty in overcoming the language
barrier, however, also gave Mrs. Godínez the notion that it would help
her become a better guide for Latino families with whom she shared immigrant origins. "I was always behind. . . . I knew how it was to not know
the language. I felt that I could be of some help through my experience.
Or that my experience could help me be a better teacher and help them."
Not only did she provide more aid to her Latino students, but she also
helped parents obtain services to have their precarious undocumented
immigrant status adjusted (Marrow 2009)—a particularly powerful
example of the more-than-routine service offered by Latina cultural
guardians that I will discuss in greater detail later in this chapter.

The experience of being considered limited in English proficiency
and stigmatized for their Latino heritage did not come to an end once
Latina teachers learned the English language and transitioned into middle
or high school. Rather, these women described feeling marginalized
by educational personnel such as academic counselors—at times also
of Latino origin—when seeking opportunities to continue their education (see López 2002; Valenzuela 2005).[6] Mrs. Martha Romero, a self-
identified Mexican American teacher, explained that she wanted to help
Latino youth in high school because that had been where she had felt
most excluded and in need of support and guidance. When Mrs. Romero
was attending school in the early 1990s, few Latinas in her age group
were going to college, and Latinos in education did not generally believe
they should push students, especially women, toward higher education
at the time (Gándara 1995). This pattern is changing: The Pew Research

Center reports that, among recent high school graduates, Latino college enrollment rates surpass those of whites (López and Fry 2013), and Latinas now represent a sizeable proportion of college attendees and graduates (López 2002). Working as an elementary school substitute teacher made Mrs. Romero realize that the negative consequences of inadequate academic and emotional support began to affect children during the early years, and that younger Latino students needed her to be a conduit of information as well. She said,

> I wanted to reach Chicano/Latino youth in high school because I thought that I was never reached. Nobody ever came up to me and was like, "What are you going to do with your life? What was your SAT score?" Nobody ever, *ever*! I think maybe I met with my counselor once or twice to try to get out of P.E. or change classes, but nobody ever came up to me and was interested in what I was going to do. And they were Latinos! My goal was to [affect] the youth in high school. Then, like I said, I sort of kind of started subbing [in elementary school], and I liked it, and so then I thought that this was a good way to [affect] Latino youth too.

Mrs. Romero indicates that she wants to be a source of motivation for Latino youth and assure them that somebody believes in them because, in her view, the only people who pushed her were her parents, especially her recently deceased Mexican immigrant father. Because she was rarely reached out to in school, Mrs. Romero began substitute teaching in order to pass on kernels of knowledge about schooling and the educational pipeline that she had gleaned along the way. This initial foray into the teaching occupation allowed her to see that she could carry out her socially responsible mission with Latino children.

Other Latina educators recounted similar experiences. Now that they were on the other side of the fence, their rage at the "comments that were made" and the "mistreatment and misunderstandings that a lot of teachers have about the Latino community" served as motivation for them to work collectively and provide aid to co-ethnic children. Mrs. Robles, a fourth-generation Mexican American teacher, grew up in a middle-class home. But, despite having grown up middle-class and having college-educated parents, she still suffered the effects of racial discrimination in college and felt that her parents, although educated, did not concertedly cultivate (Lareau 2003) or help her learn how to navigate U.S. educational institutions. Others, such as Mrs. Becerra, a teacher born in Mexico, explained that "As a teacher, you don't want your students to go through hurt or struggles, so you do what you can" because, she said, she was often mocked at school by U.S.-born Latinos for her accent. Such negative experiences in schools also prompt teachers to want to continue working for racial or ethnic minority schools. Many of them were adamant that they did not want to work in more affluent districts because they did not have "anything in common" with the students who attend those schools or with their parents; rather, they wanted to work in schools where their services were needed and places where they could help more.[7] These teachers are passionate about filling in, through their individual work, many of the gaps in the educational structure for the children at those schools.

Latina Teachers as Agents of Ethnic Mobility

Sociologist W. E. B. Du Bois proclaimed, "The Talented Tenth of the Negro race must be made leaders of thought and missionaries of culture among their people. No others can do this work. . . . The Negro race, like all other races, is going to be saved by its exceptional men" (Du Bois 1903).[8] Thus, Du Bois argued, Blacks should be missionaries in the promotion of racial uplift for poorer co-racials. I argue that college-educated Latina educators took their unfortunate schooling experiences and made themselves into knowledgeable experts and conduits of information that could help Latino children and their families navigate the U.S. educational system. One of the ways they did so was by overseeing children and families through the educational institution via ethnic-based strategies. This does not mean that these schoolteachers are merely providing students with inspirational messages; rather, they are trying to change the structure of education by going above and beyond their professional duties to establish programs in their schools to provide supplemental educational resources to Latino children. These Latinas explained that they stayed in the teaching profession because they felt that they could connect with Latino families and wanted to "help the community" and "help Latino kids." As Vallejo and Lee (2009) show, many professional Latinas/os from working-class backgrounds who join the middle class "give back" monetarily and socially to their parents and extended kin. Middle-class Latinas/os give back socially to their own families by driving their parents to medical appointments, translating, or filling out important documents for them. With Latino families within their reach in schools, Latina teachers spread their mission of giving back socially to extended kin and develop it into a collective eagerness and enthusiasm to uplift the Latino community, especially within the school-workplace. As upwardly mobile Latinas with working-class roots, they share the same class trajectory as other Latinas/os—from working class to middle class. This shared life course explains the obligation they feel to give back to Latino students and families through the development of a cultural guardianship by providing social support and, in some instances, financial support to Latino families in their schools. They often do so by overextending themselves, providing services that are not a formal part of their job description, such as filling out immigration forms or helping people prepare for their naturalization tests (Flores 2011a). Their teaching services go beyond what is required of them by schools and their jobs because they themselves experienced social exclusion and want to shield Latino students from similar experiences.

For instance, Ms. Erica Maciel, a first-grade teacher, was born in Rosemead in the early 1970s and was the daughter of Mexican immigrants. Her father had worked in a warehouse and her mother was a homemaker. She arrived on campus at 6:00 a.m. every day and stayed until about 6:00 p.m., explaining that she felt she had a social responsibility to help her Latino students. When prompted about this, she said, through tears,

> Because—why am I getting like this [referring to her tears] I think because growing up, we didn't have that. And as an adult, I experience it now, and I can appreciate that, but growing up, there was nothing like that. Some of these kids, they don't even go anywhere. They just stay home. Some of these kids, dad works at the car wash, they live in apartments where you spend $600 on rent and they're all—there's ten people living in a one-bedroom apartment. They're not gonna get that chance. They're not gonna get that opportunity to see things or do things that are different. That's why you do what you do, because you want them to get those experiences.

Ms. Maciel reflected on the poverty of the children as part of doing her job. Many of her Latino students lived in cramped quarters with parents and extended kin, a survival strategy implemented by newer immigrant arrivals who do not have the financial means to provide better housing, let alone supplemental experiences, for their children. Latina teachers gave back socially to school families because they wanted working-class Latino students to have experiences that they otherwise would not—the experiences that they themselves did not have when they were children.

Not only did these schoolteachers give back socially to Latino students so they could get through the system, they also gave back financially in unconventional ways. In their book *Teachers Have It Easy: The Big Sacrifices and Small Salaries of America's Teachers* (2005), Moulthrop and his colleagues argue that the teachers in their study believed teaching was a financially satisfying career if they remained single. Many of the teachers in their study described leaving the job for higher-income occupations or working side jobs to make ends meet. I found that Latina teachers gave back financially to their own families, as previously explained, and to school families that were in a financial crunch. As Mrs. Cadena, a teacher at Goodwill Elementary, explained:

> [I have] kids [that] have never gone to a restaurant, and they'll go to a restaurant with me, or they'll go to a movie with me. . . . I let the parents know, and if they can't meet here at the school, I'll go to their house. They'll do things with me. Not all the time, because I can't afford it, it comes out of my pocket. The parents try and give the kids some money, but I tell them I invited them. I don't want the parents to feel that they have to pay. Because I know they don't get to experience it. They don't get to do it with their family.

Like Mrs. Cadena, other Latina professionals also gave back financially, especially to the children of undocumented parents. Mrs. Madrigal, a 1.5-generation immigrant born in Mexico, would pay students in her class to complete odd jobs in her classroom after school on school grounds. In one instance two fourth-grade Latina students helped her clean up her room, by sweeping the floor. One little Latina child had finished sweeping up the classroom and the other was holding a *recogedor* [dustpan] so she could scoop in the dirt. Mrs. Madrigal explained that the young girls stayed after school to help their teacher clean at the behest of their mother. Mrs. Madrigal would pay them a small monetary fee and drive them home at 6:00 p.m. once their mother returned home from work. Sometimes the sisters would stay in Mrs. Madrigal's home and spend time with her daughter until a legal guardian was able to pick them up. Although Mrs. Madrigal had not been asked to pay the girls, she did so because she said, "*A esa señora ya le llevaron su* husband. *Trabaja mucho y no le sale mucho dinero*" [That mother's husband was deported. She works a lot but doesn't earn much].

Local governance structures, such as school districts, can develop their own policies when a child is not picked up from school at an appropriate time. In some cases, educational personnel call the police if children are left on school grounds after school hours. Mrs. Madrigal took it upon herself to help the family so that they would not face more legal trouble. Because Mrs. Madrigal's husband was a police officer in Compton, she would often use his help to protect undocumented Latino parents from social workers and school police by having him drive the children home if no one was able to retrieve them on time.[9] Mrs. Madrigal's unsanctioned tactics reflect what Lisa Dodson calls the "moral underground"—where middle-class professionals engage in balancing acts in their jobs simply to try to secure the well-being of others because they identify with their plight. Here, Mrs. Madrigal attempts to help a family subject to deportation.[10] Knowing the danger their students' parents were in (and their students too) made Latina teachers overall more frightened to help in Compton. While many white teachers may also identify with their students of color and Latina teachers could also want to help their non-Latino students, the situation is especially racialized for Latina cultural guardians because they or their extended families are of the same or similar communities, and they have lived, shared, and witnessed the issues first-hand. As a result, Latina cultural guardians did these balancing acts frequently.

Poverty was more acute in Compton than it was in Rosemead, but teachers in Rosemead still noticed a structural disparity between their Latino and Asian students. I was with Mrs. Cadena when she treated both Latino and Asian-origin students to lunch. On the walk around the corner to a nearby Burger King restaurant, she emphasized that all of her students "deserved it" but that her Latino students often had parents who could not "afford" to treat their kids on many occasions. Mrs. Cadena and Ms. Sánchez, a self-identified third-generation Mexican American teacher, alternated paying for the students' meals, which they offered at least twice a month. Ms. Maciel, Mrs. Cadena, and Ms. Sánchez were not the only teachers at Rosemead who provided extra support and exposed Latino students to social experiences; rather, this school had a collective mission to help all students in the school and had earned the reputation of a school that went above and beyond for students. Latina teachers at Rosemead, like Mrs. Arenas and Mrs. Franco, would often join forces to engage in massive fundraising efforts so all of their Latino students could attend their field trips. When a Latina mother said she was unable to fund her child's trip because she needed the money to buy diapers for her newborn child, Mrs. Franco had her entire class raise funds for that child's trip. At other times she has covered such costs herself. Education scholar Linn Posey-Maddox (2015) explains that some educational personnel fundraise for activities and items that schools and the educational system should provide all students. Mrs. Franco amazed me by the amount of money she was able to collect: She planned at least six field trips for all of the fourth-graders in her school, more than any other teacher in her district. Often, she solicited outside organizations to help her finance those trips. The students went on educational field trips to locations such as Disneyland via their Disney Youth Education Series; La Purisima Mission State Historic Park in Lompoc, California; and the University of California Los Angeles, Mrs. Franco's alma mater.[11] The cost of each trip was approximately $50 per student.

Some Latina teachers circumvented school-workplace policies about going off campus to provide supplemental experiences. In the United States, teachers are allowed to take students off school grounds only with a permission slip signed by a parental guardian, but not all Latina teachers followed this protocol at all times, especially with children whom they perceived to be lacking in middle-class experiences. Mrs. Becerra, a Mexican teacher in Compton, indicated during her interview that she would often take children who had accumulated a certain number of points in her class to her new home in Orange County, which had a backyard pool, for a visit that spanned the weekend. Although her daily commute to Compton was roughly one hour, Mrs. Becerra would take children in her own vehicle to her house every week so that the "kids could see other things." Most Latino children in Compton had never seen a swimming pool. She also had a unique relationship with Latino immigrant parents, often displaying elements of *familism* (Segura and Pierce 1993)—the importance of both the nuclear family and extended family members—in her interactions with them. Blood ties were not necessary for Latina teachers to treat Latino immigrant parents as extended family members, as cultural elements bound them together (see Flores 2011a). Mrs. Becerra did not get a school permission slip signed by parents or notify the principal. Instead, she would call parents and ask them to sign a permission slip she had devised. Sometimes she would pick the children up at their houses, taking the parents with her as well because she wanted them to learn to swim, a vital skill in her eyes. These trips reflect the unconventional ways in which Latina teachers give back to poorer co-ethnics.

It is important to note that not all Latina teachers engage in cultural guardianship of co-ethnic children. This difference is largely attributable to school context, generational level in the United States, and holding meritocratic ideals—the notion that all students can pull themselves up by their bootstraps despite structural limitations. While I would venture to say that most Latinas in education are cultural guardians, others who do not subscribe to this mission expressed resentment that nobody guided them through the lower or higher rungs of the educational hierarchy—neither their parents nor educational personnel—and thought that this new generation of Latino students should struggle in the same ways that they did. For example, in a previous study I conducted with twenty Latina teachers in the Santa Ana Unified School District, a district in which most teachers are Latina or white, I found that only one Latina teacher, who was fourth-generation Mexican, expressed anti-immigrant sentiments. She said she would call Immigrant Customs Enforcement (ICE) herself if she thought she knew of a violation of the law. Sociologist Gilda Ochoa (2004) and political scientist Lisa García Bedolla (1999) also explain that in communities where there are both newcomer- and later-generation Mexican immigrants, there are severe rifts over language use and fears of not being allowed to incorporate fully into the United States. Among the Latina teachers included in this comparative study, only one teacher, Ms. Tiscareño, the U.S.-born daughter of Mexican immigrants, indicated that she had reduced her efforts to help students. She said, "To be honest I used to do a lot more [in] my community, but like I said I focus more now on my parents. . . . because they have run across racism and stuff like that." In this case, Ms. Tiscareño was focusing more on protecting her aging parents from discrimination in public arenas than on protecting her students. And while she did speak to parents in Spanish and act as a cultural guardian in other arenas, she also suggested that Latino immigrant families had "no excuse" not to succeed, because she had done so despite coming from similar circumstances. But, by and large, Latina teachers who worked in multiethnic communities did provide extra care to Latino co-ethnics.

Spanish-Language Strains

While some studies have found that upwardly mobile Latinos are sanctioned for speaking Spanish in the work world (Vallejo 2012; Chávez 2011), others have found that second-generation Latino young adults make adept use of their bilingual and bicultural skills to take advantage of unique "strategic holes" that nobody else can fill (Marrow 2011: 19) in jobs available in new immigrant gateways. For instance, Morando and Hernández-León (2013) find that second-generation Latinos in Dalton, Georgia, have found an occupational niche in carpet manufacturing, where, they say, speaking Spanish is an asset. López-Sanders (2009) has coined the term *embedded brokers* for bilingual co-ethnics who are charged both with mediating relations between employers and workers and with using their authority to socialize employees into serving the aims and accepting the norms of the companies they work for.

But there is a paradox regarding language in American educational institutions (Alba 2005). We encourage white native-born Americans to learn another language, but we see it as a deficit for immigrant children that are imagined as lower class to maintain fluency in their native tongues.[12] Unlike previous scholarship, which notes that Latinos were admonished for speaking Spanish in school (Ochoa 2007), I found that the Latina teachers here vehemently encouraged Latino students to retain their native languages. These teachers did not perceive the home language as a hindrance to children's success but rather as an asset, especially if children were already literate or had conversational Spanish skills. Many of the Latina teachers at Rosemead espouse the belief that the transition to English would be much easier if children became literate in Spanish first (Hakuta 1993). They encouraged students to hold on to that language and even told parents to help their students at home. Of course the comment I heard often was, *"El español en la casa, pero que no se les olvide"* [Spanish in the home, but make sure you don't forget it] because of state requirements.[13] It was much easier for Latina teachers to encourage students to keep their native languages at Goodwill Elementary in Rosemead, because multiple languages were spoken at this school daily. Often, just by sitting in the front office while doing observations, I would hear conversations begin with, *"Hola"* [Hello in Spanish], *"Nin hao"* [Hello in Mandarin Chinese], *"Xin chào"* [Hello in Vietnamese], and sometimes *"Konnichiwa"* [Hello in Japanese].

This was a drastic change from what Ms. Maciel's parents had told her about speaking Spanish when she was in elementary school. She said, "My mom tells me stories that—like, when I would speak Spanish, they wouldn't admonish me, but they would say, 'You need to talk English.' She remembers it. I like it when they [the children] speak a different language. It doesn't bother me. It's better if they keep it." Latina teachers in Rosemead also encouraged Asian students to retain their native languages and ethnic cultures. Because most of the teachers at Goodwill Elementary shared immigrant origins, they did not admonish students for speaking another language. Mrs. Arenas added, "[I teach my students] to appreciate one another for who we are and where we come from and all other cultures. It is your responsibility to teach the kids that all cultures are great. None of this ethnocentricity where mine is better than yours. I try to teach the Asian kids that. I'm proud of my Latino culture but you be proud of yours. I tell them I wish I could speak Chinese." Although Latina teachers in Compton also encourage students to retain their languages, there were rifts regarding foreign-language maintenance in this school, stemming from the belief on the part of some that Latino immigrant children were better served by learning English than by retaining Spanish, because English was deemed necessary to succeed within the context of the United States. Larger power structures, such as the various rules and programs implemented in these schools, shape the strategies and practices that teachers can use to help their students. They also determine the lengths to which teachers must go in order to reach underprivileged children. Latina teachers could not be as open in this context about native-language use. At times, they were admonished for using Spanish to communicate with children. Mrs. Madrigal noted, "The state doesn't want us to teach bilingual education . . . . They say don't talk Spanish. I talk Spanish. [The] principal, she addressed me one time because I was talking to the [students] in Spanish. This principal that left, he talks Spanish and he understands that 'Hey, you need to be bilingual.'" I would often see Mrs. Madrigal's own children on campus. They understood Spanish but rarely spoke the language. When I asked her about this, she said that she did not want her children to assimilate into white America but thought that they needed to learn how to learn to be proficient in English so they would not go through some of the hardships she and her parents had.

Many Latina teachers explained that both Caucasian and African American teachers insisted that this was not Mexico and parents, as well as children, needed to be forcibly assimilated into the English language. For instance, a Caucasian teacher who taught the same grade level as Mrs. Madrigal was overheard by Latina teachers saying, "If you're going to come to America, you have to learn the language. If I ever moved to another country, the first thing I would do is learn the language." These sentiments were also echoed by African American teachers, both men and women, whom Mrs. Godínez overheard saying, "*Dicen que están en los Estados Unidos y que tienen que hablar el inglés*" [They say we are in the United States and we need to speak English]. There were a handful of African American and Caucasian teachers who were more empathetic to Latino students and families who had not quite yet grasped the language, often going out of their way to try to translate documents themselves. For example, Mrs. Prim, an African American woman teacher, would spend extra hours after school to enter text in English into Google Translate to translate into Spanish forms to be sent home. And, Mr. Gordon, an esteemed white male teacher who could not articulate himself well in the Spanish language, would rely on his first-grade students to triangulate a conversation between himself and immigrant parents in a graceful and respectful manner.

Mrs. Quiroz noted the difficulties of navigating Spanish use in her job because Goodwill Elementary School did not have a formal bilingual program. She used Spanish anyway because she recognized how her Spanish fluency had benefited her: She had had a little bit more support as a result of her parents' ability to help her more with the transition from Spanish to English because Spanish was allowed in her public school when she was younger. "It is much more of a challenge for the students that I have now because I can't teach them in Spanish. I've had students that don't speak any English and that come to my class with only some education in their home language. I do try to speak a little bit outside of the classroom with them, just at least to give them some directions in Spanish, but I know that bilingual education doesn't exist, so I realize that I did kind of have it easier growing up." Rules and policies concerning foreign language use in schools directly affected Latina teachers' role as cultural guardians. Maria Chávez explains that "for first generation Latino professionals, the Latino culture is critical for survival and success and is the foundation and motivation for all that they do" (Chávez 2011: 34). While most Latina teachers urged parents to encourage native-language use, they were also heavily monitored by their institutions, which urged them to transition children into the dominant language. Studies have shown that students who speak two languages rather than just one, or whose culture is infused into the learning experience, perform better on certain academic and cognitive-based tasks, and grow up healthier because they have a positive self-concept (Portes and Rumbaut 2001).

Agents of Tradition and Change: Student-Gendered Transitions

Latina teachers note that they are better equipped to understand Latina/o family dynamics because they experienced similar, often gendered constraints in their own households (López 2002; Smith 2006). Through their roles as teachers who interact with Latina/o students, they complicate the messages those students receive at home from their immigrant parents who are not yet aware of the opportunities available to their children. These daughters and granddaughters of Latino immigrants took what they experienced in their own Latino families and worked as cultural guardians of their tradition—and as agents of change in the case of gender—but these processes were slightly different for their Latino boys and girls. I argue that Latina teachers are cultural guardians—not in the sense of being traditionalists but rather in that they choose elements of both American and Latino cultures to use to care for their co-ethnic students and families. They manage gendered cultural items for the benefit of their students. Teachers worked as cultural guardians to show Latina students that other options and pathways were available to them. They also attempted to address stereotypes of the Latino population and encouraged Latino boys and girls not to fall into those paths. Latina teachers saw themselves as role models for Latina/o youth and attempted to steer Latina/o students away from downward trajectories. Personal knowledge of the dynamics of Latino families, in most cases without harboring negative judgments of those dynamics, allowed Latina teachers to better connect with their students and parents.

Latinas in the teaching profession attempted to rupture the kinds of gendered practices that they experienced in their families while they were growing up with their students. It was not always easy to do so, as a hidden racialized gender curriculum ran rampant throughout their schools (López 2002). For example, although a Latino teacher in Compton, Mr. Durán, had good intentions in teaching his students about money, his lesson plan was filled with gendered images. As I conducted observations in his class, he posed the harmless-enough question: "To get a PlayStation, what must you do?" The kids were silent. He gave them a hint. "Work!" he said. The children started responding, and Perla, a young Latina, said, "You can sell things." Then he prompted, "What kind of work can you do? I know girls can do one thing." "Cook?" Pedro, a Latino boy, shouted out. Perla condescendingly sneered at him. "Clean the house," yelled out Maria. Then the teacher asked, "What can a boy do?" He waited and then answered his own question with, "Fix lawns, do people's lawns." Jesus responded, "Pull out weeds." "What else can girls do?" the teacher asked. "Girls can baby-sit. They can baby-sit nephews, cousins," answered Pablo. Keisha, an African American girl in the class, said, "You can sell lemonade."

After the incident referenced earlier between the two Latina children who were helping Mrs. Madrigal clean her room, Mr. Durán walked into the classroom and jokingly said, "*Miren que bonitas. Al rato les voy a traer un burro y una plancha*" [Look how cute. Later I'm going to bring you an ironing board and an iron]. Mrs. Madrigal quickly interjected, "Don't listen to him, girls. This will not be your future job."

In another example, as she walked her students to recess, one of Mrs. Arenas's former students came to visit her in her classroom. He appeared to be of middle-school age and was carrying an infant. Mrs. Arenas said, "That better not be your kid. You are too young for that. You need to finish school first." The young boy laughed and said, "No, Mrs. Arenas, this is my baby brother." "Oh, okay. I'm glad you are on the right path," she replied. In these ways, Latina teachers attempted to chip away at gendered, racist images of Latino boys and girls. They tried to counter what they perceived to be limiting expectations within Latino culture, often using themselves as examples of other paths available to boys and girls. As Mrs. Díaz said,

> Girls have a fantasy of what their life will be, projected ten years out, which is married with children. It's an expectation in our culture. I just want them to know, if you want that, great, but there are alternatives. You don't have to get married, you don't have to have children, or you don't have to do it right away. I just share that with them because they always ask me, "You don't have kids?" I'm like, "No." And their moms go, "But you are married." I go "Uh-huh! You can be married without children. It is possible . . . ." They say "Why?" And I just say, "Well, it's not time," or "I wanted to finish college first." . . . I like to promote that as much as I can. I'm not saying someone can't be with family and married and still go to college, but it is that much harder.

Mrs. Romero echoed these sentiments, saying, "I don't want them to see themselves as just getting married and having kids. I want them to be able to see that they can be and do anything else. Anything that men can be."

And about girls, Mrs. Arenas said,

> This is a different era. The girls are not quiet anymore. When I was little I was the one that would have to get up in the morning and make *tortillas* for the family and make sure the kids were off to school. And I couldn't do this and I couldn't do that because I was the oldest girl so I couldn't do things that my brother could do because I was a girl. . . . I think it has changed and these generations now, because most of the girls they want to be doctors, they want to be lawyers, they want to be teachers and they

have goals and we are role models for them. . . . I'm a Latina and they see that I am a teacher.

Thus, Latina teachers advocate for higher education of their girl students based on the gender inequalities they were exposed to as young women in their families. It is important to note that these gender inequalities, however, are not static and are influenced by region. For instance, immigration and sexualities scholar Gloria González-López (2004) notes that Mexican immigrant fathers from urban locales expressed more concern about their daughters' socioeconomic futures and life opportunities than the preservation of their virginity and coins the concept of "regional patriarchies" to explain this phenomenon. In some cases, fathers, particularly those of rural origins, are extremely protective of their daughters' virginity (González-López 2004).[14]

I suggest that here, as elsewhere, "the feminist outlooks and practices articulated by women were not simply by-products of assimilation into U.S. society; they were part and parcel of the lived feminist legacies of strong foremothers, including mothers, grandmothers, and great-grandmothers" (López 2002: 140) who are nonwhite. The reference group for many of the women in López's study and in this book were their Mexican and Central American mothers, whose race-gender experiences in their homes and in the labor market were vastly different from those of Anglo American women.

In her book *Gendered Transitions* (1994), gender and immigration sociologist Pierrette Hondagneu-Sotelo argues that Mexican immigration to the United States can alter gender dynamics between men and women. Migration and settlement among Mexican immigrants to the United States may change long-held ideals and lifestyles. Often, traditional patterns are reassessed, and new egalitarian relationships may emerge. Mexican women, in particular, tend to gain greater personal autonomy and independence as they participate in public life and gain access to both social and economic influence that they did not have in the home country. More important, changes in gender relations result from experiences in the home rather than from a "modernizing" Anglo influence or the acculturation process (Hondagneu-Sotelo 1994). In this case, changes in gendered expectations for Latino boys and girls result from experiences in homes and in the classrooms of college-educated Latinas. These teachers witnessed these transitions and promoted egalitarian relations between their younger Latino boys and girls. Within the context of their workplaces, Latina teachers attempted to expose their Latino students to the wider occupational and educational opportunities available to them through higher education. They would also explicitly unveil nontraditional gendered patterns for their children. Mrs. Rivas explained how she bridged the gap between children's experiences at home and her own goals for them:

> A lot of the mothers, they, if they only have one son they tend to baby them and they tend to give them everything and they tend to raise them up as you're the head of the household even though you are the youngest and you are only six years old. None of your older sisters can tell you what to do. . . . I understand that because I remember that. That's what my mom used to tell me with my brother. "No, he's your brother. You have to listen to him." Now I realize that's not right. I tell the moms, "No, that's not right." I feel because I understand that I can come in and say, "No, you need to get on him just like you did with your daughter and make sure that he understands that there are rules that he has to follow and not just because he is a man that he can get away with it."

Mrs. Díaz also explained how her own upbringing helped her within the classroom context:

> You understand the family dynamic. As a Latina, I understand the upbringing. . . . You understand how males in the family are treated differently than women in the family. I can see it in my students. The boys don't have to do certain things and you are like, "Well, that's old school. You are in the United States and you may marry an American one day and these gender roles are not as defined as they are in Latin cultures." And, we talk about that. "What are their responsibilities?" And they go, "Oh, we don't cook, we don't do laundry." "Oh, but you can!" I take what I knew [in] my family, because we had very defined roles, gender-wise. . . . It's the same thing: The girls do this, the boys do this. And I kind of try to educate them on it. I understand your perspective but here is another

perspective. . . . And, so they are like, "Ohhh." . . . It helps during conferences with parents because you kind of have that upper edge of how their
family works, how the discipline works.

In her study of Caribbean men and women, Nancy López (2002) finds
that whereas men spent most of the time outside of the home playing
sports, women were subjected to stricter social control by their mothers,
served as institutional brokers, and developed a "dual frame of reference"
wherein they compared their experiences to those of their mothers.
Thus, second-generation Caribbean women created their gender identities against the backdrop of their immigrant mothers' experiences and
struggles. Much like these Caribbean women, independence from men
is what college-educated Latina teachers gleaned from their immigrant
families' gendered experiences. "Among women, the intention to delay
marriage and child rearing was always discursively linked to the stig-
matization of their sexuality and importance of acquiring educational
credentials for dismantling those stereotypes" (124).

Latina teachers were polite when addressing these issues with Latino
parents but were also miffed and perturbed when it seemed that those
parents did not heed their advice. Student-gendered transitions were a
daily struggle for Latina teachers as they attempted to promote gender
equity among boys and girls in their homes and in school. Latina teachers at Goodwill Elementary were more successful at addressing this issue
with their Asian students as well because their co-workers would share
the gendered practices they experienced in their Asian immigrant families (see Espiritu 2001, 2003). Although Latina teachers in Compton also
pushed college and higher education on Black boys and girls, they felt
more comfortable addressing Latino family gender dynamics because
they had experienced them directly.

Parents' Reactions to Teachers

The difference between the reactions of Latino immigrant parents to
non-Latina/o teachers is an important aspect of cultural guardianship for
Latinas. Many Spanish-speaking Latino immigrant parents feel shame
when entering English-only educational spaces, and they are relieved
when they encounter a Spanish-speaking or Latina/o teacher. Some

parents clam up when they encounter monolingual English-speaking teachers whom they perceive as not cultural guardians for them. In this section I demonstrate what this looks like at the everyday micro-level.

One warm March day, I arrived for Compton Elementary's open house at around 3:45 in the afternoon. There was much hustle and bustle, with teachers running around trying to get their rooms ready. "Oh, hey," said Mrs. Madrigal as I entered her classroom. Her students, two Latino boys and two girls, were scrambling to put items on the table, sorting everything out. Mrs. Madrigal was sitting at a computer, translating into Spanish a list of twenty items parents had to cross off while participating in her open house event. "OMG, OMG, OMG!" she remarked as she typed as fast as she could.

Latino parents started trickling in. Josefa, a Latina immigrant mother, and Martha, a U.S.-born Latina mother, entered the room. "*Agarren una hoja y lean las instrucciones*" [Grab a sheet and read the instructions], she advised. Mrs. Madrigal explained, "*Decidí darle a todos los padres una tarea para este evento. ¿Quiere las instrucciones en inglés o en español?*" [I decided to give all parents an assignment for this event. Do you want the instructions in English or Spanish?]. "*En español*" [In Spanish], replied Josefa. "*Muy bien, cada mesa tiene un número y en este papel está escrito lo que tiene que hacer. Por ejemplo, en el número uno su niña tiene que escribirme una postal. La muestra está en la mesa. Cuando termine cada objetivo, le tiene que poner una palomita o una estrellita al número para indicar que ya lo hizo. Si tiene mas preguntas, aquí estoy para ayudarle*" [Great! Every table has a number, and on this paper are the directions for each station. For example, for number one, your daughter needs to write me a postcard. The sample is on the table. When you finish each objective, you should put an asterisk next to the number to indicate you finished it. If you have any more questions, I'm here to help you], Mrs. Madrigal said as her voice trailed off. The children gleefully walked their mothers to their desks. The second item read, "Read your child's short story and sign it when you are done." One station was labeled *Centro de Computadoras*/Computer Station, at which the parent had to create an e-mail account and send an electronic message to Mrs. Madrigal. Of course, Latino immigrant parents had some difficulty here. Miguel, a Latino immigrant father, had an e-mail address ready but was unsure of what to write. "*¿Que tengo que hacer aqui, señorita?*" [What do

I have to do here, young lady?], he asked me. I explained, "*En la cajita donde se esribe el mensaje, le puede escribir algo como 'hola maestra Madrigal. Soy el papá de Nancy. Me dió mucho gusto venir a este evento. Es solo un ejemplo*" [You write your message in the little box. You can write something like "Hi, Mrs. Madrigal. I'm Nancy's father. I was overjoyed coming to this event." It's just an example]. "*Ah, gracias, señorita*" [Oh, thank you, young lady], he said. He sat at the computer and began to type his message, looking for the letters on the keyboard.

Most Spanish-speaking Latino immigrant parents were extremely nervous about completing this task. I helped several Latina immigrant mothers open a Yahoo! Mail Internet account because they did not have one. "Mrs. Madrigal, what if parents don't have an e-mail account?" I asked, thinking that maybe they could skip that item if they did not have one. "No, they have to do it. Don't let them get out of here, girl, without them sending me that e-mail!" she remarked. Mrs. Madrigal helped several parents do this as well. Some of them were extremely timid and apprehensive about using the computer or entering their information. I assured them, "*No se preocupe, señora. Todos sus datos son confidenciales. Mi mamá tiene uno también, y ella es de México*" [Don't worry, ma'am. All of your information is confidential. My mother also has one, and she's from Mexico]. "*Ah okay. Esta bien pues*" [It's fine then], remarked a Latina immigrant mother.

To another Latina immigrant parent Mrs. Madrigal said, "*Mire aquí, en esta caja escribe su primer nombre*" [Look here, in this box you write your first name]. She placed the cursor over the box and let the parent input her name. The mothers were very apprehensive as they circled their fingers in the air trying to find the letters. "*Aquí se escribe una clave que nadamás usted va a saber*" [Here you enter a password only you will know]. One mother entered "*pansas*" [stomachs] the nickname she had for her son, and another entered "*Tepechi*," the name of her hometown in Mexico. Their children watched excitedly. "*Ahora, en la cajita, nada más me escribe un mensaje*" [Then, in the box, you just write me a message]. The teacher required only a "*hola*" [hello], but several parents, although it took them a bit to find the letters, wrote extremely appreciative comments to her. Although they wrote them in Spanish, some words were misspelled; it was still possible to decipher the messages, however. There were some capitalization errors, but that was because the parents did not know how to use the Shift key to capitalize. While glancing over their shoulders to make sure they were doing all right, and as I talked to other parents, the parents wrote messages like *"estimada maestra le agradesco todo lo que a hecho por mijo. Espero que saque buenas calificaciones"* [Dear Teacher, I appreciate everything you have done for my boy. I hope he gets good grades].

Another station was titled, "Suggestion Box." Here parents had to give Mrs. Madrigal a comment and place it in this confidential box. At the end of the day I read over the suggestions. Those that came up the most were *"más tarea"* [more homework], *"si se porta mal, me llama por teléfono"* [if he misbehaves, call me on the phone],[15] providing the phone number, and *"Gracias por su evento"* [Thank you for your event].

I ran to the copy machine two or three times to make more copies of the Spanish form. The parents were highly entertained. At the end of the event Mrs. Madrigal had a very good showing; about thirty-five parents had come to her classroom. Most of her students came, and some from the other classrooms came as well. "I think I would do better with one [a checklist form] in English," said one U.S.-born Latina mother.

When an African American mother, Pamela, walked into the room with her daughter, there was a pile of English forms left on the table. She was one of the two African American parents with children enrolled in Mrs. Madrigal's class. She and her daughter did not need any help getting through the instructions. Rather, they took the paper, the mother read the instructions out loud, and she and her daughter completed the list together. "'Find your work on the subject board and place a sticker on your work.' Where are the stickers?" Pamela asked. I found some stickers and gave them to her daughter. "Here you go." They continued with minimal help. When Pamela and her daughter were done, Mrs. Madrigal spoke to the mother and asked her if she knew where the mother of her other African American student was. She was having trouble keeping contact with this mother. "Hey, do you keep in contact with her? It's very important that she come to things like this." "I'll let her know that it's important for her daughter's education," Pamela said.

Among the several classrooms I visited during open house, Mrs. Madrigal's was the only one that had such a massive showing. While Mrs. Best, an African American teacher, had just returned from maternity leave, very few parents were in her room for the open house event.

She was standing outside of her door in front of her classroom waiting for parents to come in. Mr. Gillespie, a white teacher, had two parents in the room. "Aw, nobody is in there. Oh, that makes me so sad," remarked Mrs. Madrigal.

I walked over to see what preparations Mr. Durán, a teacher of Mexican origin, had made for the event. His classroom looked much cleaner than usual, but the floor was still a mess. Mr. Durán said that some of the Latina immigrant mothers had offered to clean the floor for him because it was so dirty. I asked if the custodians ever cleaned the room. He said that they would just take out the trash, but that even if you asked them to clean, they did a very superficial job. I walked with him to get some red licorice out of his car and he said he was going to change in the bathroom. Later, Mrs. Madrigal sent me over to his classroom to give him some pretzels to liven up his classroom.

Rosa, a Latina immigrant, walked into Ms. Beasley's room at around 6:55, when open house was almost over. The mother looked very tired and was wearing a black and purple shirt with the Taco Bell logo emblazoned on it and the little hat. She took off her hat as she walked into the classroom, showing her hair pulled back in a tight bun. "Hi, Ms. Beasley," she said as she walked in. "Oh, hello, how are you doing today?" Ms. Beasley asked her questions about her son, but Rosa, in her broken English, replied "*Ai dono*" [I don't know]. Ms. Beasley instructed Rosa's son to show his mother his work as she stepped out of her class and walked over to Mrs. Madrigal's room. "Wow, you guys just had a party in there. You had so many people in your classroom," she said to Mrs. Madrigal. Mrs. Madrigal left for home at 7:10 in the evening.

The reactions that Spanish-speaking Latino immigrant parents have toward Latina teachers are an important aspect of cultural guardianship. Latino immigrant parents themselves react in different ways to non-Latina/o teachers who do not speak English, forcing Latina teachers to become cultural guardians for them within school grounds.

Conclusions

This chapter shows the ways in which Latina teachers, who come from mostly working-class origins, serve as cultural guardians in the schools.

These educators guard their students' cultural roots and their fragile identities and self-esteem. At the same time, they are regulated by the institutions and the schools in which they work. As sociologist Lisa Dodson (2009) shows, the world of street-level work is fraught with tensions, ambiguity, and difficult choices and judgments. In some cases, teachers must use their street-level skills in their professional lives in order to help the children of Latino immigrants navigate the school system. Their devotion develops once these cultural guardians are established in their new careers as teachers: Seeing the needs of poorer Latino students and families in light of their own experiences, they came to the realization that they could serve as a valuable resource for their lower-income co-ethnic students.

The Latina educators gave vivid examples of their own negative schooling experiences as the children of immigrant and working-class parents and did not want their own Latina/o students and families to endure similar hardships. They focused on countering negative experiences in school, empowering students, especially Latinas, to get through the system. Latina teachers explained that they stayed in the profession because they felt that they could connect with Latino families and wanted to "help the community" and "help Latino kids." They also noticed the scarcity of professional Latina and immigrant role models for Latino students once they started to work in their schools.

Latina educators adopt many of the functions of street-level bureaucrats to subvert a system that disenfranchises working-class, racial/ethnic minority youth, especially Latinos. In myriad daily ways, these cultural guardians exercise the substantial discretion that characterizes the teaching profession to guide Latino children on an often-difficult path through the educational system, even when this requires them to resort to non-institutionalized means like Latino ethnic-based strategies. While, at first glance, it appears that Latina educators give special preference to Latino children, administration and state policies that reward successful "Americanization" have left these students out in the cold. Latina teachers aid their Latino students by using Latino culture, non-institutionalized, and other non-official mechanisms. They work around the rules, or add their own flavor and treatment, by using institutional "loopholes" to help undocumented Latinos (Marrow 2009).

Here we see that Latina teachers are highly aware of state regulations and school policies and break the rules to help poor children whom they perceive as having limited opportunities that the school and the larger society are not seeking to expand. In the next chapter, I show how this process played out in each school.

4

Co-ethnic Cultural Guardianship

Space, Race, and Region

Compton Elementary is a predominantly Latino immigrant school located in the historically Black-majority city of Compton in Los Angeles. Images of south Los Angeles as majority Black persist in southern California and nationwide, led by cultural images from the hip hop group N.W.A. (Niggaz Wit Attitude);[1] John Singleton's 1991 film "Boyz N the Hood"; and the recent film "Straight Outta Compton" (2015). When I asked teachers what they knew about the city of Compton before working there, several began singing Tupac Shakur's single "California Love,"[2] waving their hands in the air in imitation of dance moves historically associated with African American culture. Yet African Americans have been a numerical minority in the area since 2000 as it has Latinized. Other regions in California such as Rosemead in the San Gabriel Valley have also experienced demographic change, influencing the ways in which racial-ethnic minority communities are branded, represented, and racialized in larger society. However, the controlling images[3]— hegemonic racial ideologies that permeate social institutions—in Compton were distinct from those present in Rosemead.

In chapter 3 I described how the dire need for Latina role models at Compton and Goodwill and the structural limitations Latino students faced over the life course prompted Latina teachers to exhibit social responsibility to co-ethnics. In this chapter I explore Latina teachers' approach to Black and Asian students, families, and colleagues. I show that Latinas I spoke with expressed racism toward Blacks and saw opportunities with Asians. Their approach to cultural guardianship and its absence toward Black or Asian students by teachers of any ethnicity also reflects context. I found that the macro-structural racialization forces that have created Latino south Los Angeles affect Latina teachers' perceptions of racial positioning in their places of work. While both Compton and

Goodwill are in greater Los Angeles, the controlling images (Collins 2000) applied to each city—such as the Black underclass or the ethnoburb—drive distinct perceptions of race, immigration status, and region. Research has addressed the role of controlling images in relation to racial/ethnic minority groups and individuals, but not to space. Findings reveal that larger macro-structural forces such as representations of communities affect local racial hierarchies and in turn serve as the impetus for the development of co-ethnic cultural guardianship.

This chapter reveals that *controlling images of space*—racialized images of physical geographic locations—set the tone for the ways in which the individuals who participated in my research interact at work institutions. I make two arguments about these interactions. First, the controlling images that respondents have over these locations seep into educational spaces. Second, prevailing views of America's racial/ethnic hierarchy, which place Latinas/os in the racial middle along with Asians, and between Black and white, oversimplify reality. By relying on the outlooks of middle-class and upwardly mobile Latina teachers, I argue that Latinos hold fluid racial positions in multiracial schools. The position of Latinos in an urban school (Compton Elementary) differed significantly from that of the school in an ethnoburb (Goodwill Elementary). While Latina teachers have achieved intergenerational class mobility, they perceive Latino immigrant parents as below both African Americans and Asians in terms of political power and decision making within the district. Their perception of relative valorization of these groups in the U.S. racial landscape influences these evaluations, as do space and region. Immigrant Latinos' racial position in educational spaces is shaped by racial controlling images applied to each city. This difference influences Latina teachers' approach to cultural guardianship.

How are school district spaces racialized? How do the controlling images of space set the tone for how Latina teachers evaluate racial positioning in multiracial workspaces? And how does this process help explain the absence of guardianship directed toward Blacks or Asians in multiracial environments? As this chapter will demonstrate, Latina teachers perceive immigrant and unauthorized Latinos to be below African Americans and Asians in southern California regional racial hierarchies in terms of relative valorization and political power.[4] I show that controlling images of space enact racialization of educational workspaces in ways that amplify problems of school governance structures. Controlling images of space are a major instrument of power because they have the ability to guide behavior and, when internalized, can profoundly influence perceptions of the marginalized and rearrange local racial formations. This process has a profound effect on the development of Latina co-ethnic cultural guardianship in multiracial organizations and spaces. As historian Josh Sides (2005: 104) notes, "We are extraordinarily sensitive to the consequences of stereotyping people, ethnicities, genders, and races, yet we remain insufficiently skeptical about what we imply when we think we are simply referring to a place."

A brief historical overview of these regions will help contextualize the dynamics of how racial positioning operates and unfolds in majority-minority communities. While Compton and Rosemead are only a few miles apart, historical residential segregation, racial covenants, restrictive immigration policies, and racial discrimination against people of color construct distinct histories and distinct controlling images (Camarillo 1970; Sides 2005; Saito 1997).

Historical Transformations of Compton and Rosemead

Compton

In the 1950s, 45,000 people lived in the suburb of Compton, among them fewer than 50 African Americans and an even smaller Mexican population (Sides 2006). Strict racial covenants and neighborhood residential segregation maintained the racialized boundaries of urban space by keeping African Americans out of Compton as late as 1948. Reflecting their middling racial status, Mexicans could live in Compton but were not allowed to buy homes outside of their *barrio* on the northern tip of the city (Camarillo 1970; Straus 2009). According to historian Josh Sides (2005), white hostility toward Mexicans was milder than animosity toward Blacks. Middle-class African Americans were willing to pay more for homes in Compton and white homeowners sold their homes to aspiring Black suburbanites, who were willing to buy homes at higher prices than white middle-class buyers (Sides 2005).

Compton became a Black utopia; by the 1960s, Blacks dominated the city and schools. But the effects of deindustrialization and the Watts riot of 1965 had deleterious effects on the city (Strauss 2014). Southern

California's floundering economy and the outmigration of jobs undermined the pillars of Black prosperity (Sides 2005). Unemployment soared in the 1970s, especially among poorer African Americans. The prevalence of Black street gangs also grew. By the 1980s, Compton had become, according to Sides, "a metonym for the urban crisis" (Sides 2005). Hollywood's film and music industries exploited the growing regional notoriety of the city, cementing the image of Compton as an urban battleground for poor Blacks.

The reputation persists even as the African American population has declined to 32.9 percent (U.S. Bureau of the Census 2015). The most recent census figures indicate that 65 percent of Compton's 98,597 residents are of Latino origin, primarily Mexican immigrants and their children (U.S. Bureau of the Census 2015). Non-Hispanic whites are 0.6 percent of Comptonites. These demographic shifts have also manifested in schools and classrooms. While Latinos formed 37 percent of the student body in 1985 (Camarillo 2006), nearly 80 percent are Latino now, with most of the remainder, 19.4 percent, African American (CDE 2013). All the adult members of the school board are African American,[5] and this has been a source of racial cleavages over equal political representation (Fabienke 2007; Vaca 2005; Strauss 2009). The racial/ethnic minority group that is in power and control has not changed since the mid-1960s. Thus, Latina teachers are operating within a racialized structure that African Americans continue to maintain even as their numbers drop.

Rosemead

Rosemead is a smaller city in the west San Gabriel Valley. As in Compton, gangs, crime, and code yellows[6] afflict the school district and community, albeit to a lesser degree. Until the 1950s, most residents in the San Gabriel Valley were working-class whites, with large pockets of Latinos. At that point urban renewal programs and freeway construction attracted Asian immigrant middle-class residents to Rosemead. The 1965 Hart–Celler Act, which eliminated the last vestiges of Asian exclusion and provided for family reunification, increased the flow.[7] Many Chinese- and Vietnamese-origin people opened ethnic restaurants and stores (Zhou 2009; Saito 1997).[8] Luis J. Rodríguez, the son of Mexican immigrants, describes these patterns in his novel *Always Running La Vida Loca: Gang Days in L.A.* (1993):

> The Mexicans who came to live in the San Gabriel Valley worked in the fields, the railroads or the encroaching industry which soon dotted the valley. . . . It didn't take long for middle-income Anglos, primarily feeling L.A.'s inner-city as it filled up with people of color, to move in and around these *barrios* and create the first suburbs. . . . In later years, large numbers of Asians from Japan, Korea and Taiwan also moved into the area. Sections of Monterey Park and even San Gabriel became known as Little Japans or Chinatowns. . . . The *barrios* which weren't incorporated, including Las Lomas,[9] became self-contained and forbidden, incubators of rebellion which the local media, generally controlled by suburban whites, labeled havens of crime. (pp. 40–41)

Rodriguez's account accurately depicts the racial and class heterogeneity of the region.

Today, the San Gabriel Valley has several collections of U.S. suburbs with large foreign-born Chinese-speaking populations, ranging from working-class residents living in Rosemead and El Monte, to wealthier immigrants living in Arcadia, San Marino, and Diamond Bar (U.S. Census Bureau 2010). Asian families are more than 60 percent of the population in Monterey Park, Walnut, San Gabriel, Rowland Heights, and Rosemead (Saito 1998; U.S. Census Bureau 2010).[10] In the 1990s, Rosemead ranked among the top six U.S. cities listed on immigration applications as destinations for Chinese immigrants (Fong 1994). Vietnamese immigrants and other Latino nationalities to the city increased in this period as well. Of around 55,000 residents, Latinos constitute 34 percent, non-Hispanic whites are 4.7 percent, and Asians are 58 percent and growing. In the Garvey district, which includes Goodwill Elementary, 56 percent of students are Asian, 41 percent are Latino, and only 1 percent are white (CDE 2015). While the Asian-origin population is class-heterogeneous (Zhou 2009), Mexican immigrant and later-generation families have remained working class. Prior to Asian immigrants' moving into the area, the region was racialized as "dirty" by the media because of its Mexican residents (Rodriguez 2005). Asians dominate the school board in the district. Mrs. Prado, the Latina principal, referred to Asian students in this school as the "Asian super group" because of the achievement gap between Latino-origin and Asian-origin students.

According to geographer Wei Li (1997), ethnoburbs such as Rosemead are different from Chinatowns because of their residents' demographic characteristics, such as higher socioeconomic status and thriving economic structure. However, "ethnoburbs"—ethnically diverse suburbs— (Li, 1997, 2009) have begun to attract less-skilled immigrants from the Chinese mainland and other Asian countries. The growing ethnic economy's demand for cheap labor has driven a growth in low-skilled and undocumented immigrants.

Controlling Images of Space

The very first time I drove to Compton Elementary, I parked my car on the street outside the school. An older African American man was raking up the leaves in his yard. I walked toward the entrance of the school, passed the ten-foot chain-link fence, and stood by the flagpole. The U.S. flag that hung on the pole was ripped and tattered. The California state flag was somewhat faded, but you could make out the figure of the bear. Still standing by the pole, I turned around and looked at the homes that stood at the front of the school. The street was quiet. The occasional car would pass, but for the most part all you could hear was dogs barking. At the house next to where the African American man was raking, a younger Latino man had come outside and started working on his car. Both houses displayed flags—the African American man's house had the Stars and Stripes in front of the window, vertically draped; a Mexican flag bedecked the door of the Latino man's house. They remained visible for the duration of my research, as visual symbols of the shrinking African American population and the growing Latino population.

"Ugh! You Need to Move out of There": Latina Teachers and Their Families

Latina teachers told me they were afraid to work in Compton at first. It quelled their anxieties to learn that the African American population had dwindled in size and that working-class Latino immigrant families had come to dominate the region and Compton Elementary's student body. Mrs. Estrada, a U.S.-born Latina teacher, explained that before arriving in Compton she thought it would be "like gang banging and African Americans and hostile . . . afraid to go in." But she felt differently later:

> Once I arrived I saw that there were more Latinos than I thought. At first I thought it was mostly African American. So I ended up liking it because I felt like, "Oh, this is like my community, when I was growing up." I stayed because of that. . . . I thought it wasn't so bad. . . . I took a drive and it seemed very normal, just families [and] kids. I didn't see very many [Black] gangsters hanging out. Like I thought I would find [gangsters] in corners.

Similarly, Mrs. Gutierrez, a Mexican-origin teacher, noted, "In the beginning I had misconceptions about Compton. I thought it was mostly African American. They are probably gangsters. . . . But then I saw it was mostly Latino and it was okay." The anti-Black racism of Latinas/os reflects in part their unfamiliarity with African Americans: All but one Latina teacher indicated that they had known few African Americans prior to working in Compton. The one exception, Mrs. Madrigal, had grown up in Compton, and her impressions were negative. Through a cracking voice and tears she told me, "We weren't respected by the opposite [Black] race . . . and that was also a feeling from my mom. She [blowing her nose and wiping her eyes] didn't tell me directly like 'le tengo miedo a los morenos[11] or whatever' [I am afraid of Blacks], but that was definitely the feeling with the way she expressed herself." Mrs. Madrigal's parents migrated from Mexico City because they were in a dire financial predicament when she was five. She attributed her determination to leave Compton to these early experiences.

U.S. media representations of Blacks also contribute to these racial attitudes (Stuesse 2015; Zamora 2016). Latina teachers' parents also influenced their attitudes. In incorporating into the U.S. system of racial hierarchy, Latino immigrant parents bring with them the remnants of Spanish colonial rule and the Spanish *casta* [caste] system.[12] Their Latino children become exposed and socialized to this form of racial hierarchy and categorization at an early age.

Latina teachers described their parents and other relatives' expressing fear about Compton when they went to work there: "I remember when I told my mom [I was going to work in Compton], she was like, 'Oh, my god, you are going to get shot. What are you doing working over there?'" said Mrs. Gutierrez. Similarly, when I asked Mrs. Díaz how her friends and family members responded to her becoming a teacher, she replied, "I got a lot of negative feedback. I still do! I just talked to someone yesterday and they were like 'Ugh! You need to move out of there.' So I don't think they ever questioned my career choice; they questioned my location. . . . [My family's] apprehension is that Compton has more crime, Compton has gangs. There's a connotation that the students are unmotivated and they feel that that would make your teaching experience much more difficult." Mrs. Diaz's husband, a Cuban attorney in Orange County, was very supportive of her. While he was initially apprehensive that she would be working in Compton, he recognized that the students she was helping were mostly Latino and did not question her motives for staying.

Similarly, Ms. Tiscareño, the U.S.-born daughter of Mexican immigrants, remarked: "When I told people that I got hired here [Compton], my best friend is like, 'Oh, you need a bulletproof vest. I'll buy you one.' Someone else told me to buy mace. And someone else's comment was 'Get a taser.' It was all very negative. Like, 'Where in Compton are you going to work at? What area? What does it look like?'"

While Latina teachers' attitudes about Compton have changed, their attitudes toward Blacks have not. This is one reason they do not practice cultural guardianship toward Blacks.[13] As the research of Paula McClain and colleagues (2006) argues, they socially distance themselves from Blacks. They express racist stereotypes about their Black students and some colleagues and assert the supposed academic superiority of their Latino students.

However, unlike McClain and colleagues' respondents, Latina teachers at Compton do not identify with whites and do not want children to adopt a white racial identity. In fact, they specifically discouraged this. For example, Mrs. Díaz, a Salvadoran-Afro-Cuban teacher, explained, "The light-skinned Latinos think they are white. They go, 'I'm white and you're not' [to Black students]. I go 'Sweetheart [laughs], where are your parents from?' [The children] are little. I get that, but race in America is a pretty important subject to understand." Mrs. Rivas echoed this sentiment: "I wanted them to understand that they weren't white. I think they don't understand that. . . . They think they are white because they compare themselves to the African American students and it was almost a culture clash to tell them, 'I'm sorry, you're not white.'" Contrary to conventions there is no actual answer to this as Latinos can be of any racial category.

When I asked Latina teachers about their African American students, they often said that they tried to help their African American students as much as they could but indicated that they had many more "social problems" than Latino children and that they (the teachers) did not completely understand "their culture": "Honestly, I don't think I understand that culture [enough] that I would be able to even suggest how to help them. I know they are struggling a lot," explained Mrs. Estrada. Thus, in the Black/brown school, Latina teachers were cultural guardians for Latino students but not for all students of color. Latina teachers had special insight and skills for guardianship of Latino students.

Goodwill Elementary in Rosemead: "Where Is That?"

As I pulled up to Goodwill Elementary for my first visit there, an older Latino gentleman sitting on his porch across the street greeted me cheerfully in Spanish. Approaching the school, I saw a Latina office worker hurriedly placing a fat chain-link lock on the tall yellow metal gate and shoving a key into the keyhole. I stood outside the gate, hoping she would let me inside, but she seemed not to notice me. I could see several children behind her. They were running to their classrooms and being ushered in by Latina teachers. The woman finally acknowledged me. She gave me a panicked glance and said, "I can't let you in. We are having a code yellow. I'm sorry."

I rushed back to my car, locked the doors, crouched down in my seat, and waited for the order to be cleared. I knew from my experience in schools that a code yellow means that some type of criminal activity was occurring within or beyond school grounds. I was afraid there might have been a suspect with a gun. The noise of a helicopter blared over my car and circled the school. The gentleman who had wished me "*Buenos días*" [Good morning] looked up at the helicopter but seemed unrattled. For me the next twenty minutes seemed like an eternity.

Code yellows seem to happen at Goodwill at least as often as they do at Compton. The teachers explained that their school was often caught in the crossfire between a Latino gang and an Asian one. But when I asked Latina teachers who worked at Goodwill Elementary the same question I had asked Compton teachers about their friends' and family's reactions to their taking a job in the Garvey district, I found that very few had been told it was dangerous.

An influx of Asian immigration to the city of Rosemead since the late 1970s had eroded the stigma the city bore when Latinos were a larger majority. However, that stigma persisted in a pervasive feeling among Asian teachers that the Latino students at Goodwill Elementary were low-achieving because of a culture of poverty.[14] Racial cleavages had emerged between Asian-origin and Latino-origin racial/ethnic groups, a phenomenon other research has documented as well (Cheng 2014; Ochoa 2014). Longtime residents of the area, including some Latino teachers and parents, lauded the increasing presence of Asian immigrants. Mrs. Perez noted that Asian migration was "getting rid of all of the Mexican riff-raff." Mrs. Abigail Perez, a Mexican American teacher whose parents had been born in Texas and moved to the San Gabriel Valley when she was eleven years old, was one of the few Goodwill Elementary teachers who had been told Rosemead was dangerous. She began teaching at a Garvey school in the 1980s, and she noted that when the city of Rosemead had a larger "Hispanic" population, her extended family members had discouraged her from working there. Mrs. Perez described herself as a "Tejana." She was severely obese, relying on a cane with green tennis balls affixed to the bottom for mobility. At times she also wheeled around an oxygen tank. She was a very dedicated teacher and was one of the first Latina teachers hired at Goodwill Elementary. She explained, "At the beginning [my parents] weren't very pleased about it. Rosemead had a shady, had a bad reputation. It wasn't looked upon as the greatest area to work in. It had its background and its history [of Mexican gangs]. It has changed now because of the influx of the Asian people moving in and buying houses and stuff like that." Yet, she stays because she has seniority in the school and was nearing retirement.

When queried about how their friends and others replied when they said they worked in Rosemead, the younger wave of Latina teachers, many of them like Mrs. Quiroz, from Central America, said that most people had never heard of Rosemead. Seven of ten of the teachers I interviewed at the school had been raised in Rosemead or around the larger San Gabriel Valley, but it is a far smaller city than Compton and less known. The controlling images of Rosemead are different in degree and kind. Others said that their families were longtime residents of the area and had extended familial networks that included Rosemead residents. Mrs. Franco had been raised in Rosemead, and her Mexican immigrant parents witnessed the transformation of their community. She said, "Growing up in my neighborhood it was primarily Hispanic. Now my neighborhood is primarily Asian. This whole community is like that. We used to have a lot of Latino markets; now, especially as you go further down Garvey toward Alhambra, [it] is just engulfed in little Asian supermarkets and furniture stores and little delis and cafés. So it's changed." While she had bought a home in Baldwin Park, her parents remained in the home she had been raised in, in Rosemead.

In contrast to Compton, district size was also salient in Rosemead. Latina teachers explained that they were drawn to this educational space because of its relatively small size. As Mrs. Robles explained:

> I didn't really have any negative responses or that it wasn't a good profession to get into. My parents were very excited for me. I had a lot of friends who are also in the education field [who] were very supportive and told me things that I want to look out for and—'cause at the time when I was working as an instructional aide, I was working for LA Unified, and it was such a big, big school district. They had kind of said maybe you should try looking—'cause I live out in the San Gabriel Valley—"Maybe you could look out this way, there's smaller districts."

The size of the district played a direct role in mitigating interactions at the micro-level in Rosemead between Asians and Latinos. Mrs. Debbie Larry, a Mexican American teacher in Rosemead, spoke about her safety's not being a major concern for her on campus: "I get that from my fiancé now, now that we've driven through the area and we've seen that it's in a portion of town that's in a low socioeconomic neighborhood, and I've talked about how there are these rival gangs in the area. So there isn't a whole lot of concern that's been brought up. . . . It's not like it's a major issue. I've stayed here late on numerous occasions."

Goodwill Elementary was more economically heterogeneous than Compton—both in terms of the teaching staff and the students. There were second-, third-, and fourth-generation Latina teachers working at Goodwill Elementary. They were also acutely aware of intra-class differences within Asians at the school. As Ms. Sánchez explained, "Most people are working class, but we do have some [Asians] who are wealthier. . . . I think they probably own their own businesses or they you know, 'cuz we have people that come to school in like really nice cars, and, well I mean . . . . Generally I think most of the Latino students are the ones getting the free lunch, but we do have some Asian students who are low income."

Although 85 percent of children who attend Goodwill Elementary were considered socioeconomically disadvantaged and receive free or reduced-price lunch, previous flows of Asian migration have brought with them foreign investment power, Chinese ethnic business enclaves, and human capital. Latina teachers addressed the socioeconomic disparities between recent Asian immigrant working-class arrivals and Latino families, who had a much longer history in the region. While they told me that the growing Asian population had improved perceptions of the region, this dynamic maintained negative stigmas and racialization processes for Latinos. In the Los Angeles area, many people perceive Rosemead as calm in spite of the gang violence that triggered code yellows.

Teachers did not perceive Rosemead as necessarily free of danger, however. For instance, one hot spring day in the teacher's lounge, which doubled as a lunchroom, Mrs. Dávila spoke about an Asian student who had stabbed the principal at a local high school. On another occasion, teachers were extremely upset that their school was running the risk of being considered a persistently dangerous school. Ms. Maciel, a Mexican American teacher, downloaded the district's official description of the designation and brought it to the lunchroom. She went through a list of the things that had happened on their campus, raising a finger for each: "We've had discipline problems for the past two weeks. We've had expulsions. Brandishing a knife. We had that last year. A firearm. We had a fourth-grader that brought a BB gun. A robbery. They took a laptop and they brought it back. As Asian student just brought and popped a 'fart bomb.' That was a suspension." She didn't mention the code yellow I'd experienced in my first visit to the school, but it also might be identified on an evaluation of the school. Nonetheless, the racialization of space was different at Goodwill from what it was at Compton.

Teachers' Attachment to Compton

Mrs. Rivas had been teaching at Compton Elementary longer than any of her Latina teacher colleagues. She explained,

> During that time when I got hired, we got hired with people that wanted to be actors. They just needed teachers so badly that they were hiring, it didn't matter what your major was. They just really needed teachers and they hired people from Spain, bringing them over. And they were look-ing from different places. They hired a lot of I want to say people from the Philippines and actually would go and bring them and there was this program called Teach for America and they kind of pretty much brought you over from different parts of the states and an incentive was $10,000 to come work for Compton for two years. Then, after two years you could go ahead and do what you wanted. There were so many incentives. They re-ally needed teachers. My concern was if I leave this district, what are the chances that you are going to get somebody that really cares. So I stayed and I'm really glad I did.

Mrs. Rivas felt that the different incentives the district implemented to recruit teachers might contribute to low-quality teaching at Compton. She added, "When we go to conferences and we put Compton Unified [on our badges] they are like, 'Whoa!'. . . . When I told people that I was going to be a teacher they were worried that it was going to be in Compton. I think everybody assumed it was going to be a steppingstone. I was going to work here for maybe a year or two and then eventually go to LA Unified or go to Long Beach." But once Mrs. Rivas started to work at Compton Elementary she "never wanted to leave" because she was helping Latino children. In 2010, she was the only Latina fifth-grade teacher at the school.[15]

Aware of the stigma attached to Compton, Latina teachers often spoke warmly about the school and their jobs and said that Latino chil-dren were motivated to learn. Mrs. Godínez described an experience on a school field trip. "I'm really used to that reaction. Then she [a woman staffing the museum they visited] said [of Mrs. Godínez's job], 'Kind of rough, isn't it?' And I said, 'Well, yes, but it's okay as long as you stay at school.' I get some strange comments from people that don't work here. . . . There's a lot of teachers who I've met throughout the years who say 'I don't know how you work in Compton. I cannot work out there.'"

Latina teachers at Compton felt it was considered a reservoir of unqualified and mediocre teachers who could not find work elsewhere. The talk at a pool party Mrs. Becerra threw for the teachers of Compton Elementary referenced this dynamic. Mostly Latina/o and African American teachers attended even though white teachers were also invited. Unlike Rosemead, Compton employed only two Asian teachers. I was standing next to a table with two African American teachers and Mrs. Romero, who was using her ring to pop open beer bottles for everyone. The teachers were talking about gossip within the district, the removal of their previous African American principal, and about their relatives who were looking for work as teachers. One of the African American teachers said, "I told [my friend], just come to Compton. They are always hiring in Compton." Mrs. Romero said, "Yeah, I tell them to come to Compton too, but they don't want to come. I hate it that they think we are bad teachers here."

Compton does have a high turnover rate. According to Latina teachers, white teachers drive this. They use Compton as a steppingstone in order to secure a job at a more prestigious or affluent district. The Latina office secretary who had lived in Compton for more than thirty years told me that the school employed many teachers from Spain and through Teach for America at one point because of its high turnover rate. In one academic school year the school had seen at least forty teachers transition out of the school and they "scrambled" to find replacement teachers. The general perception was that if teachers could survive two years in Compton, they were adequately trained to work at another school and doing so would be a piece of cake. Teachers who stayed behind and were committed to the students and families in Compton felt others thought they had low aspirations or a lack of options because of poor performance. As Mrs. Madrigal said, "Compton is always the one to pick up whatever they can pick up. . . . Very few people are like, 'Oh, let me go work in Compton.' That's not the first place you think. You just don't!" None of the other Latina teachers explicitly expressed that as well.

The experiences of Compton teachers reflect a larger ghettoization of the teaching profession. Work and occupation sociologists have argued that as more racial/ethnic minorities and women enter occupations, the prestige that the job holds is devalued (Charles and Grusky 2008; Reskin and Roos 1990; Tomaskovic-Devey 1993; Abbott 1988). Charles and Grusky (1990), in particular, refer to the worldwide occupational segregation of women and men into different occupational niches as leading to the formation of "occupational ghettos." This contributes to a perception that teachers in the United States are people who performed poorly in college and therefore could not find more prestigious employment. However, on average, high school teachers come from the top half of their college classes. Similarly, while elementary teachers' SAT scores fall just under the college median nationwide, physical education teachers are the only group whose members have scores that fall well below the college median (Gitomer 2007).

Social Capital

Blacks in Power: "Compton es una Mafia" [Compton Is a Mafia]

Latina teachers at Compton Elementary explained that they felt that as Latinas they held a lower social status than their African American colleagues because of language, political exclusion, and unequal representation in the school district. African Americans controlled the school board, and Latina teachers rarely got involved in district politics. While they encouraged Latino immigrant parents to lobby for themselves at the district offices, most did not because of the language barrier and because they lacked American citizenship and thus feared they might get deported. In her research on Asian Americans, Claire Jean Kim (1999) speaks of the feelings Latina teachers described as civic ostracism. Latina teachers and Latino immigrant parents suggested that they did not trust Black authority in the district and questioned Blacks' commitment to Latino students.

Latina teachers seemed anxious about discussing their feelings about African American colleagues and administrators on campus. In an interview at her home, Mrs. Madrigal explained,

This district is so racial. This city is very racial. This city wants to keep Blacks in power. I don't care what race you are as long as you possess the knowledge to run this city. Do it! But, *aquí* [here], no! It has to be, you have to be Black. If you are not Black, I'm going to give you hell. . . . It's about who you know and it's about who you know that happens to be Black. . . . If it wasn't because *hay mucho Hispano* [there is so much Hispanic], I mean I wouldn't be here. Nobody other than Blacks would be there.

Latina teachers filtered political problems they perceived in the district through the lens of the controlling image of Compton as an African American space. Mrs. Madrigal explained that she felt Compton was run by nepotism and favoritism and that Black administrators intentionally deprived Latinas of political power. In this instance, reality and controlling images of space intersect and influence Latina teachers' negative perceptions of Blacks. Mrs. Madrigal makes a factual observation about Blacks' overrepresentation on the school board, and this observation affects her appraisal of Backs and their purported desire to maintain control of Compton. "There is a strong hold. *No lo quieren dejar ir*" [They don't want to let it (Compton) go], Mr. Salinas, a Mexican teacher, shared. The school, Mrs. Madrigal said, was as "an urban battleground."

Other teachers agreed with Mrs. Madrigal. During Back to School Night, a parent asked the third-grade team about changing district policies regarding class placement. Mrs. Shah, an Iranian American teacher, responded, "We are just the messengers. So please don't shoot us. . . . We are just like little marionette puppets, doing what we are told." She curled her fingers and wiggled them to represent the hands directing the marionette. Mr. Vega, a Latino teacher, added, "You as parents have a lot of power. If you go to the district, go as a group, not just as two or three parents." Mrs. Brady, an African American teacher, agreed: "[Y]ou as parents have more power than us as teachers. We work here but we can't change it unless you make your voice heard." Mrs. Díaz added, "Our third-grade team is very close. Our test scores have improved." Tensions over controlling images of the region between Latino and African American parents at this event were clear.

Latina teachers felt politically ostracized because of the Black domination of the school board. They felt that the board did not provide them the resources they needed to help their Latino students succeed academically. They also felt the district was insensitive to the need of parents who lack English skills.

All of the Latina teachers and Latino parents in Compton wondered why the majority of the school board and administrators were African American when most of the students in school were Latino (Camarillo 1970; Strauss 2014). They felt that the representation on the school board and administration should be even. Latina teachers expressed that this was a primary way in which Latinos held less school district power than African Americans because they were politically ostracized as a result of their legal status. Mrs. Ybarra said,

> They always want to keep it pro–African American at all times. . . . It's kind of ridiculous because it should be half and half. They don't want Latinos to be in charge of anything. It's very surprising that they don't want to give us an opportunity to be part of it. That's what I said about working in this community. Latinos can't hold office here because I feel like some African Americans belittle Latinos. "Why should you be a part of this community since the majority of people who are living here are trying to get their papers, become citizens or residents?"

Educational spaces can be the center of racial contests, and they are also emblematic of entrenched systems of local power (Straus 2009). Tension between Latinos and African Americans was most palpable during Parent-Teacher Association (PTA) meetings, events that Latina teachers rarely attended. Many Latina teachers explained that when they started working at Compton Elementary they attended one or two meetings, but they completely avoided the PTA once they were exposed to the racial dynamics between African American teachers, immigrant Latino parents, and a few English-speaking second-generation Latinos. Black parents did not regularly attend these meetings. In fact, *las mamás voluntarias* [immigrant Latina mother volunteers], all members of the PTA boasted and were content that the majority of their membership was Latino. When I asked about their participation in PTA, Latina teachers said they would pay the $5.00 fee but that was all: "Have you gone? It's crazy over there!" exclaimed Mrs. Estrada. Mrs. Madrigal said, "PTA is another story. I stay away from PTA because it is so political. The less drama I have the better."

Regular PTA members were *las mamás voluntarias,* mostly Latina immigrant women and one 1.5-generation Latina mother. Similar to Latina teachers, they believed that the district was not there to help Latino children academically because there was no Latino representation on the school board. All six representatives were African American. Because these executive positions are elected and many unauthorized Latino immigrant parents cannot vote, not even legal permanent residents, several of the Latina teachers agreed with Latino parents that there was some "corruption" going on in the district, further reflecting civic and political marginalization of Latinas/os. Felicia, an immigrant *mamá voluntaria*[16] and PTA member, explained her hesitation to go to the district to ask for aid. She said, "*Compton es mafia, es pura corrupción. Fijate cuanto niño moreno hay aqui, la mayoria es niño Latino. . . . El distrito esta lleno de puros morenos. . . . Los morenos todavia piensan que ellos son los esclavos, pero los únicos esclavos somos nosotros*" [Compton is a Mafia, it's pure corruption. Look at how many Black children there are here, the majority are Latino children. The district is full of pure Blacks. Blacks think that they are still the slaves, but the only slaves are us]. School boards are often elected, but undocumented Latino residents of Compton cannot vote.

Racial Triangulation

In her theory of racial triangulation, Claire Jean Kim (1999) shows that Asian Americans occupy a field of racial positions. This field of racial positions profoundly shapes the opportunities, constraints, and possibilities with which subordinate groups must contend, ultimately serving to reinforce white dominance and privilege. Racial triangulation occurs by means of two types of simultaneous, linked processes: (1) relative valorization and (2) civic ostracism.[17] However, I argue that unlike Asian Americans, Latinos in Compton experienced these processes differently because of the controlling images applied to space.

Lacking citizenship posed an enormous barrier for Latino immigrant families in Compton. Mrs. Godínez explained,

> Many [Spanish-speaking immigrant] parents are not willing to go to the district and fight for their rights. Many of them don't want to go over

there and fight for their children's education. The ones that end up doing it are the African Americans. Some of the parents say, "I don't want to go over there." I tell them, "You have to go and fight for your child's rights." They say, "No, I don't have my papers. I can't go over there." I'm like, "Okay, but they are not going to ask you if you are a citizen." They kind of degrade themselves. "I don't know English." And I say, "There are people that speak Spanish over there." "No, but they are going to find out I'm not legal here." So I just let it go.

It is completely reasonable for Latino parents to feel that it is better to let something go than to fight for it. In *Deported*, Tanya Golash-Boza (2015) demonstrates how rampant deportation is in seemingly innocuous interactions—for example, getting stopped for a speeding ticket—parents risk going to detention and abandoning their kids if they get deported. A tiny hypothetical risk is worth paying attention to for them. If parents felt they could not agitate for their children's rights, Latina teachers feared that if they did it themselves they might lose their jobs. Latina teachers used the controlling images that contrasted African Americans, who are far from the top of the racial hierarchy, with co-ethnics who appeared at a relative disadvantage to justify the cultural racism they express toward Blacks.

Goodwill Elementary contrasted with Compton in that it provided an abundance of social resources to both Asian and Latino students. The school had partnerships with various community organizations that donated money and other resources to both Asian and Latino families and teachers. Panda Cares, a community involvement program of the Panda Restaurant Group (Panda Inn, Panda Express, and Hibachi-San), which is headquartered in Rosemead, provided much of this funding. The program donated food for school meetings and fundraisers. I first became aware of these resources during a Pancake Breakfast Fundraiser at Goodwill Elementary on a Saturday morning. Latina teachers were collecting tickets and monitoring the children outside. Asian and Latino workers were in the kitchen preparing the batter and plates with pancakes. A Latino family was sitting next to me and an Asian man brought them plates of food.

Panda Cares also provided training for Latina and Asian American teachers. They offered teachers conferences on the "7 Habits of Highly

Effective People," based on the teachings of Stephen Covey. While some teachers, like Mrs. Dávila, described the book as a type of "cult," Covey's teachings were widely professed on campus. Teachers would use Covey's strategies in their classrooms, especially when they noticed discord among their students. They even explained them to parents during Back to School Night. The main premise of applying Covey's work to schools is that establishing an "abundance mentality" or "abundance mindset" makes them more successful. If there are enough resources for everyone, success can be shared as well. The idea was to celebrate the success of anyone in the school rather than feel threatened.

The stated objective of teaching Covey's work was to ameliorate race and inter-class relations on campus between Asian and Latino students. Administrators felt that Latina and Asian teachers would have a better understanding of one another as well as cross-ethnic students and families because of the "7 Habits" strategy. Given greater feelings of goodwill—which prompted me to select its alias—at Goodwill than at Compton, it seems possible that the program had some good effects in ameliorating everyday interactions. Although these Latina teachers at Goodwill Elementary implemented the strategies they learned in the program, inequality between Asian and Latino students persisted. Asians were thought to be outperforming their Latino counterparts, which led to resentment and competition similar to the racial dynamics Ochoa (2014) documents in her work.

Latina teachers explained to me, however, that Latino families had the opportunity to take advantage of many of the resources that the wealthier Asian population provided. In fact, throughout the school day, a rolling chalkboard was set at the front of the school. The chalkboard was festooned with flyers of different resources, and news of extracurricular afterschool activities offered in the city were pinned to it that all parents could take advantage of such as activities for their children. The school also regularly set up booths at the entrance of the school to introduce parents to services that might benefit them. For example, a Nuvision Federal Credit Union offering bank accounts for kids brought an Asian and and a Latino representative to the school.

Sharing information did not guarantee that a Latino family would have the money to pay for extracurricular activities or the means to transport their children to them. Latina teachers, recognizing this, created after-school programs for free or nominal cost at the school, specifically directing them to the needs of their Latino students. Mrs. Franco remarked that some of the after-school programs, such as a reading program she developed, were open to Asians, but she and her colleagues specifically wanted to help Latinos. She also said that she and Mrs. Cadena would joke that they were going to start a Spanish-speaking school for Latino kids because Asian students had extra resources such as the Kumon Learning Center or Chinese school on the weekends. Mrs. Cadena said,

> Asian parents actually take advantage of extra things. And they're not all academic. They have drawing and arts and science, reading comprehension. If I tell them, "Look, they have this—" And some have just taken the kids and gone without anybody saying. But some of my Hispanic parents, I've offered. I say, "Look, your child needs some extra help. They already stay after school and in the summer. Here they're offering these classes, $40 for 10 weeks." Some of them just don't take advantage of the opportunities. I think in this area, you'll notice they do offer a lot of after-school programs and a lot of the Asian kids do participate.

At Goodwill Elementary, citizenship status and language did not exclude Latinos or Asians from participating in school events such as the PTA as it did at Compton. But Ms. Maciel and Ms. Dávila, both active volunteers in the PTA, noted that Asians were more likely to hold leadership positions. I overheard the outgoing PTA president, Tammy, encouraging Latina immigrant mothers to join. Tammy, who is Asian, said to them, "Come on, come on, we need new blood, new faces." The women seemed uncomfortable; they said they were reluctant to join because of the language barrier. (Goodwill Elementary's PTA does not have a translator; neither does Compton's.) However, one of the Latina mothers said she se animo [was encouraged] by Tammy. She became the new PTA vice president; the new president was an African American man. The mostly Asian PTA board was a matter of contention. However, Liz, who participated in the Spanish-speaking Latina immigrant focus group, expressed doubt that Latina/o parents had the time to join the board. "A mí se me hace que los Asiáticos son más organizados" [It seems to be that Asians are more organized], she said. In Compton a white male teacher became president during my research, which seemed to have generated unity between Latinos and African Americans. While Cheng (2014) notes that shared experiences of exclusion can be a source of unity and commitment in "non-hierarchical" spaces, controlling images of space in Rosemead created opportunities for inter-ethnic cooperation. In Compton, however, the underclass controlling image divided Latinos and African Americans.

Education scholar Jonathan Kozol (1991) discusses the disparities in education between schools of different classes and different races. Not all schools and school districts provide the same resources for all of their students. While Asian immigrant families provided resources and opportunity at Goodwill Elementary, at Compton Elementary school Latina teachers struggled to get resources. They felt that they did not have the necessary resources, such as instructional supplies, to aid the community. Mrs. Romero said, "Working here in Compton is a little bit . . . it kind of shatters your hopes a little bit about what you thought you wanted to accomplish." Bureaucratic mayhem and the lack of resources had frustrated her desire to provide enriching field trips. On one of my visits to the campus, I observed an hour-long faculty meeting in which teachers took turns arguing that they needed paper for their classrooms. Mrs. Becerra pleaded with the school staff person in charge of providing school supplies, "Ayy, come on, Mrs. Stuart, we need more paper. Get us more paper." Mrs. Stuart is African American. Unlike Goodwill Elementary, Compton Elementary did not have formal music, science, art, or theater programs. Their visual and performing arts were limited to only ten minutes of the school day, one day a week. A formal Gifted and Talented Education (GATE) program was also not available. Unfortunately, most of Compton's limited resources were spent on getting children to learn the English language.

Historians have noted that conflicts over bilingual education have often driven a wedge between African Americans and Latinos in school governance (Vaca 2005; Strauss 2009; Brilliant 2010). Compton schools were considered Quality Education Investment Act (QEIA) schools,[18] meaning that extra funding was provided for so-called at-risk students, namely Latino, African American, socioeconomically disadvantaged and English Language Learner students. Some Latina teachers at

Compton also said that they received "combat pay"[19] for working in a low-performing, undesirable urban public school.

School Choices for Latina Teachers' Children

I asked the Latina teachers I interviewed about their own school choices as a way to compare their impressions of the schools that employed them with their ideals. They all expressed a desire to send their children to the best schools possible. While working at Compton Elementary made them feel needed, controlling images associated with Compton greatly influenced their decisions to enroll their children in other districts. By contrast, teachers at Goodwill Elementary chose to educate their children at Goodwill.[20] They perceived it as a source of good opportunities; they felt their own children would have a high likelihood of success in Rosemead.

Historically, it has been common for middle-class Mexicans to send their children to Catholic parochial schools instead of enrolling them in schools with immigrant and poorer co-ethnics (García 1991; Telles and Ortiz 2008). Many college-educated and middle-class African American families also opt to live in communities that have school districts known for their superior academic achievement and enroll their children in urban public schools (Posey-Maddox 2014). Dual immersion language programs favored by middle-class white families have been increasingly popular with upwardly mobile and middle-class Latino families (Muro 2015).

When I was in the schools, none of the Latina teachers who worked in Compton enrolled their children in the Compton Unified School District. Many of them said that they wanted to shield their children from racial conflict at the middle school and high school levels. I observed an interaction in Mrs. Madrigal's classroom which demonstrates that African American teachers shared these concerns.

Mrs. Rhodes, a fifth-grade African American teacher, was carrying her infant. The baby was her second; her son was enrolled at Compton Elementary. Mrs. Madrigal told her that she was contemplating enrolling her seven-year-old daughter in a Compton school (not Compton Elementary), because doing so would make it easier to pick her up from her current school in Paramount, but she was hesitant. As it was, Mrs. Madrigal's husband, a Los Angeles police officer, would pick up their daughter and drop her off at around 2:00 p.m. at Compton Elementary.

"I don't know if I want [my daughter] to come here. It's a bad area. Plus you hear all these things in the news. You have your son here, how's that? Gimme some advice?" Mrs Madrigal asked Mrs. Rhodes.

Mrs. Rhodes, who takes advantage of a program that permits teachers at Compton to enroll their children regardless of where they live, told her, "It's not a big problem when they are small. They're young. They don't take notice. The problems start in middle school. Here, I know where he is and I choose his teachers. He's not coming here for middle or high school though."

Mrs. Madrigal agreed. "Aww, heck no! I just don't know if this is the best environment for my daughter," she said.

Cheng (2014: 68) argues that at the middle and high school levels "racially segregated groups were easily perpetuated and naturalized." Latina educators recognized that these processes began at much younger ages, however. Eventually, Mrs. Madrigal enrolled all three of her children in a school that had higher test scores than Compton Elementary, in the Paramount Unified School District. I got the impression she was not happy with that school either, and, when I told her about my other research site, she said, "Awww, I want my family with the Asians and the whites, like the Asians and the whites in the suburbs. To me, the Asians are kind of like whites now. How did they make it? How did they get in there?" She was referring to the notion that many children of Asian immigrants were attending schools in more affluent areas that she perceived to be very class-heterogeneous, and she noted that as a Latina she did not have the same access. This statement also suggested her impulse to distance herself and her family from Blacks.

The teachers thus recognized that poor Latino immigrant families that enrolled their children at Compton had little alternative. They did not blame immigrant Latino parents for sending their children to schools in Compton, but they saw their doing so as an outcome of structural discrimination and larger patterns of residential segregation. Mrs. Romero had enrolled her young son at Compton Elementary because she was going through a divorce. If he attended Compton she could take care of him after school, and she had minimal resources. But she took him out as soon as she could, after nine months. She said,

[My son] did first grade here, but I sent him back because we live in a really good school district. The school that [all of my children] are at right now, it is the 20th top school in the state. I was like, "I'm going to take them over there" because even though he was with Mr. Gordon [an esteemed white teacher at Compton] . . . your best teacher is only really as good as your district. If the district doesn't have the music program or the P.E. program or the science program or the art program then my child is not really getting everything that he deserves. That is why I switched him back. People would kill to get into that district. . . . It's sad that all the districts aren't the same. They should all be the same. Like these kids [her students] deserve just as much as those kids [at ABC Unified].

According to Mrs. Romero, her son deserved "a well-rounded [education]" and to be in a "good district." Like other middle-class parents, teachers strategize to find the school they think will position their children for success, but their resources and racial perceptions define these practices. Latina/o immigrant parents were aware of teacher choices and also wanted their children to emulate the mobility patterns of their teachers. Similarly, Mrs. Becerra, a 1.5-generation Latina teacher who lived in Tustin in Orange County, an affluent and mostly white school district, enrolled all four of her children in schools in Tustin Unified. A primary reason she did not want her youngest child to go to Compton Elementary even though it would have been more convenient for her was that he was physically disabled and the schools did not provide adequate resources to accommodate his needs. She said that to send her youngest to Compton would be unthinkable because Compton would not fulfill the individualized education plan Tustin Unified had laid out for him.

Some Latina teachers went to great lengths to enroll their children in schools away from Compton. When I interviewed Mrs. Rivas, she had dyed purplish hair, long acrylic nails, and hoop earrings. As she spoke, I could see her tongue ring. She also wore a Tiffany bracelet with many charms. Our interview was cut short because she had to pick up her daughters from school. She explained that she lived in Riverside County and would drop her daughters off at her mother-in-law's house in the city of Downey, before arriving to her job at Compton Elementary. The commute from her home to her daughters' school took roughly sixty minutes, Monday through Friday, in addition to the twenty minutes she commuted from Compton to get them. She used her mother-in-law's address[21] to enroll her daughters at "a private school in Downey Unified" in a city in southern California with a large and thriving middle-class Latino population. Even though she was middle class, Mrs. Rivas felt that this was one way to secure a better education for her daughters. Her own maternal grandmother was from East L.A. and Mrs. Rivas did not want her daughters to attend schools where she had. The interest of Latina teachers in Compton in helping Latino families did not change their preference for having their children attend schools with more middle-class people, including non-Hispanic whites and Asians.

In stark contrast, all Latina teachers who worked at Goodwill Elementary recommended the school to their close relatives, and those with children enrolled them in the school, taking an active role in teacher selection and programs for the gifted and talented. Four of ten Latina teachers who worked at Goodwill Elementary had grown up in Rosemead. They said that their own parents worked tirelessly and endlessly to send them to Catholic school for their own K–12 education because they did not want them to attend Rosemead schools. However, as adults and having obtained middle-class status, they felt the schools had turned around. They pointed that Goodwill Elementary had been deemed a California Distinguished School. Mrs. Robles, for instance, enrolled her son and daughter at the school and ensured both were placed in Gifted and Talented Education (GATE) classes. She explained:

A while ago we were a Distinguished School, a little higher than we have been the past few years. But the area where I live, this is a better school than the schools my kids would have to go to. So it's a little more convenient. My husband [works down the street]. He works there, I work here, it's just easier to bring the kids here than if they were to be over there in El Monte by themselves. I don't have any family that could help me pick them up or anything. So I think that would also limit the time I'd be able to be here and what I'd be able to do here. I'm just fortunate that they're here.

Mrs. Robles and her husband, also a teacher, also lived in El Monte, a much larger city that is more than 60 percent Mexican (U.S. Bureau of the Census 2010). Their children also attend Goodwill.

Mrs. Cadena spoke of her desire to have her young sons attend Goodwill Elementary. She looked forward to having them experience the fourth grade with Mrs. Arenas. The principal allowed Goodwill's teachers to choose their own children's teachers, an advantage they might not enjoy at their zoned residential schools. At a faculty meeting, I overheard the principal say to Mrs. Cadena, "Don't worry, we got him in GATE," regarding her older son's placement. Months later I found out that Mrs. Cadena wanted her older son to attend a diverse middle school in Temple City after Goodwill Elementary that has a larger white and Asian population than Rosemead. The Temple City Board of Education calls their school district "A District of Distinguished Schools" because every school in the Temple City district has been designated a Distinguished School by the state of California at some point. Distinguished Schools are rated high for academics, deportment, and extracurricular activities. Temple City High School was also ranked #209 in *Newsweek*'s ranking of America's Best High Schools in 2011. When I asked Mrs. Cadena why she wanted to move her older son to that district for middle school, she said that moving him to Temple City would "keep him out of trouble" with Latino students enrolled in Rosemead schools. She also hoped he wouldn't interact with the Latino students in Temple City, because he would be placed in advanced classes where most of his classmates would be Asian and white. She felt that the stereotypes of Latino students got worse at the intermediate level in Rosemead and wanted to protect her son by enrolling him elsewhere.

Latina teachers at Goodwill Elementary also thought their children would have more opportunities in the future if they went to school with Asian children. They relied on controlling images to affirm their position and were adamant that they did not want their children to go to school with Black children. "I don't know if I would send my child to schools in Compton. I would rather they stay here with Asians," said Mrs. Robles. Latina teachers also felt that Goodwill Elementary was a good school for their kids at the elementary level. Most college-educated Latina teachers echoed the sentiments that Dolores, a Latina immigrant mother who participated in the Spanish-speaking focus group, expressed:

Mi hijo dijo, "papi no nos muevas para allá [a Watts]. Yo estoy muy cómodo y tranquilo aquí. Prefiero estar aquí. Es que yo creo que con los Afro-Americanos hay más conflicto. Los Asiáticos son más calmados. En esta escuela los niños se llevan muy bien. Conviven muy bien juntos. Es muy tranquilo aquí." [My son said, "Dad, please don't move us over there (to Watts). I am very comfortable and at peace here. It's because I believe that with African Americans there is more conflict. Asians are calmer. At this school the children get along. They got along really well. It is very tranquil here"].

Dolores's son played a deciding role in where he would go to school and was explicit that he would prefer to be with Asians than with African Americans.

In her book *Academic Profiling*, sociologist Gilda Ochoa (2014) argues that in multiracial high schools a binary racialization process emerges in which Asian students are labeled as "intelligent" while Latinos are perceived as "average." Similarly, ethnic studies scholar Wendy Cheng (2014) suggests that a concomitant binary of Asian valorization and Mexican inferiority emerges in these contexts. I found that Goodwill Elementary conformed to these studies. But Latina/o parents still wanted their children to attend multiracial schools. They felt that their own children would pull through and succeed in spite of potential assaults on their self-esteem.

Ms. Maciel did not have children, but she encouraged her sister to enroll her biracial (Mexican and Black) niece at Goodwill. She directly emphasized the school's diversity: "I wanted and my sister wanted her to be with people where there was diversity so that's why we brought her over here." Ms. Maciel felt that enrollment at Goodwill would protect her niece from racism and from being tracked into lower classes, which Latino and African American children can encounter in schools (López 2002).

Mrs. Franco also did not have children at the time of our interview. She was the only Goodwill teacher who said she would not enroll children there. While believing that the school offers a good education, she thought it might be awkward to enroll her child at the same school where she worked. She also pointed to a conflict that had arisen between an Asian teacher and Latina teachers at the school over a Latina teacher's accent. As Mrs. Franco described, the Asian teacher turned to her and asked, "Would you put your child in a classroom with a teacher who had a very heavy accent?" Mrs. Franco found the remark offensive and did not want to expose her children, when she had them, to such attitudes. Unlike the other Latina teachers and Latino parents who actively tried to get their children enrolled in Goodwill Elementary, Mrs. Franco felt that racial tensions on school grounds were a valid reason to avoid the school.

Conclusions

Within the last couple of decades, the cities of Compton and Rosemead have experienced major shifts in the proportional representation of racial/ethnic groups in their regions. While traditional race scholarship assumes a Black–white hierarchy with Latinos falling somewhere in between the two poles, I find that the controlling images applied to school districts affect Latina teachers' perceptions of racial positioning. The data presented in this chapter offers a complex and nuanced portrait of Latina teachers' experience of racialization along multiple axes of power, community, and exclusion. I show how their constituents racialize schools districts, and how Latina teachers object to what they see as anachronistic control in educational spaces, especially Compton. Racialization of these districts affects relationships at the school. Latina teachers who work in Compton are often asked about their personal safety and are encouraged to leave Compton by friends and family for districts that are not associated with the controlling image of the "Black underclass" even though the majority of pupils are now of Latino origin. Yet Latinas also express ambivalence about having their own sons and daughters attend schools in Compton. Latina teachers who work at Goodwill Elementary in Rosemead, on the other hand, enroll their children in the school, live near the community because of their familial networks, and are able to access resources that the more socioeconomically diverse Asian immigrant population provides, although Latino children are not on an equal footing with Asians.

Given that Compton is racialized as a Black masculine space and is associated with the urban underclass (Wilson 1987), Latina teachers see it as undesirable and attempt to socially distance themselves from Black people. In addition, Latina teachers in Compton feel that the school district authority is in Black hands, and they do not trust that they are working for the benefit of Latino children and families because their voices remain unheard and their views unrepresented. This negative context of reception disadvantages Latino students, which hastens Latina teachers' predisposition toward them. Latina teachers see Rosemead's substantial Asian American population as an attraction, and as an opportunity for mobility for their own children. Although Latina teachers and poor Latino families are able to access the resources that the more socioeconomically established Asian American population provides, they do not have parity with Asian Americans. Latina teachers perceive that they are below their Asian colleagues in terms of relative valorization in the U.S. racial structure. As college-educated professionals, Latina teachers make distinctions between themselves and undocumented poorer co-ethnics. They see undocumented Latinos as below African Americans because of language, citizenship, and power within the district, and below Asian Americans on indicators of class resources, educational success, and racial stigma.[22] Because of these perceptions, they direct their teaching efforts to reaching the children of immigrant Latinos, with whom they feel an ethnic affinity, and whom they perceive to need more aid because of their precarious and stigmatizing status in regional racial hierarchies. In the next chapter I explain how Latina teachers reach co-ethnic students through alternative forms of cultural capital, and how these practices are received by their African American and Asian colleagues.

5

Bicultural Myths, Rifts, and Shifts

An important aspect of cultural guardianship is *Chicana/Latina cultural pedagogies*—alternative forms of Latino ethnic capital that Latina teachers exercise and transmit daily. They include communication codes in Spanish, immigrant narratives, and alternative mathematical strategies. The focus of this chapter is twofold. First, I define Chicana/Latina cultural pedagogies and illustrate their differences from the symbolic forms of Latino cultures of the heroic folkloric variety that appear in schools occasionally. Second, I elucidate the resistance Latina teacher cultural guardians faced, especially in Compton Elementary, to their use of Latino cultural resources[1] to facilitate Latina/o student progress. While informality might have made them invisible, I observed that both non-Latina colleagues and school administrators challenged or denigrated Chicana/Latina cultural pedagogies.

The common conceptions of Latino cultures in U.S. schools represent important context for Chicana/Latina cultural pedagogies. A 2008 news story in the *Los Angeles Times*[2] provides a good example of how this conception confines teachers. The story described the firing of Karen Salazar, a second-year English teacher at Jordan High School, who worked for the Los Angeles Unified School District in the city of Watts. At twenty-five years old, Mrs. Salazar was a fairly new and young teacher. She held a political science degree from UCLA with minors in African American studies and Chicano studies. She worked at Jordan High School for two years before, a year away from tenure,[3] she lost her teaching position for including *The Autobiography of Malcolm X*, an approved text for high school students, and poems written by African American and Latino poets in her classroom—as well as approved texts, materials appropriate for culturally relevant teaching (Ladson-Billings 2005; Banks 1993).[4] Administrators speaking to the *Times* said they dismissed her on the grounds that her choice of material for her largely

Black and brown students was too "Afro-centric" and that she was too politically "militant."

Mrs. Salazar's dismissal stems from debates over the significance and importance of ethnic cultural capital in workplaces such as schools. Some cultural resources are of the heroic folkloric variety—such as the symbolic and nonthreatening forms of cultures like cuisines, famous icons, and celebratory holidays (Washburn 1996; González, Moll, and Amanti 2005). These are usually celebrated in schools occasionally during certain days or months of the year.

But Bourdieu and Passeron (1977) use the concept of cultural capital to explain how high-class elites transmit the attitudes and knowledges their offspring need to succeed in the current educational system. In most cases, this transmission of cultural capital results in advantages for higher-status whites, reproducing their high social status in schools. This also comes at a cost to poorer and lower-status whites. Chicana/Latina cultural pedagogies, on the other hand, consist of cultural elements such as communication codes, immigrant narratives, and alternative mathematical problem solving—cultural resources many lower-status Spanish-speaking immigrant parents transmit to their children. Most of the Latina teachers who participated in my study grew up in working-class or immigrant homes, and they find they subvert normative and explicit workplace rules[5] regarding Latino cultural resources in teaching. As this chapter will describe, they foster navigational skills for Latino families through this subversion.[6] I observed these pedagogies as non-institutionalized teacher practices that are not formally taught or officially evaluated. Interviews revealed that many teachers used these tools with their own families, as well. As I explained in chapter 3, Latina professionals use these techniques when they begin interacting with Spanish-speaking Latino immigrant parents and their children once in the workplace. I found the pedagogies to be similar across Compton Elementary and Goodwill Elementary, but they produced different responses from colleagues and administrators in the two sites, with Latina teachers experiencing far more friction at Compton Elementary than at Goodwill. Beyond the exercising of Chicana/Latina cultural pedagogies on school grounds, this chapter provides a multifaceted and nuanced understanding of Latino cultures and shows how Latina teachers attempt to create a positive context of reception for Latino children and their families even as they meet acute nativism and antagonism in schools and in society in general.

Chicana/Latina cultural pedagogies differ from symbolic celebratory Latino culture that takes place only certain times of the year of the heroic folkloric variety. They occur daily in work interactions with both Latino students and Latino parents as measures to make schools more welcoming places for Latino families. I begin by showing examples of celebratory cultural events that occur on specific days of the academic year and then move to an alternative set of practices Latina teachers use to bring Latino cultural knowledge into the classroom on a more consistent basis, and how the teaching staff as a whole and the respective administrations receive these practices at Compton Elementary and Goodwill Elementary.

Heroic Folkloric Latino Cultures

A Diego Rivera painting with white calla lilies hung above the teacher's cluttered desk. An ensemble of various Mexican crafts such as *Día de los Muertos calacas* [Day of the Dead skeletons] playing guitars, colorful papier-mâché flowers, Mexican *lucha libre* [free wrestling] masks, and a poster of César Chávez with "*¡Como Siempre!*" emblazoned across the middle surrounded the paintings. Sections of the room were partitioned off and with similar items as the design focus items. The room belonged to Mrs. Emma Cadena, a self-identified Latina teacher whose Mexican-origin grandmother was born in Santa Ana, California and Mexican-origin grandfather was born in Hidalgo, Texas. Mrs. Cadena had blond hair and green eyes. Her mother was Irish, but she was raised by her father's family in Santa Ana. She teaches the fifth- and sixth-grade combination class at Goodwill Elementary. In asking Mrs. Cadena about how she incorporates Latino culture into her teaching and as a part of the school culture, I referenced the decorations specifically. She said,

> I think it's important for students, whether they're Asian or Latino, more so for my Latino kids, because I know with their previous teachers, they don't know when Hispanic heritage month is. When they get to sixth grade . . . it's like, "How come we never knew this?" . . . I think it's important to them. It's their culture. They need to know that all Latinos

can't be labeled as gardeners and dishwashers and things like that. There are famous Latinos. You may not hear about them, but there are. They're amazed!

Other Latina teachers at both sites made remarks much like Mrs. Cadena's. They boasted about the elaborate festivals that they held yearly, and the planning committees that they willingly signed up for or that they were assigned to by their principals. When it came to planning ethnic cultural events on school grounds, Mrs. Gutierrez, one of the organizers of the Latino Heritage Festival and a first-grade teacher at Compton Elementary, said that this festival and Black History Month were the school's main festive events.[7]

Figure 5.1 demonstrates what "food, fun, faces and festivities" (Washburn 1996)—a symbolic form of culture—looks like in many elementary schools and workplaces. I captured these images at both Goodwill and Compton Elementary. As we can see from figure 5.1, this is a perfect example of heroic folkloric Latino cultures associated with popular icons, symbolic decorations, and foods. Latino culture has been "canned" and reproduced in schools in very contained ways (Washburn 1996) that are celebratory in nature (see Gans 1979; Waters 1999). In the era after the civil rights movement of the 1960s, socially sanctioned multiculturalism,

Figure 5.1. Heroic Folkloric Latino Cultures

a derivative of a culturally relevant teaching, is celebrated in schools, and teachers are encouraged to expose children to the safe parts of ethnic culture such as cuisines, Latino icons, *Ballet Folklórico*, dances, and popular festivals. This helps students learn about important historical events and traditions and serves to validate Latino children's traditions, but these aspects of Latino culture are largely symbolic (Gans 1979). This symbolism, although important, is limited in that it does not capture daily interactional forms between upwardly mobile Latina teachers and lower-status Mexican immigrant families that are also crucial to student learning.

Goodwill Elementary celebrates *Cinco the Mayo* and the Chinese New Year,[8] and it also held an International Day Festival toward the end of the school year, reflecting the Asian and Latino cultures of the student population of the school. The International Day Festival at Goodwill Elementary included cultural garbs and dances that were all recycled from years prior, and each grade level had its own dance assigned so as not to overwhelm the teacher and detract from the school work schedule. These cultural aspects fall under what I call "Heroic Folkloric Latino Cultures." This is the version of Latino culture that is expected, reproduced in the media, symbolic, and often stereotypic. It is also lived, but I consider the advantages it offers rather limited.

I would argue symbolic demonstrations of tolerance of foreign culture have replaced the Americanization programs I detailed in chapter 1. The more subtle processes and pressures of assimilation still linger in schools today. Americanization programs of the 1920s and 1930s were based on the idea that Mexican culture was an obstacle to academic success; the objective was to assimilate children into a white mainstream (González 1990; Urrieta 2010). Various historically oppressed groups challenged practices such as Americanization in public institutions during the civil rights movement, leading to the institutionalization of celebratory multiculturalism of the folkloric variety in the U.S. educational system by the 1970s (Banks 1993). Teachers are encouraged to promote diversity in the classroom and to expose students to various cultural customs and traditions (Delpit 2006; Nieto 2005). As in Goodwill and Compton, however, occasional celebratory approaches dominate (González 1990; Nieto 1999). To address how teachers can include culture in classrooms on a more regular basis, education scholars González, Moll, and Amanti

(2005) suggest a "cultural funds of knowledge" frame and argue that teachers should attempt to learn and understand the political, historical, and personal situations of their students and look to their students' home lives, which often contain rich cultural and cognitive resources. According to them, teachers must be willing to go into their students' homes and learn and uncover their local knowledge base. For example, they propose that teachers observe signs of cultural identity such as Mexican candy in their students' homes, and that using such objects in math lessons is a powerful tool (Moll, Amanti, Neff, and González 1992). The researchers do not answer some practical questions their recommendations naturally raise, however. For example, how can a teacher enter students' homes without seeming intrusive? How many homes would a teacher need to go into? When is a busy teacher to make time for such fieldwork?[9] My observations in Latina teachers' classrooms with their students and families revealed that teachers who come to their jobs with Latino cultural knowledge sidestep some of these issues.

Chicana/Latina Cultural Pedagogies

Chicana/Latina cultural pedagogies have historically been unwelcome in the teaching profession (González 1990; Ochoa 2007). Latina teachers at both sites counter this by encouraging one another to incorporate and address Latino cultures in their classrooms and workplaces. Their approach reflects the fact that Latino culture is not monolithic or static. Historian Vicki Ruiz (1997) describes the ways in which immigrants and their children pick, borrow, retain, and create distinctive cultural forms as "cultural coalescence." Mexican culture consists of a set of permeable cultures that, while rooted in generation, gender, region, class, and personal experience, evolve based on Latinos' new experiences and new ideas as we engage the ethnically heterogeneous society in which we live.

I discovered that Latinas are using Chicana/Latina cultural pedagogies and practices in their daily work interactions with both Latino students and Latino parents to make schools more welcoming places for Latino students and families and to facilitate the learning process. I define Chicana/Latina cultural pedagogies as the subtle ethnic cultural cues that Latina teachers are able to duplicate, discern, and communicate because of their own connections to immigrant origins and their struggles with language and communication styles and mathematics.[10] These are fluid cultural practices that teachers adjust to the needs of differing Latino communities within the school. I find that many Latina teachers have the prior situated knowledge that allows them to discern hints about how they should alter their teaching and interactions in particular circumstances in order to effectively reach and communicate with Latino students and Latino immigrant parents. Much as how the women flight attendants whom Hochschild (2003) studies smile and exhibit jovial demeanors on planes, an act of *emotional labor* that requires a worker to induce or suppress her feelings in order to sustain the outward countenance that produces the proper state of mind in others, Latina teachers invoke ethnic capital in their jobs. This is an act of emotional labor that requires an empathetic understanding of the daily expressions that are a vibrant part of Latino ethnic culture. As we will see in the next section, teachers convey information (*amabilidad, personalismo*, and *simpatía*), endorse values (immigrant narratives), and employ an alternative curriculum (the math) in these expressions.

Language and Communication Codes: (*Personalismo, Simpatía, and Amabilidad*) [Personalism, Sympathy, and Kindness]

"[I] know how to talk to them," Mrs. Rivas, a Latina teacher with dark purple hair, said of Spanish-speaking immigrant parents in the Compton community. Born in Sacramento, California, and raised in East Los Angeles, Mrs. Rivas is fully bilingual. She said, "You just need to learn to speak to parents . . . to be able to adjust to speak to different parents. . . . It helps being bilingual that they actually come up to you." She was highly cognizant of communicative forms of speech in the Spanish language exhibited by Latino immigrant parents. This was more than sharing the language; it was also understanding forms of expression. She described having an advantage with Mexican immigrants that could also apply to other Latino subgroups such as those from Central America.[11] Beyond shared language, she described an understanding of conversational etiquette that made it possible for her to establish rapport with Spanish-speaking parents.

Mrs. Becerra came to the United States as a young teen from Mexico. She says, "I'm able to communicate to most of the parents. . . . Not only because of the language but because of where I come from, Mexico. I relate to their struggling to come across. They have issues like 'Oh well my husband was taken in [deported].'" It was common for teachers to cite their understanding of the immigrant experience as an asset in communicating with foreign-born Latino parents.[12] Although they are college-educated, Spanish-speaking Latina teachers are able to subtly modify their interactional modes in response to language cues and generate comfort and ease in the classroom or parent–teacher meetings (Bourdieu and Passeron 1977) without relying on children to serve as cultural brokers. African American parents at Compton Elementary rarely used their children as cultural brokers, while Asian immigrant parents often had to do so at Goodwill Elementary as well (see Kwon 2015).

Interactional rituals were an element of Latino immigrants' habitus that Latina teachers used to communicate with Latino families and help them navigate the school's culture. Mrs. Estrada, a thirty-four-year-old U.S.-born Latina teacher at Compton Elementary, for example, described Latino parents who approached her seeking clarification of letters that had been sent home or trying to find their child's homeroom classroom. Mrs. Estrada said that many of these parents were wary of approaching monolingual English-speaking teachers because they could not advocate for their children effectively: "A lot of parents would come to me to go and translate to the teacher they had now. They were embarrassed or something. Like intimidated that they couldn't speak the language, so I think they kind of like don't defend their kid like they would if they could."

Similarly, Ms. Lizet Tiscareño, a U.S.-born teacher of Mexican origin, said,

> I am bilingual. [Parents] see that I am of the same culture and that I speak their language. That alone has helped a lot of parents approach me because they have said this to me. Like, "Oh, thank goodness that you can speak Spanish because I remember when I came to see the other teacher and asked how the student was doing I couldn't understand what he or she was saying. I couldn't speak to them." Or they would say, "I am so glad that you can understand me because I have concerns and I couldn't get these concerns across to other teachers."

At the time of the study, neither Compton Elementary nor Goodwill Elementary had a formal bilingual program, a reflection of California's "English Only"[13] movement. While Goodwill Elementary's teachers and the principal did not police the use of Spanish, Compton Elementary took a formal position on Proposition 227 that teachers should communicate with all students only in the dominant language. In this environment, anxious parents frequently approached Latina teachers because they felt nervous, embarrassed, or intimidated when trying to interact with monolingual English-speaking teachers. Ms. Tiscareño elaborated, "[Mexican immigrant] parents are nervous to talk to teachers because sometimes they feel hesitancy or even low self-esteem. . . . I know that when my [own] parents would go to my meetings with my teachers it was scary for them because they didn't know how to communicate with them and they didn't feel they were up to par with their English and the professional level the teachers had." This finding complements that of Guadalupe Valdes (1996), who found that Latino immigrant parents purposefully missed parent–teacher conferences with monolingual English-speaking teachers because they were fearful of being judged negatively because they did not speak English fluently. Bilingual teachers offered an important resource for parents in a similar bind.

A few non-Latino teachers at Compton Elementary also speak some Spanish, but Latino immigrant parents feel more at ease discussing their children's academic progress with a native or fluent Spanish-speaker. For instance, I heard Nina Robles, a Latina immigrant mother, say to Mrs. Yolanda Ybarra, "*Ay, hablas Español*" and when Mrs. Ybarra replied, "*Sí,*" she said, "*Me siento tan afortunada que me callo un ángel del cielo. Estaba tan perdida. Tenía tanto miedo de esta junta. Me puede ayudar*" [I feel so fortunate that a guardian angel fell from the sky. I was so lost. I was so afraid of this meeting. Can you help me?]. She was referring to a meeting with Mrs. Miller, her son's teacher. He was showing poor progress, but she did not want him to repeat the grade, believing the social consequences would be grave. Mrs. Ybarra is a U.S.-born teacher of Mexican origin. Mrs. Miller is primarily monolingual, but she has some Spanish conversational skills. I joined them for the meeting, and I found that even as Mrs. Miller addressed Ms. Robles in Spanish, they seemed to be miscommunicating. "*¿Se siente comfortable*[14] *con* *mi español?*" [Do you feel comfortable (in English) with my Spanish?], said Mrs. Miller. The parent looked at her quizzically, scrunching her eyebrows. She did not know the word *comfortable* (a Spanglish word) and therefore asked Mrs. Ybarra to translate for her.[15] In the meeting, Ms. Robles spoke extensively about her migration story, which involved fleeing an abusive husband. Mrs. Ybarra duly translated, but Mrs. Miller showed little interest. Ms. Robles believed late enrollment in the term and lack of English fluency were the reasons her son was behind. Mrs. Miller actually rolled her eyes at one point during the narrative when Ms. Robles turned to talk to Mrs. Ybarra in Spanish about migrating with her young son while pregnant and crossing the mountainous terrain with the *coyote* [smuggler], nervously laughing about the ordeal. Mrs. Miller seemed resentful of Mrs. Ybarra's presence and that Ms. Robles joked during the meeting. She wanted the meeting to focus on the student's academic achievement rather than on any of the social challenges he or she was facing. Vice principal Quinn was also present in the meeting to moderate.

Mrs. Franco, a second-generation Latina teacher, sometimes felt nervous using Spanish with Latino immigrant parents, describing her command of the language as "choppy." Nonetheless, when she received a phone call from the grandmother of one of her Latino students, she used Spanish:

MRS. FRANCO: *Mijo* [Son], can you answer the phone?

CALLER: *Sí, es la abuelita de Mayito. Namás quería saber si se iba a quedar después de escuela.* [Yes, it's Mayito's grandmother. I just wanted to know if he will stay after school.]

STUDENT: It's Mayito's grandma.

MRS. FRANCO: (grabs phone) *Mayito se va a quedar en la clase.* [will stay in class]

(Goodwill fieldnotes, 10/12/2009)

Research shows that bilingual Latina teachers often code-switch between Spanish and English during informal conversations with one another (Flores 2011a). Spanish conversational language codes among working-class Latino immigrant parents and Latina teachers, most of whom were children of immigrants or, if they were not born in the

United States, came here as children, contain a wide range of such switches. Most of the Latina teachers I studied had some understandings of Latino forms of cultural expression in Spanish-speaking countries. The use of *mi-jo* and *mi-ja*, contracted forms of *mi-hija* and *mi-hijo*, as in the above example, reflect this knowledge. Mrs. Franco's addition of -*ito* to the name Mayo likewise indicates her comfort with Latino cultural expression. Mrs. Franco explained that she did not know speaking Spanish was an asset for her in her job until she experienced it first-hand in her interactions with parents, noting that it was a "big deal to be Latina and to be able to communicate to the kids and with the parents."

Mrs. Madrigal is proficient in Spanish and English, the child of Mexican immigrants who migrated with them at the age of five to the United States. I observed a parent–teacher conference with Mrs. Romelia Martínez, a Latina immigrant mother whose son, Cristian, was doing very well in Mrs. Madrigal's fourth-grade-level class.

She always had coffee brewing in her classroom for herself and any potential parent visitors. Mrs. Martínez paused at her door with her green baby stroller and two children, Cristian and Luz, hesitant. She said tentatively, "*Hola maestra*" [Hi teacher].

Mrs. Madrigal responded: "*Pásele, pásele, Señora Martínez. Con confianza. ¿Gusta de un cafecito?*" [Come in, come in Mrs. Martinez. With trust. Would you like some coffee?]. Mrs. Martínez does not speak or understand English fluently, but Mrs. Madrigal might have conducted the conference in Spanish in any case.

Mrs. Martínez declined the coffee pleasantly: "*No Gracias*" [No, thank you].

"*¿Cómo ha estado?*" [How have you been?].

"*Muy bién, gracias. ¿Y usted?.*" [Very well, thank you. And you?].

Mrs. Madrigal replied as she gestured Mrs. Martínez to sit in a chair, "*Pues, nadamás contando los días. ¿Cómo sigue su esposo de su diabetis?*" [Just counting the days. How is your husband's diabetes?].

"*Pues no muy bien pero hay la llevamos*" [Not too well but we are hanging in there].

"*Me da lástima de oir eso. Ojalá que todo salga bien.*" [I'm sorry to hear that. I hope everything turns out well]. Mrs. Madrigal turned to Mrs. Martínez's baby, asking, "*¿Cuántos meses tiene?*" [How many months is she?].

"*Ocho*" [Eight] was the response.

"You're going to college. Yes, you are!" Mrs. Madrigal said to the baby.

The mother chuckled. I could see she was very at ease because of the use of Spanish and common refrains. The other children smiled.

Mrs. Madrigal signaled the conference would begin. "*Cristian es un niño agradable. ¿A si se dice verdad? ¿Agradable?*" [Cristian is a pleasure to have in class. That's how you say it, true? A pleasure?].

"*Sí!*" [Yes!] the mother replied.

Mrs. Madrigal confirmed her usage of *agradable* with Señora Martínez first and then expressed that Cristian always paid attention and was doing well in her class but would talk too much when engaged by his classmates. While the two women had only just begun to discuss Cristian's excellent academic and behavioral record, Mrs. Madrigal had already employed several Spanish communication codes, blending formal and informal interactional forms. First, she addressed the parent as *Señora* Martínez. Several non-Latino teachers, instead of addressing parents by honorific and surname, would say, for example, "Cristian's mom" or "*la mamá de Cristian.*" While using "Cristian's mom" may not be disrespectful to Latino immigrant parents, this emphasizes the student and not her status as an adult parent. Second, Mrs. Madrigal uses the formal form of *you*, *usted* [you], rather than *tú*, which connotes respect. By using it, Mrs. Madrigal bows to convention and shows her respect for Mrs. Martinez's role as a more significant figure in her student's life. English does not make this distinction, so non-Latino teachers may be unaware that they are not being formal in this way. Some Latino immigrant parents, especially those from rural backgrounds, may feel that this is disrespectful. Offering Mrs. Martínez *cafecito*, the diminutive of coffee, makes the mundane object delicate and graceful and adds warmth to the offer. The word *confianza* [a form of confidence] signifies trust. By confirming her use of the term *agradable* [a pleasure] with Mrs. Martínez, she demonstrates that communication codes are not unidirectional, but reciprocal. This means that it was common for Latina teachers to use the parent as a Spanish-language resource to enhance the communication between them, evident when Mrs. Madrigal says, "That's how you say it, true."

The conversational elements and cultural codes and signals Mrs. Martínez employed are at the disposal of Latina teachers when they use

Spanish. The Latina teachers communicated in Spanish with Latino immigrant parents, invoking language codes that sociologist Prudence Carter (2003) would characterize as "non-dominant" forms of expression in marginalized conversational etiquette in institutions that privilege English and Anglo ways of "talking the talk." British sociologist Basil Bernstein (1971, 1973) refers to these sociolinguistic patterns among working-class groups as the "restricted code" that is common knowledge shared among families, children, and extended kinship and friendship networks. In using *mijo* Mrs. Franco also exhibits use of the restricted code. I deem these necessary tools to build a cultural comfort zone with working-class Latina/o immigrant parents that Latina teachers exercise daily.

Dominant Language and Behavioral Codes: Mr. Goyette's Classroom

Mr. Goyette, a white male colleague of Mrs. Madrigal's with whom she team-teaches, met with Mrs. Romelia Martínez to speak about Cristian as well. I was present not only in my participant-observer capacity but also to serve as a translator. Mr. Goyette determines the language scores for both his students and Mrs. Madrigal's, and Mrs. Madrigal felt that Cristian could be earning a better language score. Mrs. Madrigal determined the math scores for both classes.

Mrs. Martínez was waiting by Mr. Goyette's classroom when I arrived. I was in Mrs. Madrigal's room observing a parent–teacher conference when he walked into her room and mouthed, "Can you help me translate?" I walked over to his room and asked Mrs. Martínez if she was comfortable with my being there. She agreed. Cristian; her daughter, Luz, who was in the third grade; and her infant were with her. Mr. Goyette motioned to us both to sit down at a semi-round table in the back of his classroom. Cristian sat in the middle, between his mother and me, while Mr. Goyette sat across the table. Her daughters were to her left. Then he prompted me to ask Mrs. Martínez if she had any questions about Cristian in his class.

She looked at me, saying, "*A sí vine a preguntar por qué Cristian está tan bajo en el lenguaje. Si me puede explicar por que se saco un dos.*" I translated: "Mrs. Martínez says she wants to know why Cristian was doing so poorly in language. If you could, explain to her why he has a two out of five as his language score."

Mr. Goyette kept his eyes on me, Cristian, and Luz as the interaction continued. It was rare that he directed his glance at Mrs. Martínez.

Five minutes into the meeting Mr. Goyette turned around in his chair and picked up a chapter-book that was on a shelf. "This is Judy Blume's *Tales of a Fourth Grade Nothing*," he said, perturbed. He opened the book to the first chapter, slammed the book on the table, and demanded that Cristian "read the first paragraph out loud!"

Panicked, Cristian started sounding out the words and breaking them into meaningful syllables. "Chaaap-ter . . . one . . . The . . . Big . . . Win-ner . . . I . . . won . . . Drib-Dribble at Jim-Jimmy—"

Mr. Goyette grabbed the book from his hands and read, "Chapter One, The Big Winner" with exaggerated fluency. He began to wave his arm in a figure-eight motion to insinuate the pace of his reading style. "As a fourth-grader you need to be reading like that. Not Ch-Ch-Chap-ter One. No stuttering. It should be fluid!" (He presumably meant *fluent*.)

He pointed his index finger at Mrs. Martínez, "*MÁS LÉA, LÉA, LÉA!*" [MORE READ, READ, READ].

She stared at the index finger pointed at her, silent.

Cristian was clenching the table. His breathing became shallow. He looked at his mother, who was visibly upset. Her young daughter looked at her too.

Mrs. Martínez finally said, "*¿Qué puedo hacer en la casa para ayudarle?*" I translated, "What can I do at home to help him?"

"Tell her to turn off the TV, take away the PlayStation even if he cries," Mr. Goyette told me to translate. Unthinkingly I softened a little: "*El maestro Goyette dice que a lo mejor sería una buena idea que le apague la televisión y que le quite el playstation*" [Mr. Goyette says that maybe it is a good idea to turn off the television and take away the PlayStation].

Mrs. Martínez told me to tell Mr. Goyette, "*No tenemos televisión ni playstation en la casa*" [We don't have a television or a PlayStation at home]. Her infant was playfully clanking a pen on the table and Mr. Goyette grabbed the pen from the infant's hand and set it down on the table. I took a deep breath and translated again.[16]

Mr. Goyette again used his Spanish catchphrases, "*Estudio, estudio, estudio. Toda noches* [*sic*]" [Study, study, study. All nights]. He went on, addressing Cristian, "How come you didn't tell your mother that I have my 'Plain and Simple' after-school tutoring?" I translated again. I told Mrs. Martinez that Mr. Goyette had said he sent a paper home for her to sign so that Cristian could stay after school.

Teary-eyed, she pleaded, "*Cristian por que no me dijistes mijo?*" [Cristian, why didn't you tell me, son?].

Cristian took a big gulp and did not respond.

The meeting ended soon after that. Mrs. Martínez was still wiping away tears when Mr. Goyette, looking very pleased, told me, "You've got to be stern and direct with these parents."

Mrs. Martínez pushed her stroller past Mrs. Madrigal's door hurriedly as the teacher asked, "*Como le fue . . . .*" [How did it go?]. She didn't stop.

"What happened?" Mrs. Madrigal asked me, watching the retreating figures of Mrs. Martínez, the stroller, and Cristian and his sister gripping the two sides.

"It didn't go so well," I said. This interaction is congruent with Guadalupe Valdes's (1996) assessment about why Latino immigrant parents will avoid coming to school. Mrs. Martínez was proactive in finding solutions for her son, but dominant language and behavioral codes between her and Mr. Goyette might have made her more apprehensive about how she approached parent–teacher conferences with monolingual teachers in the future. Mr. Goyette's approach corresponds with dominant language and behavioral codes that maintain cultural hegemony. He greeted Mrs. Martínez in a businesslike manner, showed her evidence of Cristian's reading skills, and told her ways to address the problem. His "objective" language and behavioral codes established him as a "professional" and an "expert," while disempowering Mrs. Martínez and Cristian. I got the sense that we had lost this mother, at least temporarily.

Based on my observations and in interviews with Latina teachers, versions of this coarseness in language and communication codes that Mr. Goyette had subjected both Mrs. Martínez and her son to were not uncommon, especially at Compton Elementary. Mrs. Godínez, a

Latina teacher who was extremely reserved and kept to herself in her classroom at Compton, said, *"Hay maneras de comunicarse"* [There are ways to communicate], but monolingual English teachers and personnel *"No se prestan para comunicar"* [Don't lend themselves to communication]. According to her, this was the case with both her white and African American colleagues. Psychologist Nilda Chong (2002) argues that Latino immigrants and their children respond positively to politeness of demeanor, comportment, and address and favor the pleasing forms versus what they perceive as the direct, businesslike messages conveyed in interactions with English-speaking professionals. In Mexican culture, an intense emotive style and person-centered approach signals caring and appreciativeness. While English speakers may all prefer a pleasant demeanor, and conflict makes many people uncomfortable, immigrant Latinos may be substantially less comfortable with conflict and confrontation with professionals and those in positions of authority. Such conversational elements may remind parents of home and their ethnic background. These conversational elements that bilingual Latina teachers employ are at their disposal when they use Spanish.

Latina Teachers as Translators and Cultural Guardians

Latina teachers often served as translators for teachers who could not speak Spanish, and they were attuned to the differences in interactional forms between teachers of different racial/ethnic backgrounds and Latino parents. They often share the instinct that prompted me to slightly soften Mr. Goyette's implicit criticism of Mrs. Martínez. As Mrs. Quiroz, a Guatemalan teacher at Goodwill Elementary, put it, *"les trato de suavizar el mensaje"* [I try to smooth out the message] whenever she served as a translator for Asian American teachers. Mrs. Quiroz had also noticed a lack of eye contact between teachers for whom she was translating and parents; she said she specifically directs her focus at the parents' eyes. She and others also expressed sympathy for monolingual English-speaking teachers who have difficulty communicating in Spanish during parent–teacher conferences and said that to some extent the loss of rapport is inevitable: "I can see the frustration that a lot of English-speaking teachers have during parent–teacher conferences. . . .

If they don't have a translator, they can't communicate. . . . I've always seen the distance. The fact that they don't speak the [Spanish] language creates . . . the barrier." At the same time, she acknowledged other barriers such as those I observed.[17]

Third- and fourth-generation Latina teachers at Goodwill Elementary with minimal Spanish skills also face linguistic and social barriers with Latino parents, and some felt they were disappointing Latino families. Mrs. Cadena explained, "A lot of the Latino families think that I speak Spanish, and I feel like I let 'em down. I can't speak it. I understand for the most part what they're telling me, but [it] makes me feel like I'm somehow letting them down." They had to rely on translators, as well. However, they did have somewhat fewer cultural barriers.

The Role of Immigrant Narratives

One of the ways first-generation Latina teachers described connecting with their Latino students was by sharing their own immigrant origins and histories the very first day of school. The Latina teachers told of their experiences as children of immigrants adapting to a new American culture and the intergenerational and bicultural dynamics that emerged within their families. They spoke of their family's fear of deportation and separation, a topic that resonated with many Latino students whose parents and/or siblings were undocumented immigrants (González 2015; Suárez-Orozco and Suárez-Orozco 2001). Latina teachers noted that some of their young Latino students were living in daily consternation that their parents would be removed while they were in school. Teachers like Mrs. Becerra connected with their students with stories of their own transitions. They considered this a vital tool for students who had trouble understanding their teacher's directions and were embarrassed by their not being able to respond in English. Mrs. Becerra described having a tough time transitioning into an American high school.

> The [culture] shock. . . . I did not speak the language in my first two classes in high school [when] I was put back in the ninth grade, because you know high school goes from ninth through twelfth grade. I was put in ninth grade. My first two classes were ELD [English Language Development] and then I had music, art, and PE easy. I did struggle a little bit.

It was mostly a frustration I guess because I really wanted to communicate with people so I was trying to learn.

Mrs. Becerra freely shed tears remembering the rigors of adjusting to an American school.

Mrs. Becerra noted the differences between U.S.-born Mexican Americans and Mexican immigrants (see Valenzuela 1999; Ochoa 2004 in school, noting that legal status was an issue for some. At the same time, I found that later-generation Latino teachers were generally aware of the power of the immigrant narrative. Mrs. Cadena has limited Spanish-speaking skills, but she described how her Mexican grandfather's words reverberated in her head when she was in school: "'Finish school,' he would say. I would have loved to stay in school, but I didn't have the choice."

Ricardo Stanton-Salazar (2011) argues that teachers serve as important empowerment agents when they employ practices such as Mrs. Becerra's because they equalize an otherwise unequal power relationship. Mrs. Díaz, the daughter of Central American and Caribbean immigrants, could draw on their experiences in talking with her students:

[I talk to them about] how my mom was boarded on a plane with a note stapled to her shirt from El Salvador [at] four years old. . . . We talk a lot about why your parents came, about struggle, about sacrifice—because some were born there [Latin America], but probably right after they were born they came over. Once in a while you will get a kid who lived there for a little bit, but for the most part they have lived most of their lives in the U.S. We talk about why they immigrated and of course I get on my college soapbox and why [their parents] want a better life for their kids. So understanding the process of why their parents immigrated is helpful for me teaching them.

Mrs. Díaz is cognizant of the internal heterogeneity within the migration histories of the Latino population, intragenerational divides, and varying contexts of reception (Menjivar 2000; Stepick and Stepick 2009; Suarez-Orozco and Suarez-Orozco 2008).[18] She invokes stories of Latino migration to the United States and struggle in order to promote educational success, pushing her students to show their appreciation for the sacrifices their parents made for them. This mirrors the "immigrant bargain" (Smith 2006)—a process that stresses educational and occupational success and suggests that second-generation Latino young adults measure their moral worth or failure based on upward mobility. Much like immigrant Latino parents who use this strategy in Smith's study in New York, I observed Latina teachers working as intermediaries in the incorporation process for the children of Latino immigrants, instilling the immigrant bargain and parental sacrifice in their teaching to spur college-going behavior among their Latino students. A number of teachers described their parents' backbreaking jobs in their earlier days in the United States, and the effects they felt from it.

Latina teachers credited their parents' immigrant backgrounds for their own drive to succeed in school. They exemplified the findings of Jody Agius Vallejo and Jennifer Lee (2009) in regard to the children of Mexican immigrants who now form part of the middle class—that the desire to reciprocate socially to their families and poorer co-ethnic communities drives their success. If research identifies the parents' role in instilling this narrative, I found that college-educated Latinas also participated in the process to empower children to negotiate, transition, and learn dominant forms.

While Latina teachers at Compton Elementary used immigrant narratives in their classrooms, they also self-monitored in the presence of negative attitudes. Mrs. Díaz recalled how she had been particularly careful soon after the U.S. House of Representatives passed an anti-immigration bill in December 2005 but said that no matter what she experienced with her colleagues she would never stop talking about her immigrant experience in the classroom. Teachers at Compton often experienced negative reactions from their colleagues to such stories. Mrs. Díaz described a colleague who said, "They should be deported, they have no rights here." She questioned whether such a teacher could be sensitive to the needs of children who suffer from the fear of their parents' being deported.

In spite of their greater sensitivity to the issues Latino children and their families faced, Latina teachers were not necessarily unwilling to criticize Latino immigrant parents in interviews. They described a "*rancho*" or "*pueblito*" mentality,[19] meaning they made work, not school, a priority because of poverty. Mrs. Madrigal explained: "You want someone who is illiterate to be literate [the parents]. It's that wave that gets out of the ranches and gets out of Mexico and just comes here for the first time trying to make the best of their life. . . . [They think] let me get out of poverty, let me start all over again. . . . My mom and dad were part of that wave. They never volunteered [at school] because they were always working." Mrs. Romero added that her own Mexican immigrant father would tell her that immigrant parents possessed a different culture because of their poorer backgrounds. She said, "The people are coming straight from a little *pueblito* [rural community] and they are struggling. . . . They come here and don't even know they're supposed to be involved in their kids' school. They are just trying to put bread on the table and it's a different mentality." Their comments recall the research of Guadalupe Valdes (1996), who describes the differences between the Mexican educational institutions and the American schooling system, and how working-class Mexican immigrant families do not always recognize these differences.[20] Latina teachers acknowledged that Latino immigrant parents wanted their children to do well in school, but parents from more rural backgrounds often lacked the personal experiences with education and thus the knowledge to help their children succeed academically. At the same time, they adamantly challenged the script that Mexican culture and families did not value education, and they did not understand these dynamics as cultural failings. In fact, they highlighted that Latino parents would provide verbal encouragement (Gándara 1995) to their children and help them with their schooling in the ways that they could. They perceived Latino families' socioeconomic constraints and that low levels of human capital in the home country had traveled with them to the United States, influencing Latino immigrant parents' ability to participate in their child's schooling in the ways American schools expect. Instead of seeing this as a deficit, Latina teachers could resonate with these experiences, especially because they experienced it with their own parents, and integrate and build on Latino immigrants' limited human capital into a white institution. Latino families generally have lower levels of human capital (Feliciano 2005), something

Latina teachers in this study recognized and sought to address. Because of their limitations with communication in Spanish, many non-Latino teachers were at a disadvantage in this process. In chapter 6, I explain how their non-Latino colleagues, on the other hand, succumbed to negative racialization processes of Latino students.

Mathematics Is Not a Universal Language

Every year, at least one child of Latino immigrant parents would ask Mrs. Franco, a fourth-grade teacher, about methods for calculating long division and multiplication that she displayed on an overheard projector. She felt her Latino students seemed worried that she might object to the way their parents were teaching. She explained:

> [My students] tell me, "My mom learned it a different way in Mexico. Is that okay? Is that okay that she did that?" [in a worried tone]. . . . This has happened almost every year during parent conferences. I will have a parent say, "I was trying to show [my child] how to do math this way because this is the way I learned and [my child] told me 'No, No, No!' They couldn't do it because Mrs. Franco taught them." . . . So they will ask me if I can validate what they said by talking to their child. So I will explain to the child in front of the parent so that everyone hears the same thing, "It is okay if your parents have a different way." As long as they come to the same answer it doesn't matter to me.

A number of Latina teachers observed that their Latino students receive parental support with math homework. Unlike the teachers in Angela Valenzuela's (1999) study that took place in a Texas high school, and Nancy López's study (2002) of an urban high school in New York, I found that Latina teachers were very open to alternate methods. Angela Valenzuela suggests that schools are a subtractive process for Latino children because teachers undermine their linguistic abilities and cultural understandings of caring. This process in turn erodes the development of their social capital networks because they are unable to cultivate and nourish supportive relationships with school personnel. Instead of employing what Valenzuela calls a "subtractive" educational model, some Latina teachers allow an alternative mathematical curriculum to make Latino parents and children feel comfortable and validate Latino immigrant parents' local knowledge base.

Math is a key feature of Chicana/Latina cultural pedagogies. Of the twenty Latina teachers whose interviews appear in the pages of this book, fourteen made direct reference to algorithmic differences, noting that long division and multiplication equations were daily sources of contestation between themselves and their Latino students. Latina teachers draw from the nondominant cultural capital of poorer Latino families to generate parental involvement, which is crucial to educational success in schools (Valdes 1996; Ochoa 2007). More than "cultural brokers" who might facilitate communication between schools and parents, they engage in a reciprocal process to incorporate Latino parents' knowledge into their classrooms.

Ms. Sánchez, a fifth-grade Latina teacher who also works at Goodwill Elementary, said, "Oh, yeah! The Latinos solve them differently.... I let them do it. I always tell them, I have to teach you this way, but if you are more comfortable doing it the way your parents showed you, then that's fine." Ms. Sánchez is a third-generation Mexican American and she knows the method her students learn from their parents, which probably increases her comfort with encouraging students to listen to their parents.

Mrs. Cadena, a fourth-generation Latina teacher, explained:

Some of the kids will tell me, "My dad taught me like this." The only thing I tell them is, "Whatever way you're comfortable with, continue it." I teach it a certain way in class. It's gonna confuse 'em when they go home and their dad says, "No, you do it like this. This is how I learned." But whatever they're comfortable with. I can't tell them, "Your dad's been teaching you all this time, but because I'm your teacher this year you have to change it to this." It's a lot harder for them. I do run into that. The same with Chinese too, more so with Latinos. The math from Mexico. But there are some Asian [students]—from their grandparents they get it. They say, "My grandpa showed me."

In the focus group part of this study, I gave parents this prompt: Please solve the following math problem/*Por favor hágame esta operación*:

1238 ÷ 84 or 29 × 34, written vertically. Figures 5.2 and 5.3 show examples of immigrant and native-born parents' responses. Latina/o immigrant parents arrived at the same quotient but did not detail all of the steps the American curriculum requires. In Mexico long division uses the obelus (÷) symbol, while in the United States the problem is usually displayed in a tableau. One Latina immigrant parent in the group got very excited at the opportunity I gave her to demonstrate the method and her own expertise. At the same time, the multiplication math prompt in figure 5.3 posed problems for some of the immigrant parents because I wrote the problem vertically, as I did in the U.S. version. During the focus group with Spanish-speaking Latina/o immigrant parents, one Latina mother, gesturing horizontally with her arm, asked me, "*¿Me la puedes escribir hací? Es más fácil. De este modo no le entiendo*" ["Can you write it for me this way? It's easier. I don't understand the problem written that way"]. Of the ten Latina immigrant mothers included in the focus groups, eight solved the math problem the way they were taught in their home countries. The two exceptions were unable to use either method; one was illiterate in Spanish and English and the other scarcely more educated; she had received less than a fourth-grade education.

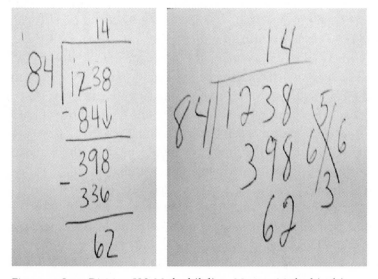

Figure 5.2. Long Division: U.S. Method (*left*) vs. Mexican Method (*right*)

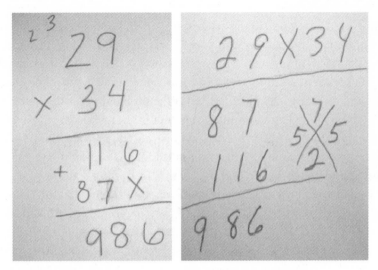

Figure 5.3. Multiplication Problems: U.S. Method (*left*) vs. Mexican Method (*right*)

I asked Latina teachers if they could show me the method that Latina/o parents were using. Some could; others said they would need to ask their own parents and get back to me. In her study of prospective Mexican American teachers, Vomvoridi-Ivanović (2012) argues that researchers cannot simply assume that teachers can use their cultural knowledge for pedagogical purposes in mathematics, even when they share their students' background. However, Latina teachers' general knowledge that a different method exists in Mexican schools and a willingness to permit their students to use it constituted a distinct advantage for their students. At Goodwill Elementary, Latina teachers described the Asian American teachers, who constitute the majority of the non-Latina teaching staff, as open to these cultural resources. I was present during a discussion of the cultural rift between U.S. methods and Mexican methods in the teacher's lounge at lunchtime.

Mrs. Arenas, a Latina teacher, remarked, "Mexican parents solve part of the problem in their head. They don't write everything down."

Dina Nguyen, a Vietnamese cultural liaison for Asian American parents, said, "That's funny, some Chinese students learn a different way too, from their parents." Asian teachers, like Latina teachers, also allowed alternative strategies for co-ethnics in regards to mathematics. This was not the case at Compton Elementary school.

Latina teachers at Compton Elementary had a different experience from that of their colleagues. Many described Latino immigrant parents who would schedule meetings with them because their children *"lloraban"* [cried] or grew "frustrated" when doing math homework. I saw evidence of this cultural mismatch myself during a "Swun Family Night"[21] at Compton Elementary, an event targeted to Latino and African American parents who wanted to aid their children with their math homework. The presenter was a Latina teacher with whom the district had contracted to make such presentations. None of the teachers at Compton Elementary attended. When I walked into the cafeteria, there were about five Latina mothers present in the room and one African American grandfather listening to the presentation on addition and subtraction.

When the question-and-answer portion began, one Latina mother, visibly upset, exclaimed, *"Mi niña se frustra y se pone a llorar porque como yo le enseño no es como le enseña la maestra"* [My daughter gets frustrated and she starts to cry because how I teach her is not how her teacher shows her].

Another Latina immigrant mother chimed in, *"A la mía ya la pusieron en clases especiales"* [Mine has already been placed in special education classes].

The presenter, in Spanish, responded, *"Nosotros queremos enseñarle la manera mas fácil para el niño"* [We want to teach the child the easiest way possible].

A second-generation Latina mother said, *"A mi me pasaba lo mismo. Me enseñaron a mi diferente cuando estaba chiquita. Y luego yo le decia a mi mamá, Hací no se hace. Le tengo que hacer como le hizo el maestro"* [The same thing happened to me. My parents taught me differently when I was small. I would tell my mother, "This is not how you do it. I have to do it how the teacher taught me"].

"Alli es donde existe la confusión" [This is where the confusion begins], said another Latina immigrant mother.

At both of the school sites, math was an everyday struggle. I observed that this subject in particular defied what Peterson (2004) termed the "cultural intelligence" of their parents (see also Thomas 2009)—that is, their ability to relate and work effectively across cultures. This was evident in an informal conversation with two Latina immigrant mothers. The older of the two, who was meeting her fourth-grade daughter at the end of the school day, had disheveled hair and looked tired. She had grocery bags at her feet. She explained that a white teacher at Compton "*Le tacho todas las operaciones a mi hija*" [marked all of my daughter's math problems wrong]. The silver crowns in her teeth shone as she spoke. "*Y allí la niña llorando por que su tarea estaba llena de rojo*" [And there the girl was crying because her homework was filled with red marks].

"*¿Qué hizo?*" [What did you do?], I asked her.

"*Pues fui ha hablar con el maestro para preguntarle por que se las tacho todas*" [I went to speak to her teacher to ask him why he marked them wrong].

She was getting angry. She felt personally attacked by her daughter's teacher because he asked if someone at home had done the homework for the daughter, or if she had copied her homework from her colleague. Like Mr. Goyette, the teacher seemed to look down on Latino families.

Latina teachers recognized the problems math instruction raised. While white, native-born parents experience problems because teaching methods have changed, the cultural rifts Latino families experience with their white teachers makes the issue far more fraught. The sense that parents and teachers doubt each other's competence gains heat across a cultural divide. Much as one of the parents at the math education evening at Compton had, Latina teachers recognized the long history of conflict over math in U.S. schools. Mrs. Godínez, a second-grade teacher at Compton, for example, recalled having been placed in special education classes as a result of the struggles she had with math. Indeed, there is a long history in the education literature of Latino children labeled as special needs (González 1990) because of a perceived language impairment, but cultural rifts over math can also lead to such perceptions. Famed mathematician Martha Civil (2008, 2009) argues that cultural misunderstandings arise between Latino immigrant families and school officials because mathematical word problems do not use examples that relate to a Latino student's home life. Similarly, education scholar Eduardo Mosqueda (2010) suggests that English-language proficiency is necessary to handle the linguistic complexity of math content. Through interactions between parents and school officials and from the voices of Latina teachers, I found that it is not only language proficiency that matters but also acknowledging and allowing alternative mathematical problem-solving strategies is crucial in the classroom for the children of Latino immigrant parents in order to succeed.

Not all teachers validated the mathematical nondominant forms of cultural capital that Latino parents brought with them from the home country. I asked teachers at Compton Elementary if they allowed Latino students to solve math problems the way their parents taught them. Mrs. Rivas said that if it "made sense to the child and they could explain it to the teacher, then it was fine." Mrs. Madrigal said that she was unaware of the method her students had learned from their parents because her parents did not have much schooling in their country of origin and she began kindergarten in the United States, but she informed me that once Latino parents met with her and "discussed the steps" she was more receptive to allowing the strategy because there was someone at home to foster the method.

Non-Latina teachers were less likely to allow Latino children to use the method their parents taught them. Mr. Colt, an upper-grade African American male teacher, told me, "They only know one way. The way I teach them." Latino immigrant parents indicated that they found non-Latino teachers immovable about teaching the method they themselves knew. Several African American women teachers indicated they might be receptive to allowing children to solve problems the way their parents taught them, but by and large they were not aware that other methods existed in Mexico. Latina teachers generally felt that their colleagues' resistance had more to do with racism and a sense that Latino children should assimilate to U.S. ways of solving long division and multiplication than concern for their mastery of mathematics. Mrs. Godínez, for example, highlighted teachers' preference for keeping the learning process "standardized."

Lisa Delpit (2012) suggests that teachers can connect math concepts to community issues relevant to African American students. Unlike Eduardo Mosqueda (2010), I find that is it not only language proficiency that matters, but also acknowledging and allowing alternative mathematical problem-solving strategies provided by Latino immigrants is crucial in the classroom for the children of Latino immigrants. The issue of children being taught an entirely different method of solving problems than their parents, and the complicating issue of cultural disconnect, differs from Delpit's research. In any case it was apparent that the issue contributes to the alienation between Latino families and non-Latino teachers.

Conclusions

Based on the ethnographic evidence presented in this chapter, I argue that there is a quiet transformation taking place in the teaching occupation in California's public schools in Latina teachers' classrooms. Research from almost twenty years ago indicates that schools operate under a "subtractive" model for Latina/o youth (Valenzuela 1999) because schools divest Latina/o students of their social and cultural resources. As I have written elsewhere, administrators and white colleagues may admonish Latina teachers who work in the token context among a majority of white colleagues in schools with majority Latino student populations for using Latino cultural resources to aid the learning process (Flores 2011a). Latina teachers draw upon Chicana/Latina cultural pedagogies, subverting standard workplace rules regarding Latino culture in teaching, and serve as empowerment agents for Latino families, but their efforts are met in different ways in each school.

Education sociologist Prudence Carter (2003) distinguishes between dominant and nondominant forms of cultural capital, arguing that most scholarship tends to ignore nondominant forms. I find that Latina teachers, the college-educated daughters of working-class Mexican immigrants, exercise Chicana/Latina cultural pedagogies—a nondominant form of ethnic cultural capital—to foster navigational skills for Latina/o families through language and communication codes, immigrant narratives, and mathematics. This chapter builds upon previous theories by demonstrating additional cultural rituals that Latina teachers who are bilingual and bicultural integrate in quotidian interactions with working-class Latino immigrant families. While American public schools have historically banned the teaching of Latina/o culture and acute nativism has typically created a highly hostile context (Portes and Rumbaut 2001; López 2003), I suggest that Latina teachers are aware of this nativism and its dire consequences and try to create a more positive context of reception for

Latino families in schools (Portes and Rumbaut 2001) so that they can curtail and buffer the downwardly mobile pathways of some Latina/o youth, serving as intermediaries in the educational learning patterns of the children of Latina/o immigrants.

I build upon the ways that education scholars have been conceptualizing cultural funds of knowledge in schools as formal, institutionalized celebratory multiculturalism is not enough because it is mostly symbolic. Because of their working-class roots and immigrant backgrounds, Latina teachers are able to tap into the subtle Latino cultural cues that immigrant Latino families bring with them from their countries of origin and to implement Chicana/Latina cultural pedagogies daily, effectively addressing a history of antagonism. Latina teachers seek to work with the cultural frames Latinos families bring to the classroom. Latina teachers also rely on their own parents' narratives and those of the parents of their students for support, moving beyond a monocultural Anglo and unilateral frame. They also use what the scholarship describes as *personalismo, simpatía,* and *amabilidad* in their communication codes with Latino immigrant parents, extending our knowledge of bilingualism and biculturalism in schools. These class-based communication codes demonstrate how most Latina teachers use restricted codes, interpreting themselves instead of using their students as cultural brokers. Last, they allow an alternate curriculum in regard to mathematics, accommodating the cultural elements that Latinos families bring to the classroom. The mathematics finding challenges the literature by urging scholars not to focus on English-language competency alone in their assessment of the challenges Latino children face but also the methods that may best support their educational development.

To their families and communities, the Latina educators at Compton Elementary and Goodwill Elementary are figures of success and honor. They are dedicated to helping this next generation reach and succeed in higher education. They have achieved intergenerational mobility, with the majority of them surpassing their working-class Latina/o parents in education, income, and occupational status, and they are in a job that allows them to "give back" socially to Latina/o children and their families in ways that might ameliorate the inferior education that has prevailed in Latina/o disadvantaged communities. I find that college-educated Latina teachers understand the oppressive and top-down "hidden curriculum" of schooling and attempt to teach their students in appropriate responses to the system. I argue that the practices of the mostly bilingual and bicultural Latina teachers in this study are not uni-directional, but reciprocal: a cooperative effort that facilitates ongoing relationships between the parent and teacher. Latino immigrant parents help Latina teachers understand their immigrant cultural background, which is evident when Latina teachers use Latino immigrant parents as a resource as well.

The different experiences of implementation at Compton Elementary and Goodwill Elementary affected the role of Latina teachers as cultural guardians. The racial tensions I identified in chapter 4 doubtless affected the level of resistance to their use of culture to facilitate Latina/o student progress that teachers at each school experienced. The model of Goodwill Elementary in which Latin teachers could more effectively incorporate the pedagogy into their daily work lives with Asian American co-workers might represent a useful model for other schools.

6

Standardized Tests and Workplace Tensions

There is [racial/ethnic] tension created because of the testing.
—Mrs. Larry, fifth-grade teacher

It was nearing the end of the academic school year. The house that I parked my car next to for over a year at Compton Elementary school had been painted a different color and completely renovated. A real estate sign with a Spanish surname and a phone number had been posted on the newly manicured lawn. The Latino family that lived next door to the African American family had removed the Mexican flag. The marquee that stood at the front of the school displayed a countdown for state tests: "*Pruebas en 3 días*" [Tests in three days].

High-stakes testing is a cornerstone of the educational structures in the United States. In California, state tests involve the application of language-grouping labels to language-minority students that fuel interracial conflicts between Latina teachers and their African American and Asian American peers. As cultural guardians within the classroom and beyond the school gates who rely on ethnic cultural resources to facilitate their students' educational success, Latina teachers resist structural inequality. This includes biased standardized testing that racializes their students and affects their students' well-being in the long term. This chapter explains the workplace tensions that high-stakes state testing creates for Latina teachers and the ways in which they shield co-ethnic children from inequitable racialization processes.

In addition to the marquee, a large banner adorned the inside of Compton to pump up students for exam week. I visited Mrs. Madrigal a couple of days prior to their big week of state testing, when she was composing a letter informing Latino parents that their children were about to take "*un exámen importante*" and asking them to ensure their children would go to sleep on time and eat breakfast a couple of days prior to the testing week. Although the California Standards Test (CST)[1] was conducted in English, and thus Latino immigrant parents would have difficulty helping their children prepare for it, the letter asked them to support their children through written and verbal encouragement (Gándara 1995).

Mrs. Madrigal looked worried. The results of the CST, which students in grades 2–5 would take all over California, would determine the fate of Compton Elementary, because it was in its fifth year as a Program Improvement[2] school. She kept a letter to a Latina student from her immigrant mother on her wall for inspiration. It read:

> *Diana,*
>
> *Quiero que le heches muchas ganas a tu éxamen. Tu saves que si puedes, quiero que me perdones porque ay veses que te regaño o te grito, pero es por tu bien. si tu le echas ganas y pones mas atención, podras lograr lo que tu quieres y ser alguien importante en el futuro y ser una profecional, teniendo buenas calificaciones y ser buena estudiante podras seguir adelante. Tu saves que tu papá y yo te queremos mucho y queremos lo mejor para ti y tus hermanos.*
>
> *Att. Tu Mamá que te quiere mucho. que dios te bendiga y te cuide[3]*

> [Diana,
>
> I want you to place a lot of effort on your test. You know you can do it, I want you to forgive me because I know there are times that I discipline you and yell at you, but it's for your own good. If you put a lot of effort and more attention, you can achieve what you want and become someone important and be a professional, having good grades and being a good student, you can prosper. You know that your father and I love you very much and we want the best for you and your brothers.
>
> Sincerely, Your mother who loves you very much. May god bless you and take care of you]

Mrs. Madrigal was not alone in her concern. All teachers working at Compton Elementary and Goodwill Elementary and their co-workers were frustrated with and stressed out by the outcome of these tests, which could potentially endanger their hard-earned jobs. This chapter addresses interracial relations between Latina teachers at these two schools and their colleagues, most of whom are women of color.[4]

I discuss the influence of standardized testing on race relations and how these interracial dynamics complicate or reflect Latina teachers' role as cultural guardians.

Mrs. Madrigal had to use Google to translate "standardized" into Spanish. The link between race relations and language among college-educated Latinas and racial/ethnic minority women in the professions slowly unraveled as she did so. She told me:

> To my principal or administration it is all about their end-of-the-year tests, their standardized tests. I do whatever I can in the class and I know it is not going to be enough because the kids are all Hispanic. No matter how much I try to teach them the standards, especially language arts. . . . they will never perform to the standards that they state. . . . Every year *me dan niños que son* [they give me kids that are] far below basic.[5] It's not because they don't have the brains for it. It's because they don't have the language. So I have to deal with other African American teachers that don't see that. I have to deal with other Caucasian teachers that don't see that. Some of them do see it, but others don't.

The special efforts Latina educators undertake to deflect racism directed at Latino children and their families gain particular urgency in relation to high-stakes testing set in place by the No Child Left Behind Act[6] (henceforth NCLB) and scrutiny as public outcry blames teachers for students' poor educational outcomes. The explicit focus of NCLB, which was established in 2001, is closing the "achievement gap" between high- and low-performing children, especially racial/ethnic minority and white students. This also led to the development of Race to the Top in 2009, a grant used to reward individual states for developing innovative policies in local district K–12 education. In California, as demographics shifted and white enrollment in public schools decreased, attention to the achievement gap focused increasingly on standardized test-score disparities between white and Asian American students on the one hand and Latina/o and Black students on the other (Cheng 2014; Ochoa 2014). The achievement gap creates a background for the analysis in this chapter; it forms the basis for California's structural policies regarding English-language acquisition that have left Latinas and their co-workers in the teaching profession to deal with racial cleavages on their own at the everyday micro-level. This ultimately affects their students, and Latina teachers feel a particular duty to protect them by resisting biased tests and their on-the-ground consequences. At Compton Elementary, I saw evidence that macro-structural forces lead to a dichotomous language-labeling process in which both Latina and African American teachers prefer to have the children of Latino immigrants in their classrooms than Black children.[7] At Goodwill Elementary, on the other hand, Asian teachers and parents blame Latino children for their perceived inferior academic performance while praising and valorizing the children of Asian immigrants. At times, Latina teachers also succumb to and accept notions of Asian racialized privilege but also resist negative stereotypes of co-ethnics.

The Impact of State Testing

Compton and Goodwill Elementary place a significant emphasis on state testing because they fear negative ramifications from the state such as job displacement or the shutting down of their school. The majority of the academic year is devoted to "prepping" for the test, and there are a range of sanctions on the schools for not meeting yearly benchmarks.

Table 6.1 shows the Academic Performance Index score and the Program Improvement Year for both of the schools in 2010. The table shows that Latino and Black students at Compton Elementary are scoring worse academically than Asian and Latino students at Goodwill Elementary. The Academic Performance Index score, the cornerstone of California's accountability measure, tracks yearly growth. Each year the benchmark is raised, heightening the stress teachers experience. For example, one year, Goodwill Elementary received a score of 783 and missed its annual benchmark by 4 points, demoting the school from a California

TABLE 6.1. State Testing and Program Improvement (PI) Scores

School	API Score	PI Year
Compton Elementary	736	5
Goodwill Elementary	783*	2

*Goodwill Elementary missed its target score by 4 points, demoting the school from a California Distinguished School to a Program Improvement school.

Source: California Department of Education, 2010

Distinguished School to a Program Improvement (PI) school. Compton Elementary, on the other hand, was in its fifth PI year, the final year that a school could have this designation before drastic measures such as complete removal of all teachers could take place. Reflecting their relative position with respect to state testing, Goodwill Elementary made an effort to maintain science and art as part of students' daily activities, but Compton Elementary focused the majority of its school day on language, and teachers often limited science and art to ten minutes a week. Latina teachers at both schools were required to test students and place them in their appropriate CELDT[8] (California English Language Development Test) level at the beginning of the year, and this is where the ruptures based on race and language on school grounds manifest for students and affect interracial relations between Latina teachers and their co-workers.

Latina Professionals and Workplace Inequities

Research into racial dynamics between Latina, Asian, and Blacks in the workplace is scant. Most studies of Latina professionals investigate their workplace dynamics with whites (Vallejo 2012; García-López 2008; Chávez 2011). Research on Latinos in blue-collar jobs in new immigrant destinations such as Georgia and Mississippi do address workplace relations between Latinos and African Americans. For example, studies have found that white employers prefer to employ Latino immigrants because they are more exploitable than native-born whites and Blacks (Waldinger and Lichter 2003; López-Sanders 2009; Stuesse 2016) and more pliable than native-born Mexican Americans (Holmes 2013). In *Scratching out a Living*, Angela Stuesse (2016), in studying poultry-processing workers, finds that employers play a direct role in exacerbating racial conflict between Latino immigrant and African American workers by assigning them to shifts by national origin and race, minimizing their abilities to communicate with one another and understand their histories and current social circumstances.[9]

The teachers at Compton Elementary and Goodwill Elementary are primarily women of color.[10] At Compton Elementary more than 60 percent of teachers are Latina or African American women. At Goodwill Elementary, 75 percent of teachers are Asian women or Latinas. To address the complex nature of their interactions based on differing minority identities in this chapter, I use the work of sociologist Joan Acker (2006), an expert in the field of women and work. She postulates that all organizations have *inequality regimes* that serve to maintain class, gender, and racial hierarchies within a particular organization and are linked to inequality in the surrounding society. This means that distinct inequality regimes may be set up and maintained in different occupational settings. Using this lens, I show that at both Compton and Goodwill state-mandated tests dependent on language act as another powerful regime that ignites racial tensions between Latina teachers, their co-workers, and students in multiethnic schools. This chapter explores how the dynamics Holmes and Stuesse identify play out among Latina professionals and their non-Latina colleagues. As I'll describe, interracial relations at the two school differ markedly.

Helping Your Own

I interviewed Ms. Ana Gutierrez, a first-grade Latina teacher at Compton Elementary, over a four-day span before she was set to take off for her first trip to Europe over the summer. "I'm going to go home and weigh my luggage because it's probably too heavy," she said ruefully. With four years in the profession, Ms. Gutierrez was working at Compton Elementary's summer school program and was also completing her BTSA[11] training for beginning teachers. Each day, I arrived during her lunch break and we spoke for thirty minutes—all she could spare. Her colleague Mrs. Del Mundo, a first-grade Filipina teacher, came to her classroom on the first occasion and listened to her responses, at times chiming in. I informed Ms. Gutierrez that I could return to interview her on another date, but she allowed her colleague to be there because they often ate lunch together. Ms. Gutierrez was comfortable sharing her experiences regarding her pathways into the teaching profession with Mrs. Del Mundo there, but when I asked, "Can you tell me how Latina and African American teachers interact in this school?" on the second day, her demeanor quickly changed. She sat back in her chair, took one last bite of her potato salad, and started to pack her items in her Rubbermaid plastic container. The bell rang and she hastily said, "and that's my cue to go."

It was not until the school's yearly Back to School Night event two months later that Ms. Gutierrez opened up about the intricacies of national origin, race, and language. As I decorated her room by climbing up onto a wobbly table and tacking up number lines[12] students had made, she said, "Off the record,[13] Blacks don't want to help their own. They just don't. Whatever happened to helping your own people?" She looked bewildered. I asked her what she meant by that. She explained, "It seems like the African American teachers want the ELLs; they don't want the EOs." A sixty-year-old African American substitute teacher, Mrs. Cheadle, who had a long history in Compton, came into her room to share her daughter's wedding album just then, and Ms. Gutierrez stopped talking. The acronyms caught my attention, and I would later find that ELLs meant English Language Learners and EOs meant English Only. In this context, ELLs were Latino and EOs were Black.

The majority of Latina teachers working at Compton Elementary, like Ms. Gutierrez, denied that racial conflict existed. They seemed uncomfortable speaking overtly about race relations in the organization directly. As the free entrance of Mrs. Cheadle and Mrs. Del Mundo into her classroom suggests, Ms. Gutierrez had friendly interracial interactions with her colleagues. All the Latina teachers I interviewed say they are extremely content to work in schools where the majority of their coworkers are diverse faculty of color. I imagined this composition might lead them to talk openly about race with their colleagues, but this was not the case. The fact that they did not concurs with the argument of sociologist Eduardo Bonilla-Silva (2003) that most work organizations are predicated on a color-blind ideology in the United States. He argues that racism and racial ideologies became subtle around 1965, describing the covert nature of these ideologies as potentially more perilous to equality because racism is less visible.

Teachers experience color-blindness as a structural mandate from their supervisors and the public. For example, teachers are often instructed that they should not "see" race and in turn admit to being intimidated to speak about color (Pollock 2005; Lewis 2003; Castagno 2014). In my research, a Latina teacher commented: "Color doesn't matter. It doesn't matter the race. It's about the child and what's inside." As education scholar Mica Pollock (2005) argues, teachers attempt to suppress "race words" by being color-mute and often contest them in schools, but in doing so they reproduce the very racial inequalities they loathe.

Ms. Gutierrez's use of ELL and EO typified the response to the top-down ideology banning race talk on school grounds. Latina teachers speak about tensions in schools in other ways mainly through language labels, which seem safer, benign, and nonracial.

Language grouping of students begins the very first weeks of school and is crucial to understanding race relations in school organizations in a post–civil rights era. In Compton Elementary, a clear binary emerged in which ELL referred to the children of Latino immigrants while EO meant African American students.[14] These labels lent themselves to racial segregation of children throughout the school day and teacher racial/ethnic preferences of students.

ELLs and EOs in School: Tracking Students by Language

It is extremely difficult for children to escape the track they are placed in when they begin school (Oakes 2005).[15] While academic tracking appears standardized, I found that the process was arbitrary and that I too, much like the teachers, could be co-opted by the process. I attended a training session one summer day in August 2009.[16] As the teachers trickled into the cafeteria and sat at the tables, they sat in mixed-race groups determined by grade levels. I sat with the fourth-grade team. "Hey, girl, lemme scootch in *aqui*" [here], said Mrs. Madrigal to me.

Mrs. Jones,[17] the principal, began her presentation. She is tall and slender and African American and was about to begin her first year at Compton Elementary. She has more than ten years' experience and had worked at other schools in the district. Her predecessor, Mr. Olson, was also African American. "Hello, everyone. I hope you are settling in. I haven't been in your classrooms yet, I'm giving you time," Mrs. Jones said with a smile as she whisked her hair to the side and spoke on the microphone at the front of the cafeteria. She said that all teachers needed to start assessment training. At this point she began a PowerPoint presentation to highlight her points about assessment. She noted, "This means that students, the English Language Learners (ELLs), are going to be tested and grouped into separate academic levels."

As Mrs. Jones turned the microphone over to the new curriculum specialist, Mrs. Peterson, Mrs. Madrigal leaned into me. "Oh girl!" she whispered, "*A ella le tengo miedo*" [I'm so afraid of her], indicating Ms. Jones. She tensed up and shuddered as she spoke. As she told me later Mrs. Madrigal had transferred from another school in Compton because of Mrs. Jones, who had been the principal there. According to Mrs. Madrigal, Mrs. Jones "doesn't care about Latino kids."

Mrs. Peterson, an older African American woman, explained that the teachers were receiving LAS[18] (Language Assessment Scales) assessment training in order to denote whether students were above proficiency or below basic on a one- to five-point likert scale. A score of five meant that a child would be designated English proficient. The separation of students according to their CELDT level also appeared to create racial tensions between teachers and reinforced Latina teachers' role as cultural guardians to Latino students. Once scored, all ELL students would be distributed so that each teacher would have a set at the same proficiency level.

Mrs. Peterson explained that teachers would give students points based on how a "native speaker" would answer the question. She showed a picture of a little girl wearing a flowery dress, raising one hand and holding books in the other. There was an older gentleman in the image taking the little girl's picture. The prompt was: Ask the student if they can tell you one thing that is going on in this image. "What would you give a student that said, 'Someone is taking her picture'?" Mrs. Peterson asked. A chorus of "three, three" responded. Mrs. Peterson praised them, "Good! Yes!" She went on, "If a student says, 'Her taking picture,' that's a two because that is not typical of what a native speaker would say. If a student says, 'she is raising her hand,' that's a three. If a student says, 'photo' give them a one. This response is on topic, they gave the correct English word but it does not satisfy the task." Mrs. Peterson also said that if after four seconds a student did not respond, teachers were instructed to give them a zero. A score of zero meant that a student had no English ability and would be placed at the lowest level. Mrs. Godínez looked at her third-grade Latino colleagues wide-eyed, and with her mouth slightly opened, as if this were too harsh a score because a student could quite possibly answer the prompt correctly in another language.

Mrs. Madrigal and I exchanged a glance. She shook her head, then rolled her eyes. She ran her pencil down a roster, examining the scores former teachers had given her new batch of students.

Mrs. Peterson flashed another picture on the screen that showed a little girl holding a pencil and a book. She asked, "What if a student says, 'She's reading his book'?" There was a lot of discussion among teachers on this one. I proposed two and so did Mrs. Romero, a kindergarten teacher. "Well, she's holding a book," she said. Others thought it should be a one because the girl was holding it but not reading it. Mrs. Peterson acknowledged the problem but said, "If on a couple of questions you are off by one point, it won't skew the test. It's all about the rubric."

Mrs. Peterson showed another image of a student holding a paper and pencil. Mrs. Romero asked, "What if a student says, 'ummm, ummm, if I can have the paper for write'?" Mrs. Peterson said that she would give that answer a two, but that the book said to give it a three. Mrs. Shah, a teacher of Iranian descent, said, "I would give that a zero or a one because it doesn't answer the question." Mr. Salinas and Mr. Durán, two Latino teachers, and Mrs. Madrigal, Mrs. Godínez, and Mrs. Díaz all turned to look at her, signaling with stares their displeasure with her response. Mrs. Shah then said, "I want the answer! I guess I just have higher standards" and laughed. Mrs. Díaz gave her the side-eye and wrote on her sheets. Mrs. Peterson added, "It is according to the interpretation of the teacher, but we are following the rubric. You kind of have to know how a kid would be thinking." She pressed teachers to gauge the ways that a "native" English speaker would pronounce English words and express themselves. When I asked Latina teachers what was meant by "native" English speaker some of them responded, "I don't know" and others said, "probably like a [white] American."

As an observer and sociologist I did not think I would easily become co-opted by the test, but I found myself shouting out numbers I thought were correct and justifying my responses. I found myself placing Latino and African American students in levels that would be insurmountable for many of them to "test out of" and overcome in the long run. Trainings like this are significant because it made me realize that these tests actually matter and affect a student's life very early on, especially if they are non-native English speakers and of color.

English-language dominance is a marker of cultural assimilation, and people in the United States often perceive a lack of language skills as a marker of one's being a perpetual foreigner. Mrs. Peterson also instructed teachers to weigh pronunciation in their evaluations of students. This reflects a broader reality in the United States in which European and Australian immigrants receive praise for speaking "American English" when they use American dialect but retain an accent, but nonwhite immigrants receive censure for sounding even slightly unlike white U.S. natives (Tuan 1998; Santa Ana 2002). While the United States has been aptly described as the "graveyard" for languages because of its historical ability to absorb immigrants and extinguish their mother tongues within a few generations (Portes and Rumbaut 2006; Rumbaut, Massey, and Bean 2006), state testing resuscitates debates around this extinction.[19]

During the training session, it got progressively hotter in the room. Teachers started fanning themselves with the handouts. Mrs. Peterson concluded her talk: "Remember, you are only testing your ELLs, not your EOs or those that have been reassigned as English proficient."[20] Immediately, Mrs. Rhodes, an older African American teacher, raised her arm to ask a question. When Mrs. Peterson acknowledged her, she said, "What will happen to the EOs? What about the EOs?" Mrs. Peterson repeated her direction, and Mrs. Díaz chimed in: "How are we supposed to do this? We don't even know who our ELLs are!"

Mrs. Peterson had no direct response. She said, finally, "Finish up by next Wednesday if you can." The meeting was over. The teachers who had been sitting by grade level seemed to sort into racial and ethnic groups as they walked out of the room, looking unhappy.

Mrs. Peterson had replaced a Latina at the school who had recently been pink-slipped because she had fewer years working in the district. My impression was that relations with her predecessor were better. Usually, newer teachers and staff who are below a certain level of tenure are first to be released. In Compton, this meant that Latinas were the first to lose their spots if a more senior African American teacher was available.

At Compton Elementary, Latina teachers did not have the authority to determine which students would be in their classrooms. The office staff, the principal and vice principal, and a Home Language Survey[21] that was sent to Latino families determined the process of assigning students to classrooms and teachers. Latina teachers acknowledged that the state of California emphasized getting Latino children to pass the language tests more than African Americans. At the same time, they understood the issues that African American teachers brought to the forefront such as less resources for them, but they were also turned off over why African American and white teachers preferred to have a class with mostly Spanish-speaking children of Latino immigrants.

The Preference for Children of Latino Immigrants

Latina teachers were more open to elaborating on the differences between Latino and African American children in their schools when I asked them if they could tell me about EOs and ELLs in schools, the language labels applied to all students in public schools, than when I asked them using race labels. In her book *Color Mute*, sociologist Amanda Lewis (2004) argues that race is not officially taught like reading and math in elementary education but seeps itself into everyday life and interactions in schools. Teachers, Lewis argues, explicitly and implicitly teach race to students in schools despite their attempts to remain race-neutral. They mute the conversation over race-related issues but find new labels to talk about them. I found that this extended to communicating with one another, and that testing language provided these new labels. As I explained in chapter 3, as cultural guardians Latina teachers institutionalized servicing the Latino community as part of their jobs and questioned why African American teachers lacked a similar social responsibility toward their own community. In contrast to other studies that have highlighted how middle-class African Americans express a linked fate to poorer co-ethnics over racial discrimination and many seek employment in occupations with a higher proportion of Blacks to uplift them (Higginbotham 2001; Ladson-Billings 2009; Beasley 2011; Gilkes 2010; Bell 2014), they felt teachers at Compton Elementary did not show a similar responsibility to African American students and families. Like Latina teachers, African American teachers racialized EO and ELL students in the classroom, and they felt that the school district allocated more resources to ELLs to help them pass state tests. Given the pressure on teachers to improve test scores, it was practical for all teachers to favor ELLs over EOs.

Latina cultural guardians prefer to have Latino students in their classrooms because of a shared ethnic affinity, and because they understand the struggles that Latino children face when attempting to incorporate into the host society and learn a new language. This is not to completely let them off the hook, as many of them perceived African Americans in a negative light too, expressing anti-Black sentiment as I described in chapter 4. But Latina cultural guardians felt that structural constraints made it harder for them to help African American children. One factor they cited was that African American children were numerical minorities in their classrooms. It was common to see classes of around twenty students with only one African American. Each grade level had at least one EO-only classroom as well, and a monolingual English-speaking teacher was assigned to it because the general sense was that if a teacher had Spanish skills she would be teaching students who might need those skills.[22] About reaching the African American community, Mrs. Becerra, a first-grade teacher, explained,

> That's probably the biggest challenge [we] are having right now at the school. I think they [African American students] are the group that is probably the worst. I wasn't exposed to enough [African American children] because I only had one out of nineteen kids, or twenty kids. It's really hard because you would normally think that I got exposed to more [African American children] in Compton but I had one. I don't think I understand that culture. I wouldn't be able to suggest how to help them. I know they are struggling a lot. The [African American] kids are struggling a lot.

Mrs. Becerra lamented that she did not have a cultural connection with African American students and was having trouble formulating strong rapport, which is crucial to academic achievement (Valdes 1996).

Mrs. Estrada concurred with her colleague and also explained that African American teachers preferred to have a class full of Latinos.

> An African American teacher took on the African American kids, the whole class was EOs, and she struggled. I think even for them [Black teachers], they would prefer to be in a class with Latinos than African Americans because they are having a lot issues with them. . . . That teacher was going crazy, like, "Never again are we putting all the EOs

together." . . . I think they may see them [children of Latino immigrants as] more calm compared to the EOs or the African Americans so I think in some ways it [ELL status] is like a plus.

In their seminal book on education, *Children of Immigration*, Carola Suárez-Orozco and Marcelo Suárez-Orozco (2001) explain that teachers generally have two schools of thought regarding the children of immigrants: (1) that they are better disciplined and more appreciative of teachers' efforts than non-immigrant students and (2) that they are intellectually inferior, "trouble-makers" who cannot assimilate into the mainstream because they lack drive. Similarly, Antonia Randolph (2013)[23] describes teachers who distinguish between minority groups in multiracial schools in the Midwest. In her research, a hierarchy of students emerged in which teachers praised immigrant minorities as "innocent" and disdained Black students as "hard." Randolph noted that even Latina teachers seemed confused by the fact that Latino students were quieter in classrooms where instruction was in English because they were not completely confident in English. They considered children of Latino immigrants as meek, docile, and sedate, but Randolph felt that the students were merely occupied attempting to learn English words. Mrs. Rivas, a fifth-grade Latina teacher, echoed this sentiment when she said, of the children of Latino immigrants: "They are more respectful. They are quieter. They don't necessarily talk back. I think that's one of the big differences."

Mrs. Godínez acknowledged that separating students by language achievement level in Compton created a bifurcation of students at the school and led to workplace conflict. She said, "When they were all grouped together like that it is like that because the Spanish students are—maybe you get the ones that are very quiet because they don't know the language so they are going to be more quiet. The EOs, they cannot stop talking. They cannot stop talking. I mean it's true. It's true. It's true."

During her interview, Mrs. Paige, an African American teacher who taught kindergarten and had mostly the children of Latino immigrants in her class, echoed the sentiments of her Latina colleagues. She said: "You're dealing with kids who are level one and level two [low levels] or in the silent period, brand-new coming here. They're getting the sensory input, input, input. They're not ready for production yet. So you end up with a quiet class [laughs]. You know what I mean?" Mrs. Bradford, a white teacher, said during a first-grade team meeting, "It's just so hard having kids that don't speak English. I'm so happy when I help them [Latinos] learn it." When I followed up with her later, I asked her if she would rather have a class of just EOs because they already speak English; she replied, "Oh no! Never. God, no!"

Mrs. Sanders, a first-grade African American teacher who was sympathetic to the negative characterization of African American students, said:

> They [her colleagues] think that they're all bad. They [Black students] talk too much. They feel like they can't handle them, in that sense. That they're too much, they don't know how to control Black kids. A lot of people don't want to have the EOs. . . . Not [that] they don't want them in their classroom, but they don't want to have them all day, or they don't want to teach them. Having a whole class full of them is what it is . . . that's the attitude.

While Mrs. Sanders did not seem to share the same attitude as most of her colleagues, she does explain that having a class composed of entirely African American children who speak English and are categorized as fives is negatively stigmatized as opposed to teaching very young Latino children who may be lower scoring initially to learn English and meet state benchmarks.

Mrs. Porter, who is African American, emphasized the resources directed to ELL students: "more attention towards the ELL learners, because they're the majority of the school. So for the school to raise their test scores, all the attention's gonna go to them because they'll raise the test scores. Whereas there's not that many EOs, so it's just kind of like they fall behind." I asked Mrs. Porter how she and her fellow African American teachers feel about this. She said:

> We don't like it. But we have to do it. It's beyond our control. . . . All you can do is try and help the EOs get higher if they're in your class later on. . . . But even here, I don't know about district-wide, but at this school, African Americans are the lowest-scoring. You would think that they would be up there with everybody else, and it's not. It shows. It does.

Mrs. Porter, who was assigned a class of mostly ELLs, elucidates that she would try to help African American students if they were assigned to her class in the future, but Latina teachers did not see it this way. Because the mission of many urban public schools is to make children proficient in the English language, state policies forced teachers to focus on linguistically assimilating the children of Latino immigrants. The preference for children of Latino immigrants has important consequences for cultural guardianship as interracial dynamics and the racialization of students can either enforce or complicate it. I am not suggesting that the feelings against "EOs" among Latina teachers was acceptable; rather, in the context of multiracial schools it bolstered their commitment to co-ethnics. In the case of Compton Elementary, the social structure enforced Latina teachers' commitment to co-ethnics but did not support African American teachers' commitment to co-racials.

Racial Dichotomies: Latina and Black Teacher Tensions

In her sociological study of Black masculinity among African American youth, Ann Arnett Ferguson (2001) argues that well-intentioned teachers and principals contribute to and reinforce negative and racist stereotypes about Black men and place them onto children, resulting in an "adultification" of young Black males. She notes how young African American boys are perceived as troublemakers and that authority figures therefore overdiscipline them. These negative and racist stereotypes are also evident at Compton Elementary School but work through language labels. While a quiet ELL may be mute because he or she has no idea what is going on in class, teachers have short-term goals throughout the day: getting through a lesson without having to stop and scold someone. Mrs. Beasley, a fourth-grade African American teacher, told me that many teachers had a "Black boy problem"—meaning that they overly disciplined or reprimanded them (see Rios 2011). Mrs. Becerra said, "*Muchos maestros dicen que los morenos son muy tremendos. Y en la realidad sí son. Sí son*" [Many teachers say that African American students are a handful. In reality they are. They are]. Mrs. Rivas said,

> Most of the EOs are behavior problems. Nobody wanted behavior problem students. . . . I don't want to sound like if I'm favoring a certain cul-

ture but if you had a group of all African Americans you knew that was just going to be a rough group. It was just going to be a rough group and that's the way it was because even the African American teachers would say, "I don't want that!" Seriously! "That's not fair! I don't want to take all of the EO's because it was a tough group." It *is* tough.

Similarly, Mrs. Godínez, a third-grade teacher, said, "Usually those [EO] classes have the worst-behaved students. . . . I don't know why that happens, but that's what a [white] kindergarten teacher said: 'I have the worst-behaved students and EOs,' and she said she is tired of it." When I asked Mrs. Godínez if she agreed with the kindergarten teacher, she replied,

> I do. To be honest with you [it's] because of behavior. Another [Black] teacher from [my] grade level almost told me the same thing because of behavior. . . . I'd rather not say names but I've spoken to some colleagues and they say, "I'd rather . . ." [smiles and pauses]. I don't think it's being racist. It's just that you don't want to have any issues with children that are not following directions or that are not on task with academics and that talk back.

Over time, I understood that because African American students could speak in English, they could verbalize responses and talk back to teachers. Their English-speaking language abilities and active interaction made them undesirable. Teachers constantly compared African American students with Latino children who were just learning the language. Mrs. Wright disagreed with her colleagues who felt that African American teachers were just as biased against African American students as Latina teachers. She herself is African American, and she said, "What I find is that if they're not a Black teacher, they feel like they can't handle them. That they're too much, they don't know how to control Black kids. A lot of people don't want to have the EOs. They're not much different than Hispanics, it's just—I don't know. . . . One teacher last year had an issue with having all of them. . . . They all cannot be a behavior problem." Mrs. Wright attests to the fact that African American teachers did look out for co-racials, but Latina teachers did not interpret their efforts this way.

Mrs. Becerra attributed the difference between students not to race or language learning per se but to the difference between immigrant parents and native-born parents. Herself a child of immigrant parents, she said, "*Tú sabes que los papás inmigrantes como nos crían. Nos crían a obedecer a los adultos, obedecer a los maestros. Son mas dóciles. Los niños [Latinos] criados por padres nacidos aquí corren el riesgo de ser problemas también*" [You know how immigrant parents raise us. They raise us to obey adults and to obey teachers. They are more docile. The Latino children raised by parents born in the U.S. also run the risk of being behavior problems too].[24]

Further complicating their view of the distinction between ELLs and EOs, teachers at Compton Elementary agreed that African American children who speak African American Vernacular English (AAVE) at home should also be considered ELLs. Mrs. Díaz, the only teacher I interviewed who had Afro-Cuban roots, explained,

> Both cultures are suffering. Why should [we] have to claw at each other to get ahead? The state gives us these resources to either share with all or share with one subculture in some ways. If you look at the budget you will see how much money is allocated for everyone. There is money allocated for English Language Learners only. There is no such thing as an African American budget. I can see why it is disturbing. . . . I think there's an automatic defense. My view is that we should all achieve this together. But just by bringing it up, walls are put up immediately. . . . When they [Black teachers] do make comments about the ELLs having more resources than African Americans I get defensive, but then I realize that is dumb. My initial reaction is like, "Wait, protect [Latinos] right?" but then another second goes by and I go, "You know what they are, right? We aren't on equal footing here." Those conversations should happen.

Mrs. Díaz recognized that African American were expected to take the California State Test at the end of the school year, without being exposed to resources that cater directly to them, even though they, like ELLs, had a language barrier.

Mrs. Rhodes is African American, and she taught the EO classroom. Mrs. Rhodes had both African American and Latino EO students in her makeshift GATE[25] class. Regarding the disparate resources, she point-blank exclaimed, "There are no resources for the EOs!" However, she did not want to talk about the challenges her African American students faced because they speak AAVE rather than standard English at home.

Mrs. Godínez, who always taught ELLs and only once in her career was ever assigned an EO class, however, said: "It would be good if they [EOs] all took the LAS [Language Assessment Scales] test. They don't give it to the African American students because they said that would be discrimination against them [because it implied that AAVE is not English], but yet they are being integrated in the class as just English Only and most of the time it's the majority, they are African Americans." Mrs. Godínez concluded, "So in a way, I think we are discriminating against them because we are bunching them up in one class," implying that they were racially segregating African American children.

The disparity between resources dedicated to African American students and those provided to students born to Latino immigrants required the teachers at Compton Elementary to deal with racialization processes on their own at the micro-level. Unfortunately, state testing and language grouping labels fueled conflict between Latina teachers and their co-workers and hurt both Black and Latino students who are struggling. These interracial dynamics at Compton Elementary result in a dichotomous racialization process that pushes Latina cultural guardians to focus on co-ethnic students who are numerical majorities. But as I'll describe in the next section, a school with high- and low-achieving students of color that can both be classified as ELL[26] changes the picture.

Goodwill Elementary

Civility between Latina and Asian Teachers

There was a convivial atmosphere in the lunch lounge at Goodwill Elementary.[27] When I arrived, I snuck in through the side door, which was propped open by a wooden block. I took a seat in the middle of the two long brown rectangular tables and perused the items on the table. A small, rectangular, glossy flyer that read, "Mando's Restaurant" caught my eye. The flyer had pictures of *tamales* and *birria* next to beef and broccoli and orange chicken. It read, "*Comida china, estilo Panda Express*" [Panda Express–style Chinese food]. On the back of the flyer was an advertisement for a carpet cleaning service. This side of the card read "Mando's Carpet Cleaning." As Asian American and Latina teachers started making their way into their lounge for their lunch period, they passed the flyer around. Each teacher took turns reading the card and there was slight banter and chuckling over the advertisement. One of the Asian American teachers, a Vietnamese woman, picked up the card and shared it with another Vietnamese teacher. They poked fun at the misspellings on the card. Mrs. Eap, a Thai and Cambodian teacher, looked at the card and started laughing. She said, "Oh, I didn't know there was a thing called *chown mein*. They misspelled *responsibility* too." The card, indeed, read "responsability." Ms. Maciel, a Mexican American teacher, walked into the lunchroom and wanted to know what all the commotion was about. "Hey, I want to laugh too. What's so funny?" Mrs. Eap handed her the card and said, "Look at your people's card." Ms. Maciel took the card. She noticed the misspelling of *responsibility*. She showed it to Mrs. Rocha, another Mexican American teacher, and they smiled at each other but looked a little embarrassed. They sat down with the others to eat. The Latina teachers were visibly discomfited, but hid it through laughter.

Mrs. Quiroz, who is Central American, took up the joke. "You can eat your *sope* [thick tortilla with vegetables and meat] with your *wonton* or your *huarache* [Mexican food dish] with your egg roll," she said, dissolving in laugher. All of the teachers in the lounge started laughing hysterically. Ms. Maciel pointed out, "If you go to a Chinese Express, the cooks are all Mexican. They are the ones making the food." Both Asian American and Latina teachers laughed and you could hear a distinct chorus of "yeah" and "mm-hmm." Mrs. Eap said, "You know how Asian people are known as cleaners, like Koreans have laundromats and mom and pop joints. Or Japanese people are gardeners? The Chinese have fast food restaurants." Mrs. Quiroz interjected, "Noooo! This is Mexican territory. We clean! We are the cleaners. We are the gardeners." Mrs. Kobayashi, a self-proclaimed *Sansei*—grandchild of Japanese immigrants—added with a slight smile, "Well, my dad was a gardener and my mom was a farm worker and then I worked at a Korean mom and pop joint." She laughed, too.

When I asked them about it later, Latina teachers explained that the immigrant experience and their ethnic origins allowed them to connect with Asian American co-workers. But there were also undertones that Asians were disadvantaged too, which Asian teachers acknowledged, and that Latinas/os as whole had no excuse for not succeeding. In the lounge, Latina and Asian teachers were able to share their life experiences and discuss the difficulties of learning a second language. After Mrs. Kobayashi's remark, other teachers contributed information about their childhood experiences with their immigrant parents and working-class parents in the United States. I focused my attention on Ms. Maciel and Mrs. Kobayashi to fully capture one conversation. The latter said, "I was surprised my mom still liked eating strawberries after having picked them in Santa Maria." Ms. Maciel nodded and said, "Yeah, there are other people that worked in the fields, not just Mexicans."

Latina teachers at Goodwill Elementary said that they were extremely satisfied in the workplace with Asian colleagues. They felt they had a lot in common because they shared immigrant origins and ties and most knew a second language, ate ethnic foods, had experienced gendered constraints within their families, were familiar with the dynamics in ethnic immigrant enclaves, and traversed dual cultures. Except for Mrs. Kobayashi, the Asian teachers were 1.5-generation, meaning they had migrated to the United States with their parents at a young age. Their gendered experiences as the daughters of immigrants encouraged the Latina and Asian teachers to form a welcoming space for each other, for parents and their children.

In contrast to Compton Elementary, similar immigrant and ethnic origins led to bonds of solidarity between Latina and Asian teachers at Goodwill Elementary. However, state testing gave rise to racial stereotypes of students of color in education, to the detriment of Latino students, and threatened those bonds. In her book *Civility in the City*, sociologist Jennifer Lee (2002) examines interracial relations between Jewish and Korean merchants with their Black customers. She argued that merchant–customer relations were not as conflict-ridden as depicted in the media but rather characterized by civility and ordinariness in everyday life. More important, she showed how both sides made great effort to make interactions pleasant, fearing racialized dramas. According to Lee, when circumstances exacerbated racial tension, Black personnel and employees tended to mitigate it. Although Latina and Asian teachers' daily interactions with one another remained civil when I observed them, as I will describe, state testing was chipping away at moments of solidarity and cohesion such as I observed in the lounge. Latina cultural guardians began to advocate for Latino students in the face of stereotypes.

"Ohhh, Diego, Our Only Latino Role Model"

Ms. Dávila, a mixed white and Mexican teacher who taught drama, was sorting the parent–teacher request sheets at the principal's request. Ms. Dávila started separating the sheets into different stacks: "One for Robles, another for Maciel," she said. Most of the parents who made requests had children in the primary grades (K–2).[28] "They talk to each other," Ms. Dávila noted. The form had a space for second choices as well, and Ms. Dávila told me that most parents would get their first choice, while a few got their second. Mrs. Wei, an ethnic-Chinese teacher who taught first grade, and Ms. Maciel, who taught second grade, received the most requests.

Ms. Dávila took the sheets to the staff's end-of-the-year meeting, which I attended. The principal, Mrs. Prado, brought to the meeting several stacks of purple sheets held together with rubber bands. "These sheets contain the names of every student in the school and their performance scores on state tests," she announced. The stacks were separated by teacher and grade level, and each teacher received his or her own. The principal said they would be assigning students to classrooms in the meeting.

Mrs. Prado instructed each teacher to take her stack and put a number on the top left-hand corner of the page in red ink. These numbers ranged from 1 to 5. "Make sure to break the classrooms down by gender, ethnicity, language, and achievement level," Mrs. Prado remarked. Mrs. Arenas hurriedly shuffled through the purple sheets and wrote different numbers of the top right-hand corner of each paper. She did this quickly, hesitating only a couple of times for two Latino students. "Jaime, two or three?" she asked herself as she tapped her red pen on the desk. She hesitated, marked three, and then scribbled over it and marked two. Several other students with Asian surnames were marked with a four, and two more Latino boys marked with a two. She then came across Diego's sheet, lifted his paper as she looked at his scores, and said, "Ohhh, Diego, our only Latino role model."

I asked Mrs. Arenas about Diego. He had migrated to the United States with his parents at the age of five. He was fluent in both Spanish and English in the fourth grade. He was very intelligent.

"I'm separating the boys by ethnicity here," said Mrs. Franco to Mrs. Arenas. "Okay, let's put these three Asian boys here and these three Asian boys here," she replied. Mrs. Robles kept sighing and taking deep breaths about more Latino students' being labeled low. I could indistinctly hear the teachers mumbling, "High, high, low, low, average. She's average. He's high. He's low."

In interviews, Mrs. Arenas and Mrs. Franco told me this labeling process was a pivotal moment in a Latino student's life. As part of the fourth-grade team, they would decide whether or not a Latino student would be designated as part of the Gifted and Talented Education (GATE) class or be tracked into the regular fifth-grade class. Latina teachers were well aware that the Asian American model minority myth—the idea of a studious Asian student—posed a risk to Latino students and tried to change the fate of a few of their promising Latino students. When Mrs. Arenas realized that Diego was not in the GATE class pile, she said, "Oh no! They missed Diego Fernández. What about Diego Fernández?" She got up from her seat and walked over to Mrs. Prado, who glanced up over her shoulder. She explained that Diego was not placed in the GATE class because of overenrollment by Asian students, and he would be given the opportunity to join the class the following year as a sixth-grader. But, it was also because Diego's mother, a Latina immigrant, did not advocate for her son more strongly. Mrs. Arenas was visibly dejected. Mrs. Franco and Mrs. Arenas are friends; she asked, "Where should we put him?" Mrs. Arenas replied, "I don't care where he goes." Both women fell silent.

Mrs. Tan, a third-grade, self-identified Chinese teacher, would have influence on whether Diego was admitted to the GATE fourth- and fifth-grade combination class the next year. Latina teachers described Mrs. Tan as "extremely strict" toward Latino families. Mrs. Prado explained that when she suggested the school have a yearly "Most Improved Award" for children whose test scores improved because Latino children were not receiving very many academic excellence awards, Mrs. Tan had remarked, "Why would we create a special award for Latino children? That's unfair." This was an interaction that Mrs. Tan confirmed during her interview. In fact no one had proposed assigning the award by ethnicity; Asian children would have been eligible although all of the teachers shared the expectation that Latino children would receive it.

An Asian teacher would also teach the GATE class—Mr. Sato, one of two male Japanese teachers on campus. While it is not necessary that students in a class and teachers share ethnicity, it was clear that Mr. Sato always taught the GATE class, which was seen as an Asian slot to teach GATE over the years and presumably, that influences enrollment, even if just subtly.[29] Mrs. Tan's GATE class was ultimately sixteen Asians—and no Latinos. As the group considered the result, Ms. Maciel remarked, "Aw, It's always Asian" in a frustrated tone. "Mmm . . . hmm . . . How sad huh? It's not my fault that it ends up being that way," replied Mrs. Tan. Mrs. Wei added, "It's the Latinos' fault. They are lazy." Then she laughed. The room was tense. In this context, Latina teachers exhibited cultural guardianship because in the larger scope of things Asians were accorded with a racialized privilege not given to Latinos.

Mrs. Prado recognized the tension in an interview when she said, "We have an Asian teacher and she will say, 'Well, I can't be a racist because I like the high-achieving Latino kids. I don't have a problem with them.'" Mrs. Prado said that Asian teachers and parents often accused her of being racist for "always focusing" on the needs of Latino students and families. However, I observed that Mrs. Prado makes a concerted effort along with her staff to create gender, racial/ethnic, and academic language achievement–balanced classrooms. Because most of the students are ELLs, the result was very different from that of Compton Elementary. I observed that Latina and Asian-origin teachers bonded over their immigrant and ethnic origins and served as translators for each other when the hired part-time translators were overcommitted.[30] But I also saw that Asian teachers often expressed a structural notion that Asians are superior to Latinos. My findings resemble those of ethnic studies scholar Wendy Cheng (2014), who states that binary discourses of "achievement" result in racialization of Asian American excellence, along with a concomitant racialization of Latina/o academic deficiency. This produced a social order that valorized Asian Americans students at the expense of non-Asians—in the case of Goodwill Elementary, Latinos. And Asian teachers resisted the school's efforts to improve the scores of Latino students who were on the cusp of meeting benchmarks in standardized testing or other measures of achievement, such as inclusion in the GATE class.

District Level 3s: Asian Supergroup and Latino Stigma

Emblazoned across the front of Goodwill Elementary in Rosemead were two logos. One read, "California Distinguished School" in blue, red, and white. Right next to it, a second one read, "Title 1 Academic Achievement School," a name recognizing disadvantaged schools for closing the achievement gap. The signs were still up even though Goodwill Elementary had lost both of these titles in 2010 and been demoted to a Program Improvement (PI) school, the designation given to Title 1 schools the first time they do not meet their Annual Yearly Progress (AYP) score. When the demotion was announced, the district[31] sent a letter home with all students at Goodwill indicating that the "English Learner and Hispanic subgroups" had experienced a drop in scores. A portion of the letter explained:

> All parents/guardians of students attending a PI school have the right to request a transfer of their child(ren) to a non-PI school with district-paid transportation. For parents who select this option, the district will pay for the transportation to the non-PI school for as long as the home school continues to be identified as a PI school. If the home school exits PI by making AYP for two consecutive years, the student can remain at the school; however, transportation will no longer be district paid. If the demand for choice exceeds funds available, priority will be given to lowest achieving low-income students. (2–2010)

Goodwill's teachers knew the contents of the letter before it was sent; the district told them to be ready for questions. Latina teachers were very concerned. They feared that Asian parents would abandon the school. Mrs. Franco told me that she had overheard Mrs. Tan remark: "Well, hopefully they [Latino families] will be the ones to transfer and then we won't have to worry about them anymore." Mrs. Larry, a Mexican American teacher, told me: "There is a concern that our Asian families are going to want to leave the school because of the Hispanic subgroup not performing high enough. The concern is that there's gonna be a lot of negativity toward our Hispanic population and that the Asian parents are gonna pull out all of their children and take them to other schools." Dora, a Latina immigrant mother who participated in the Spanish-speaking focus group, voiced a similar sentiment: "*Pues yo no entiendo por que si algo pasa que es malo, dicen que son los Latinos. Siempre le hechan la culpa a los Latinos*" [I don't understand why when something bad happens, they say it is Latinos. They always blame the Latinos]. I was in the staff lunchroom at lunchtime on St. Patrick's Day, about a month after the letter came out, when I heard teachers discussing it. A section of a wall in the staff lunchroom was covered with flyers focused on Hispanic Level 3s. The Latina teachers were very conscious of this group, who were on the cusp of being labeled as English proficient, because having many Hispanic Level 3s could garner a school a safe harbor school designation. The school had set up a Spaghetti Night to entice Latino immigrant parents to come to a meeting dedicated to their children before they took the CST.

Mrs. Franco, wearing a green headband, was speaking to Mrs. Are-nas. She was upset because a newcomer student from China named Mai who "couldn't speak a word of English" had just joined her class. "I just don't know what to do with her. If she spoke Spanish, I could help her but I don't know Cantonese," Mrs. Franco remarked. Mrs. Arenas said, "If she has gone to school, she will be okay. She just needs to make the transition and get some confidence." Mrs. Franco connected the new-comer to the letter that the district had sent out to the parents. She felt the letter had been biased and considered her new student evidence of this. "They didn't have to specify, did they? Hispanic subgroup? It pits Asians and Mexicans against one another and results in negative conno-tations of Mexicans. Do you think it was a Hispanic or an Asian parent that wanted to transfer their kid?"

"An Asian parent," Mrs. Cadena replied in a matter-of-fact kind of way. The Asian teachers ate their food silently. Mrs. Cadena explained, "These kids are walking to school because there is no car and they get free and reduced lunch. Latino students come from complex home lives and it's unfortunate that they are grouped together." Still the Asian teachers said nothing but sat huddled close together in between Latina teachers. A couple of minutes later, they left the lounge quietly.

"Asians have Chinese school. Asian parents also have some form of high school graduation,"[32] continued Mrs. Arenas.

"Why are we being judged on a test they take once a year?" said Mrs. Franco, exasperated.

Mrs. Larry added, "These test scores are contributing to negativity, just a lot of negativity."

The principal added, "For us, we are average and we need to move kids up."

"Something is wrong with the testing requisites," Mrs. Franco responded. "How many years should it take to transition [to English proficiency]?"

"There's a lot for us to do between now and May 5th. A lot of the parents are invested in kids' doing well," said Mrs. Prado, and that ended the conversation. I was struck, as I had been before, that Latino children were seen as the preferred group at Compton, but at Goodwill Elementary, Latino children were negatively stigmatized and blamed for the school's problems.

All the teachers acknowledged that Asian American students were scholastically outperforming Latino students.[33] As Mrs. Franco pointed out one day while I helped her prepare "snack-packs"[34] for her students, "You would think that because they are all mostly ELLs, they would all be doing the same." The knowledge that Asians outperformed Latino students even though they were also immigrants or the children of immigrants often led to moments of racial tension and racial outbursts in the workplace between teachers. Cheng (2014: 66) found that "the racialization of Latina/o academic deficiency—shaped students' experiences to such a degree that it was not merely an explanation for particular outcomes but productive of a social order that valorized Asian American students at the expense of 'non-Asians.' As a result, Asian American students within this social order often experienced and enacted a distinct form of *racialized privilege*."[35] This was evident at Goodwill Elementary too.

Pan-ethnic Labeling

State testing outcomes heighten racial tension at Goodwill Elementary. Latina educators often contended with stereotypes of overachieving Asian American students and underachieving Latino students. Recent educational research has shown that Asian American students, as a whole, are also outperforming all other major racial/ethnic groups on state tests (Lee and Zhou 2015). Asian students are surpassing white students in college admissions as well. Latina teachers thought the district's letter announcing the school's new status placed a negative stigma on Latino students and blamed Latino families for their poor performance. They also felt that the tests did not provide an accurate representation of Asian and Latino subgroups; they were conflicted about these pan-ethnic labels and generalizations. As Ms. Maciel explained:

> It just seemed like they were putting blame on the Hispanics. Do you have to say [referring to the letter] the "Hispanic subgroup"? Can't you just say "one of our subgroups"? They talked about how you [Latina teachers] have to take responsibility. We *all* have to take responsibility. Not all Asian kids are scoring right, either. They are not all passing, but as a group they are. We did talk about why we had to specifically name the Hispanic group. . . . They are talking about Hispanics, not just English Language Learners. That's where my question is. When they talk about Hispanics are you putting all the kids of all different language? . . . If you break it down that way . . . . If you are Hispanic and your ELL score is a one, you are not going to score well because you are clumping them. I don't know how they are grouping those. Are they just looking at surnames?

The Asian-origin children at Goodwill Elementary are Chinese, Vietnamese, and Cambodian. As a group, the Vietnamese and Cambodian kids have a lower socioeconomic status than the Chinese students, and their scores reflect that distinction.

Mrs. Prado agreed that grouping all the children of Asian descent obscured the reality of test scores at Goodwill. The Asian scores had dropped as well. She felt that the model minority stereotype hurt the Asian students who did not live up to it. Yen Le Espiritu (1992) notes that the treatment of the Asian American population as homogeneous is both common in the United States and incorrect. Subsuming Asian Americans into one pan-ethnic label can deprive poorer Asian students of the resources they need to succeed (Lee and Zhou 2015). The statistical data presented, Latina teachers felt, hid these distinctions.

Rooting for Latino Students

Goodwill Elementary held Arts on the Lawn on a Saturday in April, an event that showcased the artistic abilities and science experiments of students to their parents. Mrs. Cadena, a combination fifth- and sixth-grade teacher who is Latina, sat down with me at a concrete table during the event. As we talked, her two sons, who went to school there, came to our table to take a bite of her hot dog or a sip of her soda, and then go play or check out the booths. In between, she told me about Danny Ho, a student in her class who was doing very poorly academically. She had contacted his father on four occasions, finally asking him to sit with his son in class to control his behavior. She wanted to retain Danny because she did not think he was ready for the next grade, but she was expecting to meet resistance. "The motivation problem is reserved for Latinos. There is this belief that 'Oh, the Asian kids will snap out it.' No! I'm not just going to put blinders on and keep passing him like everyone else does because he is Asian. My kids [her Latino students] see it." Mrs. Cadena said Danny Ho's father did not want to come in to sit with his child, but he could have had an economic concern; she thought he expected the school to use harsh and physical discipline methods to force him to behave. She referred to another Vietnamese student who was darker-skinned and doing poorly academically in her class. He had said, of his grades, "I don't want to be Asian. I'm not Asian." She said she had told him, "It's okay. You can be Latino. You are one of us." This interaction is important because it demonstrates that Latina teachers rooted for Latino students because, they too, internalized messages that Latinos were inferior. In trying to claim a dark-skinned and lower-socioeconomic Asian student as Latino, Mrs. Cadena was in one way equating failure to achieve with being Latino at Goodwill but also implying that not all Asians were academically successful.

The perception Mrs. Cadena described, that Asian students would "snap out of" their poor academic achievement as they got older, or that they would eventually catch up to their peers, seemed common at Goodwill Elementary. Jennifer Lee and Min Zhou (2015) reference this kind of assumption as a hidden way in which Asian Americans benefit from racial stereotypes in schools. Being positively stereotyped as an academic achiever might at times cause stress on a child, but being expected to catch up can also lead to having the space to do so. Latina teachers such as Mrs. Cadena suggested that students who displayed similar aptitude and behavior as Danny Ho were more likely to be retained and reprimanded if they were Latino. Mrs. Franco described efforts to reverse the burden Latino kids bore: "We all are like rooting for our Hispanic kids and that's not to mean that we totally ignore our Asian kids but we realize that there is a need for some kind of extra support for our Hispanic kids. I knew that we had to do something extra for those Hispanic kids because they needed to make the grade. I'm just kind of tired of that negative stigma that gets put on Hispanic kids."

Latina teachers set up extra programs to help Latino children, as I described in chapter 3. They joked that they were going to start their own bilingual school exclusively for the Latino students because many of their Asian students attended Chinese school on the weekends.

Conclusions

State-mandated school testing intensifies interracial dynamics between Latinas and their racial/ethnic minority co-workers in the teaching profession because of the distinct inequality regimes it creates (Acker 2006). In multiracial schools and worksites, it is difficult for teachers to openly address racial inequality, and they use language as a stand-in for race, especially at Compton Elementary. This was different because the process provided neat alternatives (ELL or EO), but also because racism against African Americans is more delicate socially. While teachers at Compton preferred to have children of Latino immigrants in their classrooms, Asian teachers at Goodwill Elementary expressed a distinct preference for Asian Americans, reflecting their racialized privilege. Asian American teachers were aware of the heterogeneity within the population, yet they still repeated the error of lumping all of the Asian students together because it behooved them to do so. While the social environment at Goodwill Elementary made Latina teachers more comfortable referencing their migration experiences more than at Compton Elementary, the racial hierarchy in the United States bred tension and conflict that state testing seemed to heighten. Some of the African American teachers at Compton were more willing to expose their internalized racism than were Latinas at Goodwill. At the same time, not all African Americans teachers at Compton Elementary did that. This has important consequences for cultural guardianship, which goes beyond school walls. At Goodwill Elementary, Latina teachers serve as cultural guardians to co-ethnic students to try to equalize the disparity between racial/ethnic groups and to resist stereotypes that racialize Latino students in derogatory ways. At Compton Elementary, on the other hand, Latina teachers are cultural guardians to co-ethnic students who are racialized as meek and docile and deem African Americans as less committed to co-racials, even though that is not always the case. This has grave consequences as it comes at a cost to African American students who are excluded from the educational system, and also to later-generation Latino students who may not have the immigrant experience.

Conclusion and Epilogue

The New U.S. Teaching Profession

One day, Mrs. Cadena's students were making dolls out of yarn because they had just read a novel titled *Esperanza Rising*, a story about Mexican immigrant and Mexican American families' experiences with deportations and repatriation programs during the Great Depression.[1] To show alternate educational opportunities, Mrs. Cadena created a space where her students could ask me questions about college access and my experiences in higher education. I agreed to answer their questions and she had her students put everything away to cultivate this learning environment. Their write-ups regarding the novel served as my backdrop. The papers by both Latino and Asian students read, "Mexicans were treated badly," and "Mexican families were separated."

I stood at the back of the class and some of the students huddled at my feet while others stayed at their desks. I told them that I would be extremely candid with them and they could ask me whatever they wanted. Immediately a young Latina student raised her hand and asked, "What does *candid* mean?" I explained, "*Candid* means you can ask me whatever you want and I will tell you the truth." She snickered as she settled in between her friends. The questions started and I was caught off-guard that I would indeed have to answer very sensitive questions. Several of the questions came from Angie, a ten-year-old Latina, who Mrs. Cadena later told me "has it hard." Angie asked: "Where are your parents from? How did they come?" I answered, "My parents are both from Mexico. My mother is from the Mexican state of Zacatecas. My father was also born in Zacatecas but he was raised in the Mexican state of Sonora, right on the border with Arizona. My mother did not want to come to the U.S. because she loved her home, but my grandmother made her come over when she was older, to work. She crossed through the desert and was very scared living in the U.S. because she did not have papers." This statement made some students in the class turn their faces up to meet my eyes.

Mrs. Cadena interjected and said, "See, everyone has different experiences." The next question by Teresa, a young girl whose hair was in a long black braid and who wore around her neck a gold chain with a round emblem that had the *Virgen Maria*, took me aback: "Have your parents ever been deported?" I felt a pang in my heart and answered truthfully, "Yes, my mother was deported two times. She had a harder time. When my dad lived in Sonora the border was very different. There really wasn't a wall and people could cross to work and go back. One time, after my parents were married, my mother went to Mexico to get some paperwork fixed and they did not let her come back. My dad helped her cross over since he knew the border. I was born in the U.S. and my family wanted to stay here." The questions continued.

Angie again asked, "Do your parents have papers?" I replied, "For a while they did not." I told the class that a law, the Immigration Reform and Control Act (IRCA),[2] helped my parents and they studied to take a test to become American citizens. "The rules were different back then," I said. I told them that I would sometimes help my mother study her citizenship questions. I informed them that my father tried really hard to become a citizen. "He is what they call a legal permanent resident. He also passed the test but never received his letter to do the oath," I said.

Ricky, who chose to sit at his desk, asked me, "Do you know the football players?" The students chuckled. I smiled at Ricky's question and told him that I did have some of the football players in my discussion sections at USC, and sometimes baseball and water polo players. "They are very big and much taller than I am," I quipped. Ricky smiled, nodded his head up and down, turned to his neighbor, a Vietnamese boy, and said that he was going to try to get an athletic scholarship to go to college. "Do you think I can get one of those [an athletic scholarship]?" he continued.[3] "Those are really competitive," I said. "You would be such a strong candidate if you worked both on athletics and your academics." "Yeah! I'm good at both," Ricky said.

Flor, another young Latina with big black glasses, asked, "How did you pay for school?" "I got very lucky, Flor. I have a fellowship which is a type of scholarship and that is paying for my schooling. When I first went to college at UC Irvine, at one point I worked two jobs while I was an undergrad. I worked at a retirement home and at an elementary school working with kids like you." Flor smiled at her friend sitting next to her.

Wendy, another Latina girl, asked, "What did your parents do?" Wendy was referring to the occupations my parents held when I was younger. I answered, "My father worked in construction and then a dry cleaners for a while. My mother worked at a T-shirt factory, a McDonald's and now works as a lunch lady at an elementary school." I later found out that Wendy's father was a custodian, probably giving her the notion that her parents' occupation was tied to her own college future. After fielding questions from Latino students for several minutes, I asked, "Is there anyone else who has a question for me?" attempting to engage the Asian students in the class. But no one took the bait. Mrs. Cadena intervened and said, "Asian students?! If you have a question ask now." A little Asian American girl's hand shot up immediately and she asked: "What are your future goals, ten years from now, after you get your PhD?"

Considering the other questions that I was asked from Latina/o students, who it seemed were concerned that college and a higher education would be out of reach, this question surprised me the most. It was exactly the question graduates receive from a dissertation committee, a question that you could expect a prospective academic employer to ask, not a young child. Of course I was prepared to answer this question. I had worked on delivering the appropriate response for many job interviews, but I was surprised that a ten-year-old-girl was thinking about my future. I responded, "I hope to become a professor for a research one institution, for a college or university. My dream job would be to become a professor." Instantly, I noticed the inferiority that Latino students felt in the classroom over the questions they asked me. They looked to the floor and hunched their backs a little lower, probably thinking about what the future held for them. After this question-and-answer session, Mrs. Cadena asked her students to return to their seats. I asked Mrs. Cadena, "Do the students always ask questions like this? They were really personal." Mrs. Cadena replied, "That's nothing. They were pretty tame today."

Sociologist and education scholar Cynthia Feliciano (2005) argues that second-generation youths' achievement level is influenced by an immigrant's educational selectivity, the idea that immigrant groups are selected along multiple lines. For example, Mexican migrants have historically been a source of cheap labor for the United States, while many Asian immigrants are selected for their high technology skills.[4] While some Asian groups such as the Chinese may experience downward mobility in the United States, their college educations in the home country still allow them to procure support for their children (Zhou 2009; Feliciano 2005). The human capital some Asian immigrants bring with them from their home countries seems to promote career aspirations and educational attainment for their children (Zhou and Lee 2008). While Asian parents may also lack cultural capital, they often turn to other social networks, mainly churches and community organizations, to help them overcome their own lack of cultural capital or even human capital and to learn about school programs, testing, and college requirements. Teachers, like Mrs. Cadena, then, are often cultural guardians to their Latino students who may be lacking in these resources.

When I first began examining the lives of Latina teachers in 2006, school districts were in dire need of bilingual teachers but were also having trouble retaining younger Latinas. In fact, several of the younger Latina teachers included in this volume dreaded the end of the academic school year, because they would anxiously await their "riff notice." This means that they would possibly no longer work at their current school and spent their summer's waiting and hoping that they would be "bumped" to another school within the same district. In most cases they would be rehired, but more often than not, it was at a different school where they would have to move all of their belongings and establish new relationships. They would often have to learn a new organizational culture with a different administration and a different group of teachers. However, this trend is changing as in 2015 the New York Times published a news article[5] indicating that while many teachers were laid off during the recession and financial crisis (2008–11), where we lost about 82,000 jobs in schools, they are being rehired. Most school districts have gone from handing out pink slips to scrambling to hire teachers, even uncredentialed ones. Schools are looking for applicants wherever they can find them, out of state or out of the country. Some are even turning to Teach for America programs or are asking prospective teachers to train on the job or hiring novices still studying for their teaching credentials, prompting notions that the quality of the teaching force could weaken.

Previous studies on Latinas in the workplace focus on the work experiences of the poor and unauthorized in the informal economy and in secondary labor market jobs. Emergent studies on postbaccalaureate Latinas and their work experiences in white-collar jobs examine the obstacles they face, such as the modes of racial discrimination, sexual harassment, and cultural rifts with white colleagues in the fields of law or business. The field of education has shed some light on Latina teachers' job satisfaction using surveys that capture individual-level data on teacher attitudes and perceptions at a single point in time.

This volume, using interviews, participant observation, and focus groups, traces the upward mobility pathways of Latinas from working-class roots into the middle class, beginning with their pathways into teaching and ending with an examination of their interracial workplace relations with middle-class Black and Asian-origin teachers. This book of Latina-origin teachers working in multiracial schools allows us to see the connections between immigrant origins, class, culture, and racial/ethnic hierarchies, and these will become more salient as U.S. demographics continue to change and as Latinos spread to new immigrant destinations. Post-1965 immigration trends changed the face of America's schoolchildren, and today, one out of every four young students has an immigrant parent, and students of color constitute 44 percent of students nationwide.[6] Increased immigration from Latin American and Asian countries in the 1980s and 1990s fueled demand for bilingual educators who provided an alternative to the traditional monolingual, white middle-class teacher (Su 1996). I find that the late 1990s and early 2000s were the golden age of Latinas' entering the profession as the growing presence of Latino immigrant children in California schools created a burgeoning demand for Spanish-speaking, bilingual teachers in the 1990s, complete with both formal and informal recruitment efforts. I capture how Latina teachers, a significant wave of Latina professionals, give back to their own families and to Latino families in their workplaces and illustrate how Latinas maintain loyalties to poorer and unauthorized co-ethnics at the same time they maintain civil or tenuous relationships with non-Latino colleagues, giving us insight into the future of U.S. race relations and hierarchies.

Today, teaching is the number one occupation in the primary labor market that college-educated daughters of Latino immigrants enter. I find that dire financial constraints propelled Latina teachers to want to give back socially and financially to poorer co-ethnics because they saw the sacrifices their immigrant parents made for them and see the struggles that Latino families face in schools. Unlike previous work, however, my interviews allowed me to link socioeconomic class refracted through race, gender, and changing regional demographic trends as channels that geared Latinas into the profession. While some may deem class constraints an impediment to upward mobility, the Latina teachers in this study express a collectively informed agency, where the financial well-being of their families motivated them to stake out the quickest post-BA occupation to secure employment. Once in the profession and informed by their own life experiences, many Latina teachers become cultural guardians and provide for poorer Latino families in the community and do so in sanctioned and unsanctioned ways. These Latinas are the success stories of their communities, and once in the teaching profession, they realize that they are an incredible resource for Latino families who are trying to secure a good education for their children. This, of course, is a heavy burden for them to carry and is further promoted by unequal educational structures that disenfranchise students of color. I detail their the ways in which they outwit a system that was not intended for their students to break through. But not all Latina teachers respond in homogeneous ways. Latina teachers often reflect on their experiences in the U.S. schooling system in order to provide socially to poorer co-ethnics, but their mission takes different forms depending on the school districts they serve.

Through the comparative method, the volume also illustrates the perceptions that Latina teachers have of their abilities to effect change in their schools and how they guard but are also guarded as they implement change for Latino families. Latina teachers' experiences at Compton Elementary and Goodwill Elementary are markedly distinct. Latina teachers at Compton Elementary struggle to fight off discouragement over the prospect of advancing Latino youth through the educational system in a school district that is associated with the Black underclass. Latina teachers at Goodwill Elementary, on the other hand, express hope for Latino youth among Asian colleagues and students in Rosemead, a city where race has become almost invisible for Asians but pervasive for Latinos. We also begin to see the distinct regional racial hierarchies and positioning that emerge in their workplaces, which stem from Latino anti-Black racism and Asian valorization. With regard to regional racial positioning, I show that Latinos are a heterogeneous population whose experiences in the United States vary on markers of language, citizenship, nativity, and class. Latina teachers perceive immigrant Latinos as inhabiting different positions in U.S. racial/ethnic hierarchies within the same sociopolitical context in different regions, with immigrant Latino families positioned below African Americans and Asian Americans. These regional racial hierarchies permeate their workplaces and influence the development of co-ethnic cultural guardianship.

Because of these structural forces, Latina teachers encourage one another to actively incorporate Latino culture in schools in order to stymie the downwardly mobile paths of Latino youth and Latino families. For Latina teachers, knowledge of Latino culture is an asset in the workplace. Historically, Mexican children were forced to undergo Americanization programs and were taught that their families, communities, and culture were obstacles to schooling success. In addition, in many workplaces and institutions, knowledge and expression of Latino culture were suppressed if they were overtly displayed. I show that Latina teachers in multiracial schools encourage one another to actively incorporate aspects of Latino ethnic culture in their teaching via Chicana/Latina cultural pedagogies. There are subtle Latino cultural cues that Latina teachers are able to discern and communicate because of their own connections to immigrant origins and struggles with language acquisition and communication styles. These are fluid cultural practices that Latina/o parents and children bring with them to schools. Latina teachers alter their teaching and interactions in order to communicate effectively with Latino students and their parents. Latina teachers do this because they recognize that in our current sociopolitical context, Latinos are met with hostility and nativism and they attempt to develop more positive contexts of reception for Latino families in order to increase the likelihood of upward mobility in the future. This, however, comes at a cost for Black students and families at Compton Elementary because Latina teachers state that they do not understand how they can help the Black population. They have a difficult time connecting with Black culture. Shared immigrant and ethnic origins with Asian teachers at Goodwill Elementary, on the other hand, alleviates these ruptures. I find that non-Latina teachers can learn certain aspects of Chicana/Latina cultural pedagogies such as the math and immigrant origins. Communication codes, on the other hand, may take longer to develop and sharpen.

Last, racial/ethnic tensions between Latina teachers and their non-Latina colleagues are intensified by high-stakes testing that labels students by achievement dependent on language. Larger structural factors, such as state-mandated testing, chips away at Latina teachers' role as cultural guardians. Far from being standardized, because schools are predicated on the notion of color-blindness, language becomes a way in which Latina teachers and their colleagues feel more comfortable discussing race. Through participant observation and semi-structured interviews with teachers, I document how language becomes a proxy for race. Like studies which show that native-born employers prefer cheap, Latino immigrant labor, I show how teachers at Compton Elementary—Latinas, Blacks, and whites—prefer a classroom full of the children of Latino immigrants. At Goodwill Elementary, on the other hand, Asian students are far surpassing Latino students, and Latina teachers feel compelled to protect and defend Latino families from inferior and negative stigmas. As a result of the harsh anti-immigrant sentiment that is expressed in our current political climate, and the fact that the immigration debate is framed as a "Mexican" issue, Latina teachers, second- and even fourth-generation, identify with the plight of poorer and immigrant co-ethnics in multiracial schools. This does not mean that they identify with all aspects, but they do strive to stay connected and hope that the Mexican-origin population will no longer be negatively stigmatized as a whole. By focusing on testing and academic labels, chapter 6 contributes to the literature on interracial relations in workplaces.

Having critically discussed several of the processes by which Latina teachers socially distance themselves from Blacks and seek proximity to Asians, I find it important to highlight the policy implications of the findings presented herein. To date, there are competing empirical findings regarding the question of racial mismatch between qualitative and quantitative scholars of education. Teachers' working in multiracial contexts and race-matched teaching continues to be an intensely debated issue in academic and policy circles across the nation. I will discuss a few policy recommendations of use for teacher-education programs in the United States.

Policy Implication for Educational Reform in the United States

On August 24, 2011, an American news website, *The Huffington Post*, published an article titled, "Latino Teachers Needed for Classroom Role Models," a piece that highlighted the incongruence between the exponential growth the Latino-origin school-age population and the perceived lack of Latina/o–origin teachers. The article accentuated the cultural and linguistic gulf between many Latino-origin students and their non–Latino-origin teachers in U.S. classrooms. The Secretary of Education, Arne Duncan, was interviewed for the piece and he emphatically noted, "[R]ecruiting more Latino[a] teachers is part of our overall efforts to strengthen the teaching profession and ensure students are learning from a diverse group of teachers" (Resmovits 2011). Afterward, most of the commentators labeled the plan racist. Many were infuriated at the notion that only Latina/o-origin teachers could connect with the children of Latino immigrants, a point of view that I do not wholly subscribe to in this book. The U.S. Department of Education has made several attempts to address the racial/ethnic minority teachers' pipeline. Prior to this announcement, Duncan had proposed focusing recruitment efforts on increasing the presence of African American male teachers in classrooms.

It is predicted that within the next couple of years there will be a massive exodus of Baby Boomers who will retire and exit the workforce, creating a huge demand for teachers. Consider a report published by the Obama administration titled, "Our Future, Our Teachers," which states that over the next ten years, it is estimated, 1.6 million teachers will retire, and 1.6 million teachers will be needed to take their place (U.S. Department of Education 2011: v). If current trends continue, second-generation Latina teachers are setting themselves up to fill in those positions, and financial incentives will be crucial to ensure that they remain in the profession.

One item, however, was missing from these reports. There was virtually no mention of how recruitment efforts targeted specifically toward

Latinas would pan out in multiracial schools with diverse staff and students. While it is exemplary to diversify the teacher workforce, there are larger hegemonic ideals such as controlling images of space and regional racial/ethnic hierarchies that emerge among racial/ethnic minority groups. As this volume has shown, when Latina teachers enter multiracial workplaces, regional racial positioning within these communities may be transformed. While I find that Latina teachers exercise Chicana/Latina cultural pedagogies in schools, increasing the percentage of Latina teachers may provoke a perfect storm in multiracial schools because of high-stakes testing that primarily focuses on language acquisition.

Over the past twenty years, many Latino families have moved to new destinations and enrolled their children in schools with other racial/ethnic minority populations. Although I suggest that Latinas in the teaching profession exhibit a social responsibility to Latino families and are cultural guardians, there may be negative consequences for students of other racial/ethnic backgrounds in these schools, especially when it concerns resources for English-language acquisition. Latina and Black teachers at Compton Elementary explained that African American children also did not follow the conventions of standard American English. However, unlike resources provided to help Latino students acquire the language, Latina teachers believed that state policies and a dearth of resources for Black children to help them learn to speak standard American English were sources of frustration between Latina/o and non-Latina/o teachers. According to many of the teachers, it is imperative that national, state, and local governance structures allocate resources for African American students who, in many respects, Latina and African American teachers consider English Language Learners, too. The English Language Learner category, according to them, should also be applied to the native-born and not limited exclusively to the children of immigrants.

APPENDICES

APPENDIX A. Demographic Characteristics of Latina Teachers

Pseudonym	Age	Gen. Level	POB (Teacher)	POB (Parent)	Racial/ Ethnic Identity	Father Occupation	Mother Occupation	Undergrad Inst.	Credential Inst.	Grade Level	Yrs Teaching	Annual Income
Compton												
Mrs. Becerra	40	1.5	Mexico	Mexico	Mexican	Retired teacher in MX	Retired teacher in MX	Cal Poly Pomona (Finance)	Compton District Program* (CLAD)	1st	9	$60,000
Ms. Gutierrez	35	1.5	Mexico	Mexico	Mexican American	N/A	Retired	Cal State LA (Liberal Studies)	Cal State LA* (CLAD)	1st	4	$54,000
Mrs. Díaz	33	2nd	Orange County	Cuba/ El Salvador	Latina Cuban Salvadoran	Bank executive	Nurse	Cal Poly Pomona (Liberal Studies)	Compton District Program* (CLAD)	3rd	6	$56,000
Mrs. Madrigal	33	1.5	Mexico	Mexico	Mexican American	Welder	Homemaker	Cal State LA (Multicultural Education)	Cal State LA* (CLAD)	4th	5	$45,000
Mrs. Estrada	34	2nd	Santa Ana, CA	Mexico	Mexican American	Welder	Independent distributing company owner	Cal State Fullerton (Liberal Studies)	Compton District Program* (CLAD)	1st	5	$36,000
Ms. Tiscareño	27	2nd	Long Beach, CA	Mexico	Mexican American	Shipper/ custodian	Homemaker	Cal State Long Beach (Liberal Studies)	Cal State Long Beach (CLAD)	4th	4	$52,000
Mrs. Godínez	39	2nd	East L.A.	Mexico	Mexican	Clerk	Seamstress	Cal State Dominguez (Spanish/Mex-Am Studies)	Cal State Dominguez Hills (BCLAD/ MA in Multicultural Education)	3rd	14	$76,000
Mrs. Romero	34	2nd	Chicago	Mexico/ Texas	Mexican American	Car wash/ electronic tech	Teacher aide	Cal State Long Beach (Chicano/Latino Studies)	National University (CLAD)	K	5	$58,000
Mrs. Rivas	39	2nd	Sacramento, CA	Mexico	Mexican	N/A	Operator	Cal State Dominguez (Psychology/Chicano/ Latino Studies)	San Jose University* (CLAD)	5th	15	$78,000
Mrs. Ybarra	39	2nd	East L.A.	Mexico	Mexican	Clerk	Seamstress	Cal State Dominguez Spanish/Mex-Am Studies	Cal State Dominguez Hills (BCLAD)	K	14	N/A

Rosemead

Name	Age		Birthplace	Parents' origin	Ethnicity	Father	Mother	College	Credential institution	Grade	Years	Salary
Ms. Dávila	34	3rd	Bellflower, CA	Kansas/Iowa	Multiracial Mexican/White	Warehouse	Cashier	UCLA (Theater)	Cal State LA* (CLAD)	Drama	9	$51,000
Mrs. Robles	36	4th	Rosemead, CA	Los Angeles, CA	Mexican	Mail carrier	Pharmaceutical clerk	Cal State LA (Health Sciences)	Cal State LA* (CLAD/ MA in Arts in Education & Reading Specialist)	2nd	14	$80,000
Ms. Maciel	40	2nd	Rosemead, CA	Mexico	Mexican American	Warehouse	Homemaker	Cal State LA (Child Dev.)	Cal State LA* (BCLAD/ M.A. in Reading)	2nd	14	$80,000
Mrs. Arenas	61	3rd	San Gabriel, CA	CA	Mexican	Agriculture	Agriculture/ pre-school teacher	Cal State LA (Liberal Studies)	Cal State LA (CLAD/MA in Education & Reading Specialist)	4th	21	$86,000
Mrs. Franco	30	2nd	Montebello, CA	Mexico/CA	Mexican American	Plumber	Teacher aide	UCLA (Sociology)	University of Phoenix (CLAD/MA in Education)	4th	9	$70,000
Mrs. Larry	36	2nd	San Dimas, CA	OK/ Mexico	Multiracial Mexican/ White	Painter in aeronautics	Homemaker	Cal State LA (Social Science)	Cal State LA (CLAD/MA in Education)	5th	11	$68,000
Mrs. Cadena	41	4th	Orange, CA	Santa Ana, CA	Multiracial Mexican/ White	Welding supervisor	Factory	Cal State LA (Child Dev.)	Cal State LA (CLAD/MA in Admin.)	5th/6th	11	$67,000
Ms. Sánchez	39	3rd	East L.A.	East L.A.	Mexican American	Core maker	Teacher aide	Cal State LA (Computer Information Systems)	University of Phoenix (CLAD/MA in Education)	5th	5	$50,000
Mrs. Quiroz	29	2nd	San Gabriel, CA	Guatemala	Guatemalan	Mechanic	Homemaker	Cal State LA (Child Dev.)	Cal State LA (CLAD/MA in Reading)	1st	5	$44,000
Mrs. Perez	57	3rd	Texas	Texas	Tejana Mexicana	Warehouse manager	Homemaker	Cal State LA (Languages)	Cal State LA (CLAD)	3rd	29	$85,000
Avg.	37										11	$62,947
N=20												

*Asterisk in credential institution cell denotes if hired with emergency credential/ only marked those that explicitly mentioned it. (9)

APPENDIX B

Chronicles of a Mexican Woman PhD

When I set out to do a study of professional and upwardly mobile Latina teachers as both an "insider" and an "outsider" (see Merton 1972; Zinn 1979, 2002; Collins 1986, 2000) in multiracial elementary schools in June 2009, I did not envision that navigating aspects of occupational prestige *and* age would present methodological dilemmas. My social location as the college-educated daughter of working-class Mexican immigrant parents influenced the ways in which men and women, Latina/o, white, African American and Asian American teachers of diverse class backgrounds interacted with me during interviews and ethnography. To my surprise, respondents changed their own mannerisms and behaviors when I was in the field. Over the course of my research, it became clear to me that I possessed a type of "hidden privilege," not accorded to all Latina professionals.

Sociologist Patricia Hill Collins's (1986) concept of the "outsider within" adequately captures the struggles that race/ethnic minority scholars face in the field as they conduct research in multiracial organizations and schools. According to Collins (1986, 2000) racial/ethnic minority scholars are *outsiders within* because of their "outsider" social location in academic institutions that privilege whiteness, silencing the voices of racial others. In such institutions, outsiders within become aware of the mechanisms that keep power, systemic racism, and privilege in place. As I observed Latina teachers in multiracial elementary schools, I had to contend with my age and educational and occupational prestige vis-à-vis the teachers. Though I am a part of the second generation,[1] I do not benefit from white racial privilege in the U.S. racial structure; however, I do benefit from a *hidden privilege* as a result of the prestige accorded a doctoral degree. I term this a hidden privilege because it was not readily visible unless I revealed it verbally. It was when I explicitly told teachers that I was working toward a PhD that their interactions and demeanor changed. As an outsider within, who has experienced considerable mobility within one generation, I embodied a unique space to witness these subtle interactions and snubs in multiracial schools with both men and women teachers of various racial/ethnic backgrounds.

Although I was a native "insider" with Latina teacher participants, I was also an "outsider" with non-Latina respondents in the schools. The many debates (Merton 1972; Zinn 1979, 2001; Collins 1986, 2000) over ethnographic studies conducted by outsiders and insiders in the domain of knowledge production caused Merton (1972: 44) to call for them to "unite," instead of focusing on how intersubjectivity or "presumed" objectivity leads to greater insights. However, Merton's call for unity did not take into account how the larger context of racial/ethnic relations and the fluctuating prestige of an occupation could influence the data-collection process. This larger context can affect the research process because schools deemed to be of lower prestige may be wary of being researched as they may be under constant scrutiny to improve.

Maxine Baca Zinn (1979) argued that Chicana/o scholar insiders—and all racial/ethnic minority scholars—could engage their subjectivities as methodological tools in the recruitment of potential research participants and posed this would strengthen their analysis. Academics that are racialized others must often deal with an academic structure that does not give them the privilege of being able to study the whole world (Villenas 1996). Zinn (1979: 209) postulated that "Minority researchers have empirical and methodological advantages, but also face unique problems in addressing ethical, methodological and political concerns" such as navigating fieldwork dilemmas, the politics of identity, and their commitment to racial/ethnic minority communities and the academy. Many of these advantages are being attuned to a range of dramaturgical behaviors (Goffman 1959) in myriad settings. Drawbacks include figuring out how to navigate both frontstage and backstage race behaviors, as the backstage and frontstage may intersect, blurring the boundaries between spaces, and leading to a "spoiled performance" that is fitting for a stranger who is not white to witness (Picca and Feagin 2007). This is especially important for U.S. scholars to take into account today because racial/ethnic minorities are more likely to live in multiracial communities (Saito 1998).

AN INSIDER GAINING ENTRY TO MULTIRACIAL SCHOOLS

The field posed a unique set of circumstances for me from the moment I set foot in it, before I uttered a single word. In many respects I was an insider because I shared traits with Latina teacher respondents (gender, ethnicity), but I also remained an outsider because I was young. Age complicated my gaining social acceptance by established professionals who initially did not see me as a competent colleague, and then regarded me as an anomaly when I revealed my status. I was also an outsider to non-Latina teachers. I found that because of my subjective positioning, respondents reacted to my physical appearance with a series of assumptions, influencing their perceptions of my motives. One key informant Latina teacher warned, "It's gonna be hard for you. They [Asian teachers] are going to think that you are being biased because you are Latina." Fine (1998: 72) argues that scholars should work the hyphen—"in relation with the contexts we study and with our informants, understanding that we are all multiple in those relations." The Self-Other hyphen, according to Fine, means that researchers must explore the hyphen that both separates and merges personal identities with our perceptions of Others and to be reflexive over the story that is being told or shadowed, and its interpretation. Wagle and Cantaffa (2008) underscore that ethnographers must examine how identities shift throughout the research process in relation to the identities of the participants. The complications include self-policing of words to protect rapport, acquiring an outsider-within status of multiple identities and "a gesture of inclusion in 'whiteness'" (hooks 1989: 68). Collins (1986, 2000) notes that we can learn much from the outsider within because in spite of the hurdles they experience in the academic realm, such individuals can tap into this status in field research. This is precisely what I experienced, as my sociological training and first-hand experience in these communities gave me the insight that I had to compromise and hide my own political beliefs in order to appease all of the respondents. Although I engaged the subjectivities of Latina teachers, I was also held at a social distance from Black, white, and Asian teachers.

Obtaining site permission consent at these schools was both the smoothest and most difficult entanglement I faced when getting Institutional Review Board (IRB) approval.[2] School districts require that all volunteers and employees get a tuberculosis (TB) test and a Live Scan fingerprinting to conduct a thorough criminal background check. I was a former employee for the Santa Ana Unified School District, and so my fingerprints were on file and I had taken a series of TB tests that always produced negative results.[3] Mrs. Prado, the principal at Goodwill Elementary in Rosemead, was an amiable Latina and signed the consent form as soon as I explained the parameters of my study. Mrs. Prado was extremely supportive of my educational endeavors and immediately opened up to me regarding race relations in her school. She gave me free rein, allowing me to conduct observations at all campus events and tacked a note to the Daily Bulletin Announcements that read: "We will have a graduate student conducting interviews with teachers and doing observations." This principal also allowed me to present my project at Parent-Teacher Association meetings, provided me with a room in which to conduct focus groups, and also offered to provide me an English, Mandarin, Cantonese, and Vietnamese translator. Zinn (2001) observes that gender and ethnicity can facilitate access and ongoing relationships with informants, especially when "insiders" are conducting research in racial/ethnic minority communities. Although Mrs. Prado was third-generation and not fluent in Spanish, shared gender and ethnic background allowed access.

Gaining entry to Compton Elementary, on the other hand, was uncomfortable and sometimes demoralizing. I anticipated a slight difficulty in gaining entry considering that urban and immigrant school districts in California are under scrutiny for their performance on high-stakes tests. The Latina office secretary (who was in her late fifties), whom I later befriended, shunned me a total of four times. She was the initial gatekeeper and controlled access to the principal via phone and in person. Our connection in race/ethnicity and gender was not enough to grant me a meeting with him. While I attempted to draw connections with Latina respondents by drawing on ethnic markers (e.g., speaking Spanish), I was not always successful. This made me ponder over the higher status a doctoral degree holds that gives its owners sway but also raises suspicions for those serving and protecting minority and vulnerable populations. On the phone, the Latina office secretary would say the principal was "at a district meeting" or "not in his office." After unsuccessfully trying to schedule a sit-down meeting over the phone, I chose to drive to the school. This was my first on-site attempt. This visit was when I met the Latina secretary, who had been born in Mexico and whose family had roots in Compton spanning more than thirty years. The front office was a very small space. It could fit only about two to three people. Her colleague, an African American woman, sat adjacent to her. I explained that I had phoned and decided to come in because it sounded as if they were very busy. Again, the Latina secretary replied, "[The principal is] at lunch right now. I don't know when he will be back." I asked, "Is it okay if I wait for him here? Until he has an open spot?" Frustrated, the Latina secretary asked, "Where are you going to sit?" Stunned by her response, I said, "I can sit on this chair right here by the door." She wanted me to retreat and retorted, "After his lunch he is going to be at meetings all day." Dejected, I closed the door and made my way to exit the campus. I saw a student, approximately ten years old, who was about to enter the front office and asked her if the principal was on campus. The little Latina girl said, "Yeah. He's right there!" pointing to an African American man wearing a light green tweed coat with dark elbow patches. I did not introduce myself to the principal then because I did not want to undermine the Latina administrative assistant's power. She was someone I would have to see daily and I did not want to override her authority. I tried one last time to call the school. I devised a script I would read over the phone. Somehow I was directed to the district office, which rerouted my call to the direct line of the vice principal, avoiding the front office secretary. The African American vice principal helped me schedule a meeting with the principal. In our meeting, I explained that I wanted to understand the experiences of racial/ethnic minority teachers and their relationships with students and parents. A longtime Compton resident, he was worried I was there to cast a negative light on the school and was put at ease when I revealed I was an academic and not a journalist. An academic of a racial/ethnic minority background who had attended public schools, in his view, signified I was an *outsider within* in terms of our mutual interests as educators in finding solutions to help low-income children of color through the educational pipeline, and that I was not seeking a news story. He granted me access once I presented him with all of the consent forms and interview dockets.

Much like the Latina secretary, I found that some Latina teachers at Compton Elementary were afraid to speak with me. One Latina teacher, who at my study's onset slammed her door in my face, said, "I thought you were a reporter and I would get fired." Subtle paranoia prevailed because these teachers were working in a school that was already in danger of being taken over by the state for their low performance on high-stakes tests. Other Latina teachers agreed to the interview because of their displeasure with the district and wanted to say in confidential interviews what they could not discuss openly with their colleagues and administration.

AGE AND OCCUPATIONAL PRESTIGE

Age *and* the occupational prestige attributed to academics increased the visibility of privilege for an outsider within in multiracial settings. My experiences in the field were compounded by the fact that I was much younger than most of the respondents. Within ethnographic studies there is a tendency, not without exceptions (Sherman 2006), for scholars to "study down" rather than "study up." In sociology there is a propensity to examine the occupational trajectories of Latinos who work in "brown collar" jobs or in the informal sector of the economy (Ramírez and Hondagneu-Sotelo 2009; Estrada 2013; Hondagneu-Sotelo 2001). In this examination of race relations in multiracial organizations and schools, the power relations between studying down and studying up were less clear. I was studying "down" because I was investigating a group that works in an occupation that is devalued and is further underrated because these are lower-income, predominantly racial/ethnic minority schools. I was also studying "up" because of the age differential between us—younger interviewing older—requiring a certain mode of decorum and respect.

When I initially approached teachers for an interview I purposefully behaved deferentially because I wanted them to participate and because I was a young Latina.[4] An important component of Latina/o socialization is demonstrating respect to elders and professionals through deference, especially with regard to age (González-Lopez 2004). I was well aware that my age, in conjunction with my educational credentials, could be used as grounds to label me as arrogant in these schools with diverse staff. When I first solicited teachers I sent them a long letter detailing the study and attached a school business card to prove that I was a legitimate scholar. I explained that they were the experts and I was there to learn from them. For me this was essential because more than 90 percent of the teachers in the sample were older than I was and most of them held a bachelors degree and a teaching credential. Only four interviewees were younger than I was.

I also felt compelled to be overly deferential because being an elementary school teacher does not have the same prestige that a doctoral degree has and I did not want to appear snooty. Similarly to Zinn (1979), who observes racial/ethnic minority communities develop self-protective behaviors to deal with outsiders and to protect themselves from academic exploitation, teachers informed me they thought I might be "uppity" or "elitist" and wondered if I was coming to their schools to find fault with the ways in which they were doing their jobs. This became apparent to me when I conducted observations with the fourth-grade team in Compton Elementary. Mrs. Madrigal introduced me to the rest of her colleagues by saying, "This is Ms. Glenda. She's a real brainy." As their meeting continued, I heard her whisper to an older African American female colleague, "She thinks she's all better than us 'cuz she's getting a PhD." "Oh, stop," said the African American woman, looking over in my direction. "What?" I asked, smiling. Mrs. Madrigal jokingly said, "I'm just hatin' on you, girl! I'm just hatin' on you 'cause you're gettin' a PhD. Naww, girl, I'm just giving you props 'cuz I wasn't able to do something like that." When I told teachers I was conducting this study for a doctoral degree in sociology at USC, most Latinas told me they had aspired to more prestigious careers. Other teachers reacted with "Oh's" to signal amazement, and some immediately followed up with "How old are you?" Age was a source of needling, but it also served to curtail some of the negative stereotypes attributed to Latinas with all respondents.

As a young sociologist, however, I had to deal with older teachers' disrespecting and undermining me. While I was taking fieldnotes during a third-grade meeting, Ms. Beasley, a forty-four-year-old African American teacher, queried, "What do you take notes on over there, Ms. Glenda?" I replied, "Just words that will help me remember things." "Oh, really. Can I see what you are writing?" she said half-jokingly. I thought she was kidding. She walked over to my space and ripped the "jottings" sheet away from my hands, attempting to make out my chicken-scratch writing. She squinted at the paper but could not make it all out. She did catch a full phrase and said, "Wow, it seems like you really are taking notice of us then," as she handed me back my sheet and sat with her colleagues.

Laz (1998) argues that age is more social than chronological, suggesting it is both a process and an outcome of interactional work. The aforementioned vignette elucidates that Ms. Beasley was attempting to show me in front of her co-workers that she was the boss and expert in her classroom. I purposely downplayed my educational credentials at the sites to avoid presenting myself as elitist and did not reveal them unless they probed me for specificity, because I wanted to fit in.

Behaving overly deferential also had its drawbacks. Mrs. Madrigal said, "I just want you to get this done. You aren't going to get anywhere being timid like that." She said she understood why I was being so meek, but she feared this tactic would backfire and advised me to be more aggressive in approaching teachers. This made me aware of a hidden privilege because Mrs. Madrigal acknowledged that although we shared a similar social location as Latina educators, ultimately we did not hold the same social status in the school because of our educational levels and the prestige associated to our occupations. Because of this, she implored I be more assertive in approaching other teachers bypassing my age in a way and emphasizing the power of a doctoral degree. Over time I realized I was ashamed of and felt guilty over the prestige that automatically comes with a PhD. I attempted to minimize its significance to myself and among racial minority respondents in order to get interviews with them, but I had to overemphasize my credentials with white and Asian respondents because of the culture of poverty stereotypes associated to Latinos in education. Gauging the perceptions held by participants toward upwardly mobile racial/ethnic minorities was difficult.

AGE AND LATINA CONTROLLING IMAGES

Latina professionals have difficulties escaping gendered racist stereotypes and sexualized narratives. Peggy McIntosh (1988) compiled a list of the invisible knapsack of privilege to show how it is not distributed equally or shared by individuals of every race/ethnicity and gender. Among the items on her list is "I can do well in a challenging situation without being called a credit to my race." Unlike white scholars, Latina scholars are not immune from these overgeneralizations. My physical appearance as a brown-skinned woman played a tremendous role in the ways study participants regarded me.

I first realized at Back to School Night at Compton Elementary that upward mobility did not protect me from pejorative stereotypes applied to Latinas. Mrs. Díaz asked me to translate her portion of the presentation to the parents. Mrs. Díaz asked me to move some of the chairs in her classroom to another teacher's room. I was carrying my backpack and two chairs, struggling with one in each hand. When I walked into the room, I set one of the chairs down and tried to approach the male teacher to shake his hand. Mr. Davis, a white male teacher, forty, was short, with blonde-buzzed hair and blue eyes. He stared at me for a bit and asked, "Oh, which one of my students are you the parent of?" Taken aback, I said, "Oh, I don't have any kids." He continued, "I thought you looked a little young to have a child. You look like you are in your early twenties and I have eight-year-olds in my class. It's very common to see that in this community." I said, "I'm a doctoral student doing observations for a research project." He perked up, smiled, and exclaimed, "Oh, wow!" He took the chair I was carrying from my hands, pretended to dust it off, extended his arm motioning me to pick whichever chair I wanted, and said, "You can sit wherever you'd like." This interaction with Mr. Davis is significant because his initial assessment of me as a teenage mother was further ingrained by his comment that it was a common pattern among Latinas. His gesture of wiping down a chair for me once I revealed I was a doctoral student made me aware of the *hidden privilege* I was accorded as a young PhD candidate because it meant he was giving *me* deference and respect, even if only temporarily.

Similar events took place with other non-Latino teachers. When I first approached Mr. Goyette for an interview, he was very dismissive. The first time I tried to speak to him, he lifted a folder to shield his face and rushed past me, leaving me with words in my mouth. On another occasion, I gave him a polite "Hello" and he gave me a very perturbed "Hi," rolled his eyes, and kept walking. The notes below show how his tone changed as my time in the field progressed and when I revealed my hidden status:

Mr. Goyette has come around and has begun asking me questions about the doctoral program and my research. "I think it's great you are doing this. You are going so much higher than I ever did." On several occasions Mr. Goyette made it a point to make sure I saw him doing favorable acts in front of Latino families. If he saw me in Mrs. Madrigal's classroom, he would instantly peek inside and give me an enthusiastic, "Hey! How are you?" Once he came in and watered her plant. Mrs. Madrigal corroborated this. "Oh, how cute," she said. "He is so different when you are around." "What do you mean by that?" I asked her as I stacked some books on a shelf. "It's like whenever you are around, he is nicer to me or more helpful. Like he is trying to be that nice white man that comes to help our kids or whatever. I got that impression when I first started working here. He gave me the feeling that I'm not worth your time. But because I have that college education, it's like I'm not that Mexican [poor and uneducated]."

Mr. Goyette's behavior and impression management made me question his daily interactions with Latino immigrant parents when I was not present. Mr. Goyette took on a white savior role as impression management to a well-educated, "exceptional" Latina, making me ponder the hidden privilege I possessed and what it meant about power possessed by a racial/ethnic minority outsider within with an academic degree. My presence made him change his behavior toward other Latina teachers and the children, but only for a moment, and only with minor tasks. Moreover, some respondents changed their demeanor toward me (and in front of other Latina teachers) and gave me lauds and laurels once they knew I was in a doctoral program and not a Latina teenage mother. It was then that many non-Latino participants agreed to the interview, because they equated a higher education with social distance from my ethnic group. In Rosemead, Asian teachers and personnel were more likely to participate when I revealed my academic credentials and affiliation with an elite private university. I was able to temporarily escape the "immigrant shadow" in these multiracial schools and see not only how privilege operated for me, but how it caused others who associated me with prestige to alter their actions into something they thought I would approve of in the moment.

Not all teachers rebuffed me. One way I developed ongoing rapport with respondents was by sharing minor details about personal relationships as a young professional. This broke the ice with teachers who were familiarizing themselves with me. Because I was a native insider, this allowed me to develop an instant connection with Latina teachers who had experienced gendered dating constraints in their immigrant families (López 2002). The sample included Latina teachers who were single, engaged, married, and divorced. The overwhelming majority of them were married and in heterosexual unions. Several Latina respondents in the sample asked me if I had a significant other and when I said, "No" or "I haven't had time" some of them seemed disappointed, offering me advice in the area, fearing I might have trouble finding someone as I got older. Some urged me to postpone a relationship until I finished the doctoral program. Others encouraged me to sign up for online dating sites like Match.com and invited me to attend Latino Professional Night (LPN) events. Ms. Gutierrez, who met her boyfriend at an LPN event, shared the trouble she had dating non-Latino men who saw her as exotic, and Latino men who expected her to manage her job and cater to them. My relationship status and these women's involvement in setting me up not only helped me establish deeper rapport but also provided me with outsider within status that granted me access to and inclusion in their personal lives away from the job.

For instance, Latina teachers also set me up on two blind dates, unbeknownst to me. When I was about to depart from her engagement party, Mrs. Gutierrez informed me that she had invited a potential suitor for me. "I've known him for a while," she said. "My fiancé invited someone for you too. We thought you could pick," she added with a laugh. As I hugged her to depart, she said, "You should call him. Let me give you his number." At my next visit to the school she asked, "Have you called him?" I said, "I haven't had time." She seemed irritated and exasperated, saying, "Just call him."[5] The fact that Mrs. Gutierrez tried to goad me into calling her male friend, instead of vice versa, suggested to me the power she accorded my educational credentials and researcher role. Because of my age, it was difficult for me to traverse the relationship between researcher and friend with Latina teachers because some of them saw me as a younger sibling who needed to be protected or mentored, but also as someone who possessed influence.

Latina teachers were not the only ones curious to hear about my personal life. In one instance, a Latino teacher who was married said it would be too hard for women to find a mate in teaching. For an older and unmarried teacher he used the Spanish idiom "*No a ellas ya se les pasó el tren*" [No for them, the train has passed].[6] This was in relation to his women colleagues who were not married. Another Latino teacher inappropriately sent me a message alluding to my physical appearance after the holiday party at Lucille's Restaurant. I ignored it. He later apologized and said he "had a little too much to drink." In addition, some Latino male respondents in Compton would often expose me to jokes of a sexual nature in Spanish. This falls in line with Rosalie Wax's (1979) finding that young unmarried women ethnographers in the field were susceptible to flirtatious behavior, jokes, and propositions from men. Even though I felt uncomfortable, the boundaries between researcher and friend were less clear with Latina/o respondents because the associations to my age as a Latina affected these relationships.

NAVIGATING MULTIPLE IDENTITIES/TESTS OF
MEXICAN AUTHENTICITY

I did not anticipate the multiple labels I would be assigned by participants. Sofia Villenas (1996) notes that in her youth she had to manipulate her own identity as the daughter of professional Ecuadorian immigrants living in predominantly Mexican and Central American neighborhoods but did not expect her identity to be manipulated by the people she interviewed. At Goodwill Elementary I was mistaken for a student teacher and never for a teenage mother. I was also immediately granted an "honorary teacher" status. Mrs. Prado, the Latina principal (in her late forties) said a job would be readily available for me once I finished my research. At Compton Elementary, on the other hand, African American teachers referred to me as a "student intern," white teachers referred to me as "the PhD" once I informed them about my credentials, and some Latina/o teachers referred to me endearingly as *La Venadita* (a nickname that literally means little doe). Negotiating the multiple identities that respondents placed on me was very difficult. These nicknames and labels operated to include me, while simultaneously excluding me. For instance, an honorary teacher status emphasized my teaching experience but also signified that I was not a formal elementary school teacher because I was a doctoral candidate who studied teachers. The student intern nickname demonstrated my learning role in the school. And "the PhD" emphasized the impression my educational credentials left on some respondents, elevating the prestige accorded me. Because of these distinct labels, I felt I had to please everyone at the research sites, even if they sometimes overtly expressed anti-Mexican sentiments or associated me with urban gangs. The following vignette captures this strain:

> Mr. Goyette seemed like he wanted to strike up an urban connection with me. He often insisted I "fist-bump" him when he was about to leave the campus and go home. On other occasions he pretended to walk with a limp, emulating a *cholo* [Latino gang member] stance and posture in front of me and put his fists over his chest and rolled side to side, dancing like a gangster. Mrs. Madrigal replied, "Oh, man. That *señor* [man] is crazy."

This dramaturgical behavior demonstrates that because I was an outsider within in these schools it granted me access to the racist jokes shared in the backstage (Goffman 1959; Picca and Feagin 2007), where teachers like Mr. Goyette viewed me not as a person of color who would be offended by this racialized behavior but rather as part of their private life in the backstage where I was granted access to the racialized ideas, behaviors, and notions that these teachers have about different racial groups. This was his way of using what whites believe is benign, nonracist behavior to include me in their work life. One of the ethical dilemmas I had to navigate during the research process was interfering during interactions that dealt with race or capturing the moment. While Lilia Monzo (2014) relied on her Latina cultural intuition and advocated or intervened on behalf of the Latino immigrant families that encountered a white-dominant gaze, I could not do the same in these diverse spaces. It was imperative I not burn bridges or cause friction between teachers because these schools were multiracial, they were small, and because teachers were hesitant to talk about race relations with one another despite daily interaction. While I was internally conflicted about vocalizing dissent, as a sociologist my primary goal was to document and understand these patterns of racialized behaviors in schools. Navigating how to respond to racialized stereotypes is an additional emotional labor researchers of color who hold distinct outsider within statuses must bear in different spaces. A negative reaction to this behavior and interaction could have affected my rapport with respondents and status as a researcher and participant.

I also had to contend with multiple and sometimes problematic teacher "personalities." Because I was an outsider within, I soon realized that *personalities* was a code Latina teachers used to characterize racial/ethnic conflict between teachers and to indicate the vast array of political opinions on campus, some of which espoused meritocratic ideals and did not align with their own political views. For example, during a faculty meeting with the third-grade team, Ms. Tiscareño (twenty-seven), a younger Latina teacher, shared how her immigrant parents went above and beyond to help her because they knew the value of an education. She was angry and said, "My parents were poor, my parents didn't have an education and I made it. These parents have no excuse." A white teacher at the meeting chimed in and said, "It sounds like your parents worked hard to instill the value of an education to you." She said, "Yeah!" Mrs. Díaz attempted to defend Latino families and said, "Well, you can't really blame them. I mean they have so many obstacles to overcome." Ms. Tiscareño reiterated, "No, there's no excuse! I mean look at her [pointing to me], she came from the same place and made it!" My presence and position affirmed some teachers' political beliefs that the United States is a meritocracy and gave credence to the American belief of rugged individualism: All kids could make it if they just worked hard and pulled themselves up by their bootstraps. Teachers saw me as evidence. The same occurred at Goodwill Elementary, where some Asian teachers thought it was acceptable to speak ill of Latino students and families to Latina teachers when I was in the room. This speaks to the structural and systemic oppression that foundationally inscribes Latinos and African Americans as inferior in education and higher mobility. To be considered an exception granted me outsider within status and in the minds of some of these teachers "assimilated" me and made me an acceptable representation of my ethnic group. I suggest teachers opened up the racial behaviors they safely shared in the backstage and those in the frontstage because my PhD candidacy made me worthy of their time.

There were two primary ways Latina/o teachers tested my legitimacy and "authenticity" as a Mexican woman in the teaching field. In a climate where teachers are blamed for student underachievement, many teachers wanted to know if I had worked in a teacher capacity before. Participant observation would have been difficult to complete if I did not have a background in education because many teachers were leery of my presence. My hidden privilege helped me because teachers of color working in a devalued school understood the hardships of "making it" in marginalized communities and the struggles of obtaining a higher education. Teachers wanted to be reassured I had managed my own classroom full of students and dealt with parents, administration, and school politics. Most teachers felt a sense of relief when I told them I had worked for an urban district in southern California, and this assuaged their hesitations about my presence in their classrooms.

Second, many Latina teachers tested my authenticity by asking me about my language abilities. Latina teachers wanted to gauge my stance on the preservation of native language and bilingual education, the loss of Latino ethnic culture, and assimilation into the mainstream. Sarah Morando (2013) notes that second-generation and upwardly mobile Latinos see being Spanish bilingual as an asset in the workforce. Second-generation Latina teachers in this study wanted my opinion on third- and fourth-generation Latinos who did not have a command of their parents' native languages. All Latina teachers wanted to know about my background—where I had grown up, where my parents were from, and if I could speak Spanish. But these conversations played out in different ways. Most of the Latina teachers in Compton wanted to know that I could hold a conversation in Spanish, understood "Spanglish," and could also code-switch between Spanish and English, reflective of a "hybrid" usage of languages (Subedi and Rhee 2008). I found that most Latina teachers in Compton knew how to speak Spanish and code-switched throughout the interview and with one another. Teachers knew I was conducting a comparative study, and those in Compton asked me about Latina teachers in Rosemead, a city with third- and fourth-generation Latina teachers. They asked, "Are they coconuts over there?" or "Are they still down for the brown? Or did they forget their roots?" In this case, bilingualism and outsider within status alerted me to the politics of language and requisites needed to pass tests of cultural authenticity in this context.

In Rosemead, however, second-, third-, and fourth-generation Latina teachers were concerned I would judge them harshly and question *their* Mexican or Latino authenticity for not speaking Spanish fluently. This was new to me. As an outsider within, I was highly aware that language maintenance across the generations determines insider or outsider status within the Latino populace (Jiménez 2004) but had never considered the shame third-plus-generation Latinas felt about not knowing the language and feelings of disappointing Latino families. Latina teachers in Rosemead were timid and would tell me they "could understand Spanish, but couldn't speak it" and said their own parents did not want them to learn the language because of the stigma associated with it in the United States. My hidden academic privilege made them feel at ease and share these experiences. Because most of the Latina and Asian teachers in Rosemead shared an immigrant background, they were adamant that their Latino and Asian students retain their native languages while learning English. Latina teachers who were unable to retain Spanish felt an extreme sense of loss and wanted students to preserve theirs.

I also had to become accustomed to different communication styles in order to be accepted by all teachers on campus. Lanita Jacobs-Huey (2002: 799) maintains that native researchers, when researching communities with which they culturally affiliate, are often asked to demonstrate their communicative competence, which "entails fluency in the multiple languages and discourse styles characterizing as speech community, as well as an ability to adhere to specific discourse rules." In multiracial schools I noticed that Black teachers would pause their conversations or hesitated speaking in Ebonics vernacular once I was at ear's length of their conversations, and would speak "proper" English, highlighting my outsider status. For example, one day two African American women teachers were speaking to each other in the middle of the courtyard. I could hear the taller African American woman say to the other, "Chile [child], please! How you gone do that!" The other African American woman replied, "Man, don't hate. You gotta do, what chu gots to do!" As I approached them, their communication style changed. The taller African American teacher said, "Hello. How are you doing today? Who are you here to see?" As my time in the field progressed, African American teachers stopped self-policing the ways they expressed themselves when they realized I was an ally as a fellow educator and not there to judge their forms of speech or evaluate their teaching effectiveness.

While African American teachers initially felt compelled to self-police their communication styles around me, I also had to be aware of Spanish puns and idioms around 1.5- and second-generation Latina/o respondents in order to maintain my legitimacy in the field and authenticity in their eyes. The following vignette from my fieldnotes shows how I earned the nickname *La Venadita* and how Latina and Latino teachers spoke to me in the field:

> [Did you know we call you *La Venadita*?]. I looked at the Latino teacher quizzically and asked, "Why is my *apodo* [nickname] *La Venadita*? Little Doe? I don't get it." The Latino teacher smirked after all of my erroneous guesses and finally said, "*Noooo. Porque cuando te quitas los lentes, no ves nadita*" [Noooo. Because when you take off your glasses, you can't see anything].

This interaction with a Latino teacher shows he used a play-on-words in Spanish of a little female doe, to signify the quotidian use of spectacles and illustrates how my relationships with these teachers were contingent upon my understanding of Latino cultural puns. Over time, I came to find out that several Latina/o teachers referred to me this way when I was not present, the usage functioning as an inclusionary mechanism. It was imperative I decipher these forms of expression to maintain my insider status with them.

In Latino culture it is commonplace to use endearing *apodos* [nicknames] to refer to people (Chong 2005). Although I was given the nickname *La Venadita* by Latina/o teachers, African American and white teachers often referred to me with the more clinical "our student intern." Increasing attention has been paid to how researchers of color studying minority communities make sense of and reflect on their own experiences because their "situated knowledge," or lived experiences, can better inform the way they interpret their data (Zinn 2001). Reflexivity is the process by which a researcher understands how personal experience shapes his or her ideas and the way he or she attributes meaning, interprets action, and conducts dialogues with informants (Mills 1959: 3). My role with most African American, Asian, and white teachers was much more formal than with Latina/o teachers primarily because the study focused on the lives of Latina teachers, but also because at times I was unable to pick up on cultural cues that are a vibrant part of African American and Asian American culture. For example, when I began my study three Asian American teachers invited me to Dim sum during lunch. While a Chinese-origin teacher was translating all of the food items for me, the other two teachers were holding a conversation in Vietnamese. I felt like I was intruding. Although I became aware of different Asian dialects, language demonstrates both my outsider and insider status with these racial/ethnic groups, but being an outsider within and the hidden privilege are what granted me access to all teachers' work lives.

As a last point, Maxine Baca Zinn (1979) argues that one of the politics of conducting research in racial/ethnic minority communities as an insider is exiting the field and "breaking off relationships." When I began the study, some Latina teachers would admonish me if I left the site for the day without a proper farewell. They interpreted it as a form of disrespect if I did not personally follow through and inform them of my departure. Many Latina teachers would say, "Don't abandon us, girl. Don't become all big time and forget about your people and where you came from because I've seen a lot of Latinos do that." These cultural norms demonstrate a form of inclusion with teachers of color, but they also show that teachers were well aware I would eventually have to leave the field, as academia forces scholars to separate and exclude themselves from respondents. While teachers of color knew I would have to physically distance myself from them and the schools, they encouraged me to maintain connections to the community in other ways and not become absorbed by the academic institution. With this knowledge in mind, I waited until the end of the school year when teachers would pack up their rooms and go on summer vacation to exit the field.

NOTES

INTRODUCTION

1 Karl Marx. 1852. "The Eighteenth Brumaire of Louis Napoleon," in *Die Revolution*. New York.

2 Audre Lorde. 1984. *Sister Outsider: Essays and Speeches*. Trumansburg, NY: The Crossing Press.

CHAPTER 1. FROM "AMERICANIZATION" TO "LATINIZATION"

1 The names of the elementary schools have been disguised.

2 All teachers have been given pseudonyms.

3 Throughout this book, I use the terms *Latina, Chicana, Mexican*, or *Mexican American* and other national-origin political labels to refer to the teachers. I use *Hispanic* in quotes only if Latina teachers themselves used it. Some Latinas had an aversion to the term because it denies indigenous roots and it is a term adopted by the U.S. Census Bureau in the 1970s. *Chicana/o* was a negative political label that became reappropriated during the Chicano movement of the 1960s to signify a political identity of empowerment. It is used to identify those born in the United States who have some form of Mexican lineage.

4 Before finally landing a job as an instructional aide, Mrs. Arenas worked on an assembly line in a pickle factory and in the cafeteria of a hospital in her early twenties. Unlike credentialed teachers, instructional aides do not have to have a bachelors degree or a credential to work in this capacity. In most cases, instructional aides are on the path toward becoming teachers and work in a part-time capacity.

5 Historians such as Emily Straus (2014) and Albert Camarillo (2005) do not disguise the names of the school districts or the schools they use in their analysis. While I maintain the name of the school districts, Goodwill Elementary and Compton Elementary are both pseudonyms to protect the identities of the teachers. Because I was conducting ethnographic fieldwork in one school in each school district, the Institutional Review Board required that I change the names of the schools and teachers. I should also note that Latina immigrant mothers wanted their real names to appear in the manuscript and were adamant that I embody the style of public sociology before I spoke to them because they wanted educational change for their children. All participants were given pseudonyms.

6 Myriad bilingual-education programs were set in place by virtue of the Bilingual Education Act in 1968, but most programs were dismantled by Proposition 227, which was billed as the "English for the Children," initiative in 1998.

7 Mrs. Arenas explained that the program was eliminated because Latino parents were confused over the meaning of bilingual education. They feared that their children would be at a disadvantage if they were educated in the Spanish language in their early formative educational years instead of English. For more on the politics of language see Ochoa (2004) and García Bedolla (1999).

8 More than 8 million Mexican-origin children and youth, the largest Latino subgroup, have Mexican-born parents (Passel 2011). Additionally, one out of every four students in K–12 schools is of Latina/o origin nationwide (Fry and López 2012).

9 In recent years, Latina teachers are being recruited to work in more affluent districts in dual immersion programs (see Muro 2015).

10 Other studies have shown that Latina teachers feel that they must hide their cultural and ethnic heritage in white spaces when working among a majority of white colleagues (Ochoa 2007; Urrieta 2010).

11 Approved by voters in 1994, but still under review by the courts, Proposition 187 sought to deny social services such as education and health care to undocumented immigrants and their children.

12 Sociologist Donald Tomaskovic-Devey (1993) notes that as more women and racial/ethnic minorities enter a profession, the prestige of the occupation is further devalued.

13 Jal Mehta. 2013. "Teachers: Will We Ever Learn?" *New York Times*, April. Also see Bill Keller. 2013. "An Industry of Mediocrity." *New York Times*, October 20.

14 Two tables were run, one for second-generation college-educated Latinas and another one for third-generation college-educated Latinas. In both tables, teaching was the top occupation. This table includes the results for both second- and third-generation Latinas. This was measured by disaggregating the data based upon parental nativity status and grandparent nativity status.

15 According to the U.S. Bureau of Labor Statistics, African Americans were 10.4 percent of all elementary and middle school teachers nationwide but decreased to 9.3 percent in 2010. Teachers of Latina/o origin were 5.9 percent of all teachers in 2003 and 7.3 percent in 2010. The percentage of Asian American teachers went from 1.9 percent in 2003 to 2.4 percent in 2010.

16 Mrs. Lomeli made this remark in an interview I undertook as part of a study that gave rise to this project. I describe the project, for which I interviewed twenty-one Latina teachers in Santa Ana, in an earlier paper (Flores 2011a).

17 Also known as the California Civil Rights Initiative. This initiative amended the state constitution to prohibit public institutions from considering race, sex, or ethnicity.

18 *Double jeopardy* is used to indicate the intersection of race and gender while *triple oppression* emphasizes the interlinked nature of race, gender, and class. For more on the simultaneity perspective in organizational studies see Evangelina Holvino's work in *Gender, Work and Organizations*.

19 Within street vending, a job that is part of the informal sector of the economy, Rocío Rosales (2014) argues that *ethnic cages* more aptly describes the experiences of individuals who work in this field. This is because those who are more established tend to exploit newer arrivals who are gaining their footing on U.S. soil.

20 A note on terminology: I use the term *interracial* to refer to race relations between Latina teachers, their co-workers, administration, students, and parents. I use the terms *multiracial* or *multiethnic* when I am referring to the communities, schools, and research sites included in this study. The terms *interracial* and *multiracial* should not be confused with studies on multiracial identification and interracial dating and marriage patterns. I am not ignoring these studies. Multiracial identity and interracial dating and marriages were very small occurrences in this study, perhaps because of the large number of immigrants in these communities.

21 The Treaty of Guadalupe Hidalgo ended the war between Mexico and the United States in 1848 and led to the cession of much of the contemporary American Southwest.

22 *De jure* segregation is the deliberate planned segregation of the races through formally instituted policies and laws. Jim Crow laws were enacted between 1876 and 1965 in the American South and demanded racial segregation in all public facilities, especially schools. For example, the intellectual roots of *Plessy v. Ferguson*, the landmark U.S. Supreme Court decision upholding the constitutionality of racial segregation in 1896 under the doctrine of "separate but equal," was, in part, tied to biological determinism and the scientific racism of the era. It was deemed that African American children were biologically inferior and could not integrate with white children in schools. It was argued that separate facilities would accord both racial groups similar educational resources and outcomes.

23 *Roberto Alvarez v. the Board of Trustees of the Lemon Grove School District* (1931) preceded the more commonly known *Brown v. Board of Education* (1954), which ultimately dismantled "separate but equal" nationwide.

24 According to the Supreme Court, *Brown v. Board of Education* (1954), on the other hand, confronted the question of whether separate (but otherwise equal) educational facilities for Black and white students "solely on the basis of race" were "inherently unequal."

25 At the time they filed the suit, Gonzalo and Felicitas Méndez, a married couple and the children of migrant agricultural workers, leased a sixty-acre farm owned by a Japanese family then interned in a concentration camp. Felicitas Méndez was of Puerto Rican origins while Gonzalo Méndez had Mexican roots. Notably, four other families were also involved in the suit.

26 *Los Angeles Times*, 10 September 1996; McWilliams, "Is Your Name González?," 303.

27 The film "Walkout" (2006) depicts that Mexican-origin students had massive drop-out rates and were tracked into vocational courses and jobs.

28 For more on Chinese exclusion in schools in the 1880s, see the case of *Mamie Tape v. Hurley* in *All Deliberate Speed: Segregation and Exclusion in California*

Schools, 1855–1975. Mamie Tape was the American-born child of Chinese immigrants and was denied entry into Spring Valley Elementary in San Francisco.

29   Among other things, *Lau v. Nichols* reflected the view that language is intimately tied with national origin and argued that language-based discrimination could be a proxy for national-origin discrimination.

30   For more on *mestiza consciousness* see Gloria Anzaldua's *Borderlands/La Frontera: The New Mestiza* (1987).

31   As the stipulations of the DREAM Act show, the shift to *de facto* school segregation shows that today's teachers must traverse racial/ethnic and linguistically diverse populations.

32   A note on political identifications: I use *Latina* or *Chicana* to refer to the women in this study. *Latina* is a pan-ethnic label that homogenizes the Latino experience, but in many cases, the women in this study preferred this term over *Hispanic*. The Census Bureau chose *Hispanic* in the 1970s to identify those of Latin American origins. In some cases, as in chapter 4, I also use *Chicana*. *Chicana/o* is used to signify individuals who are of Mexican origin and was reappropriated in the 1960s as a term of empowerment.

33   I include a detailed table with the demographic characteristics of the twenty Latina teachers in appendix A because they are the focus of this study. Other interview participants were five Latino, nine Black, ten Asian, and six white teachers. Not included in the fifty interviews are informal conversations with several individuals such as a Latina speech pathologist and a Latina student teacher completing her hours.

34   The two types of training available to teachers in the Los Angeles area that focus on language are Cross-cultural, Language and Academic Development (CLAD), and Bilingual, Cross-cultural, Language and Academic Development (BCLAD).

35   Two-thirds of Latinos in the United States are of Mexican origin.

36   It was not my initial intention to select two unincorporated spaces; however, both of these schools fit under this designation and allow for standardization of the research sites.

37   Snowball sampling is a methodological technique whereby teachers who agreed to participate suggested others in the school who would also be willing to participate.

38   The raw number of teachers can change from year to year, as some teachers might be moved to another school within the same district.

39   In chapter 6, I explain how the English Language Learner (ELL) category was strictly reserved for Latino students, while English Only (EO) was used to refer to African American children.

40   In the 2010–11 academic year, the number of Latino students rose to 49 percent, while the percentage of Asian students decreased.

41   About 1 percent spoke Khmer. Most students considered proficient in the English language were Asians who had passed all required tests, or later-generation Latino families who spoke English as their primary language.

42 In 2012, the number of Latinas reached 30 percent of all teachers.

43 Teacher aides are usually, but not always, in the process of becoming teachers. Prior to this project, I had worked in a teacher aide capacity for four years. Teacher aides supplement the learning process for students and are always needed in the classroom. Most float around with different teachers within the same school.

44 Focus Group Breakdown: (Rosemead: 5 Latina Immigrant Mothers; 4 U.S. Born Parents (1 man); 6 Asian Immigrant Mothers (1 was 1.5 Immigrant); (Compton: 5 Latina Immigrant Mothers; 4 U.S. Born Mothers; 4 Black Parent Figures). All focus group participants were given pseudonyms.

CHAPTER 2. "I JUST FELL INTO IT"

Portions of this chapter are related to a previously published article: Glenda M. Flores and Pierrette Hondagneu-Sotelo (2014), "The Social Dynamics Channeling Latina College Graduates into the Teaching Profession," *Gender, Work and Organization* 21(6): 491–515.

1 All teachers have been given pseudonyms, and I have disguised details about the schools to protect the anonymity of respondents who graciously participated in this project.

2 A chapter book is a story book that relies on prose over pictures. A number line is a mathematical tool teachers use to help students learn how to count, add, and subtract.

3 Hondagneu-Sotelo notes that structural changes in the United States and Latin America gave rise to Latinas in domestic employment. As more white women entered the workforce, and the rise of dual-earner career families became common, domestics were needed in their homes. Central American women, in particular, were more likely to be live-in domestics.

4 Historically, Hondagneu-Sotelo notes that domestic jobs were held by African American women in the United States.

5 Acronyms stand for Cross-cultural, Language and Academic Development (CLAD) and Bilingual, Cross-cultural, Language and Academic Development (BCLAD).

6 This resulted in Senate Bill 1777, which provided incentives for school districts to reduce K–3 classes to a pupil–teacher ratio of no more than 20 to 1. This legislation originally provided annual incentive funding of $650 for each student in a smaller class and an option of $325 for students in a staggered session in which the pupil–teacher ratio is no more than 20 to 1 for half the day, creating the need for more teachers in the lower grades.

7 Teach for America is a nonprofit organization that aims to recruit graduating college students and place them to teach in a low-income community for a minimum of two years.

8 Teaching requires successful completion of the following tests: CBEST (California Basic Educational Skills Test), CSET (California Subject Examinations

for Teachers), RICA (Reading Instruction Competence Assessment), and BTSA (Beginning Teacher Support and Training), a program sponsored by California Department of Education and the Commission on Teacher Credentialing for professional development of newly credentialed teachers (two years). (Source: State of California Commission on Teacher Credentialing.)

9 Sociologist Denise Segura (1989) has noted that clerical work was one occupation where Latinas were concentrated in large numbers.

10 Emergency teaching credentials were popular in the 1990s when there was a huge demand for bilingual teachers. Today, teachers must be fully credentialed before obtaining a teaching job, but there are exceptions in schools that have difficulties recruiting teachers.

CHAPTER 3. CULTURAL GUARDIANS

1 Sociologists have many ways of determining upward mobility. In this case, I define upward mobility as intergenerational mobility—rising above one's parents' occupations, educational level, and income.

2 Lisa Dodson (2009) details how middle-class employers of all racial/ethnic backgrounds would break the rules to secure the well-being of their lower-class employees.

3 Suárez (2002) indicates that Latina teachers serving the Orange County and Los Angeles areas said they described teaching as a "calling" and went into the teaching profession to ameliorate the inferior educational trajectories of their students. I find that this process did not happen before employment but after, once Latina teachers had been in their jobs for a couple of months.

4 To be clear, Mrs. Díaz's parents were college-educated in their home countries of Cuba (father) and El Salvador (mother).

5 In *The Dreamkeepers*, Gloria Ladson-Billings (2009) highlights how middle-class African American teachers successfully use culturally relevant teaching techniques to reach African American children. Like Ladson-Billings's, my argument is not that only Latina teachers should teach Latino students; rather, I highlight how their interactions with Latino students demonstrate sanctioned and unsanctioned ways of reaching underprivileged youth.

6 In her book *Becoming Neighbors* (2004), Gilda Ochoa explains that the Mexican-origin population was internally divided by generational level. In communities where the majority of residents are of the same racial/ethnic origins but divided by generational levels, cultural guardianship may take different forms.

7 I want to note that this perspective is changing as many Latina teachers are increasingly being offered and are accepting teaching positions in dual immersion schools that are sprouting in more affluent areas.

8 W. E. B. Du Bois (1903) once proclaimed that the "Talented Tenth" of the African American population was crucial in promoting racial uplift for poorer African American families, who were being prepared for lower-skilled industries.

9 While Mrs. Madrigal would call her husband to help her to aid children, she also used this practice as an intimidation tactic. In one case she said that she would have her husband drive to the homes of her African American children to "scare" African American parents to "get me that homework."

10 On more than one occasion, Latina teachers expressed sympathy for children whose parent or parents were deported while they were in school. In another instance, Mrs. Ybarra consoled a sobbing child who did not want to return to school because his father had been taken away.

11 I was asked to chaperone several of these trips and contributed financially ($20 each) by paying for the field trip for parents who participated in the focus group portion of the study.

12 Persian, French, Italian, German, or Chinese immigrant parents who want their children to maintain home language fluency do not encounter anywhere near the level of hostility that Latina/o parents do when they ask for bilingual education. It is Spanish in particular that Anglo Americans see as a low-prestige language and as a cultural threat (Chávez 2008).

13 In chapter 6 I explain the role that high-stakes testing—that which tests English-language proficiency—played in cultural guardianship.

14 González-López (2004) writes about differences in how Mexican fathers protect their daughters' sexuality based on whether they came from urban or rural locations. She finds that fathers who grew up in the countryside in Mexico are much more likely to be extremely protective of their daughters' virginity not because they are culturally backward but because in their small towns, a girl's reputation had material consequences. Alternatively, fathers who had grown up in cities with more resources and information, where women worked in different careers, did not care as much.

15 In chapter 5 I explain the significance of behavior and education for Latino immigrant parents.

CHAPTER 4. CO-ETHNIC CULTURAL GUARDIANSHIP

Portions of this chapter are related to a previously published article: Glenda M. Flores, "Controlling Images of Space: Latina Teachers and Racial Positioning in Multiracial Schools," *City and Community* 14: 410–432.

1 The pioneers of gangsta rap.

2 "California Love" was one of Tupac Shakur's (2Pac) most popular songs of the 1990s, famous for its lyrics "California knows how to party" and "in the city, city of Compton."

3 Controlling images has been applied to racial/ethnic minority groups, but much less to space. For instance, the mammy, Jezebel, matriarch, and welfare queen are powerful controlling images used toward African American women. In contrast, the lotus blossom, dragon lady, and the emasculated male are common among Asian Americans (Espiritu 1997).

4 Latino identities can be mixed; however, the overwhelming majority of Latina/o students, families, and teachers included in the study were not of multiracial backgrounds.

5 In 2013, the all–African American school board appointed a high school Latino student representative to their board.

6 Code yellow is used by school officials when the facility must be locked down until the police clear the order.

7 Immigration from Latin America, Asia, and the Caribbean to the United States increased because of the Hart-Celler Act.

8 The Panda Restaurant Group, the largest Chinese fast food restaurant chain in the United States, was founded in Pasadena, California, in 1973 by individuals from the Yangzhou region of China's Jiangsu province. According to the city's 2009 Comprehensive Annual Financial Report, the chain ranked number four of the city's top employers.

9 An old Mexican *barrio* labeled one of the county's most crime-ridden for its gang activity.

10 Alhambra, Arcadia, Temple City, and Diamond Bar's, also in the SGV, residents are more than 50 percent Asian-origin families (U.S. Census Bureau 2010).

11 *Morenos* is a neutral term used by immigrant and second-generation Latinos to describe color or phenotype. This can be a nonracial and nonracist description that can become pejorative based on intonation during quotidian speech and interactions.

12 The term *pigmentocracia* or pigmentocracy, first coined by Chilean sociologist Alejandro Lipshütz in 1944, is a group-based social hierarchy based on skin hue. In Latin America, dark pigment has been met with disdain and inferiority while white skin and European features are valorized.

13 Some Latina teachers did align with Black teachers along religious lines.

14 In chapter 6, I discuss in greater detail how Latina teachers explain the racialization processes of children.

15 By the end of this study, Mrs. Rivas had accepted another position in the Long Beach Unified School District as a curriculum specialist.

16 Most members of the PTA at Compton Elementary were immigrant Latina mothers. Only one African American grandfather attended their meetings during the study period.

17 Through the process of civic ostracism, the dominant group constructs the subordinate group as immutably foreign and unassimilable with whites on cultural and or racial grounds in order to ostracize them from the body politic and civic membership.

18 The Quality Education Investment Act (QEIA) was sponsored by the California Teachers Association (CTA). The program began in 2006 and ended June 30, 2015.

19 While the term *combat pay* typically refers to military pay for deployed soldiers, teachers working in Compton used this term to reference supplements and

incentive pay in their annual income. Combat pay equates poor, urban schools with war zones. Teachers earn a stipend ranging upward of $600 for working in inner-city schools.

20 Many school districts permit teachers to enroll their children where they work.

21 Using a family member's address to access schools is not uncommon, but it is illegal in many states. School districts seek to verify that guardians are residents, not property owners. Regulations vary state by state and sometimes community by community. Violations may be punishable by a fine or jail time. A homeless African American mother in Bridgeport, Connecticut, was sentenced to five years in prison for enrolling her elementary school–age son in a district where she did not reside.

22 See chapter 6 for an analysis of how African American students are frozen out of the schooling system.

CHAPTER 5. BICULTURAL MYTHS, RIFTS, AND SHIFTS

1 I use *Chicana/Latina cultural pedagogies* and *Latino cultural resources* interchangeably.

2 Howard Blume. 2008. "School Rallies 'Round Dismissed Teacher." *Los Angeles Times*, June 12.

3 In California, teachers receive tenure after three years of working in a district, assuming their performance evaluations are positive.

4 Culturally relevant teaching was first developed in the 1980s to explain how school curricula such as books could be incorporated in schools to cater to racial/ethnic minority students. This is different from other conceptualizations such as funds of knowledge and community cultural wealth that identify resources within racial/ethnic minority populations that are often not valued or incorporated in schools by educational personnel.

5 All school districts have individual rules regarding the use of culture in schools. These district policies vary and usually depend on the school board and the political leanings of the principal.

6 Latino ethnic culture, and ethnic culture in general, however, remains unwelcome in many professional institutional work settings (see García-López 2008; Livers 2006; Chávez 2011). For example, Chicana attorneys are explicitly told to conceal "ethnic" Latino markers in their appearance in white institutional settings and with white co-workers (García-López 2008).

7 Because Compton Elementary was predominantly African American and Latino, Latina teachers also explained that they participated in Black History Month and would show their support by wearing custom-made T-shirts depicting a historical figure, such as Martin Luther King Jr. or Harriet Tubman, and would prepare an elaborate show filled with dances and poems performed by their students for their parents in the cafeteria.

8 This event is associated with the Chinese traditional holidays and is also referred to as the Spring Festival or Lantern Festival. It includes cultural elements such as

the lion dance and red envelopes that include money, a practice that Mrs. Wilson, a Caucasian teacher, always celebrated in her classroom with her Asian and Latino students. Each year is associated with an animal that will bring good fortune to those who were born in a year associated with it. For example, 2016 was the year of the monkey and 2017 is the year of the rooster.

9   The funds of knowledge model raises a number of additional questions. For instance: How many homes would a teacher need to "go into"? When would they do that? How often? Would that be part of their official duties and thus would they be paid for the time spent on such fieldwork? How would they select what to use as a knowledge? If they saw something at one house how would they know it was common in other houses? The pedagogy I propose suggests that most Latina teachers do not have to take these additional steps as many of them are already aware of Latino cultural resources.

10 A question I get asked frequently at conferences is if whether non-Latinos can learn these Latina/o cultural cues. Elements of the pedagogy such as the mathematics examples can be learned and taught in teacher training programs; however, these pedagogies also require a certain disposition and sympathy toward the Latino immigrant experience that not all teachers exhibit.

11 Latina teachers I interviewed are aware of variations in the Spanish language depending on country of origin and region. For example, Salvadoran immigrants will use *vos* instead of *tú* to say "you" and *usted* as a form of respect with parents and the elderly.

12 The analysis in this chapter focuses on Latina teacher interactions with foreign-born Latino immigrants. While Latina teachers also described communicating with U.S.-born Latino parents in English and Spanish, their assessment of these parents was in a negative light.

13 The English Only movement and Proposition 227 passed in June 1988 with 61 percent of California's electorate. The proposition stipulated that English Language Learners be placed in structured English immersion and then be transferred to mainstream classrooms taught overwhelmingly in English. These models promote a "sink or swim" educational model.

14 The correct word is *cómoda*.

15 Spanglish uses word mixtures such as this often: *lonche* for lunch, *troque* for truck, and so on. However, recent immigrants are unlikely to recognize the terms.

16 In the Methodological Appendix (appendix B), I explain in greater detail the dilemmas I faced as an *insider* and an *outsider* in mixed-race schools and elaborate on the added emotional burdens that scholars of color must contend with over capturing the data versus intervening on behalf of parents who face anti-immigrant sentiment.

17 It is important to note that Asian teachers who could speak another language expressed having this advantage with Asian immigrant parents as well. There was much more diversity in terms of Asian dialects (Vietnamese, Mandarin, Cantonese) than in Spanish.

18 The U.S. government received the first wave of Cuban migrants, the Golden Exiles, warmly.

19 A Mexican family with a *rancho* has the means to raise livestock. A *pueblo* is a poor, small village or community where most homes are made of adobe or stones.

20 Ana Rosas (2011) explains that in Mexico, many teachers serve as surrogate parents who ensure that Mexican children are *bien educado* (well-educated/behaved).

21 SWUN Math is a mathematical model developed by Si Swun, an English Language Learner who struggled with math as a student. His model is based on math methodologies found in Asia, namely Singapore. SWUN Math has spread throughout southern California and is used in schools districts with low socioeconomic, English Language Learner, and minority student populations.

CHAPTER 6. STANDARDIZED TESTS AND WORKPLACE TENSIONS

1 The abbreviation stands for the California Standards Test and it is based on the California State standards. However, in the 2014–15 academic school year, the state of California changed the exam to the Smarter and Balanced Assessment Consortium (SBAC). The exam was administered online and the scores released for the first time. These high-stakes exams tend to change every couple of years, but I argue that the tests heighten racial tensions regardless of the name of the test or its design. Instead of beginning testing in the second grade, the SBAC will be taken by third-graders. Additionally, California assigns each school and district an Academic Performance Index (API) rating ranging from 200 to 1,000, with a statewide API goal of 800 for all schools.

2 Schools that do not meet their annual yearly progress report score based on school performance on the CST receive a Program Improvement designation. Compton Elementary school had received the ranking five years in a row, meaning that if their scores did not improve significantly they were in danger of being taken over by the state.

3 I did not correct the Spanish orthography. Instead, I left the note the way the mother wrote it and translated it into English accordingly.

4 Men were numerical minorities at Compton and Goodwill Elementary. They are also numerical minorities in the teaching profession at the elementary level.

5 "Far below basic" is the lowest English Language Learner label that can be applied to a student whose first language is not English.

6 NCLB requires that states develop assessment tests in basic skills. The Act does not assert a national achievement standard but, instead, allows each state to develop its own standards.

7 White teachers also preferred the children of Latino immigrants in their classrooms over Black students.

8 The California English Language Development Test (CELDT) is still used today. Scores are assessed on a 1–5 point scale. CELDT is a required state test gauging English-language proficiency and given to students whose primary language is

other than English. It varies in four areas: writing, speaking, listening, and comprehension.

9   Mario Barrera (1979) made similar observations in *Race and Class in the Southwest*.

10 While Goodwill Elementary employed only three male teachers, Compton Elementary school employed ten. As I explained in chapter 4, the controlling images of space largely affected Latina teachers' perceptions of racial positioning in schools. I suspect that controlling images of space also lured more male teachers (both white and of color) to Compton because it was situated in a neighborhood that is racialized as a Black masculine space; they often noted that they should be able to "handle" working with the student population in Compton. For more on the contradictions of men's professional lives in elementary teaching, see *Real Men or Real Teachers?* by Paul Sargent (2001).

11 The abbreviation stands for Beginning Teacher Support & Assessment, and it is a program for newly credentialed beginning teachers.

12 A strategy teachers use to help students develop their counting skills.

13 I later asked Mrs. Gutierrez about this statement in order to include it, and also asked her if she could elaborate what she meant.

14 EO was also used for third-generation Latino students who primarily spoke English at home or Latino students who had been deemed English proficient, but they were a numerical minority. The term was mostly used to refer to African American children.

15 Education expert Jeannie Oakes (1986, 2005) describes how schools use "tracking" and "ability grouping" that determines the academic fate of racial/ethnic minority children.

16 Formal training sessions to determine classroom placement usually take place at the beginning or at the end of the school year. Although this process began in August 2009 at Compton Elementary, the practice of separating ELLs and EOs ran for the duration of my fieldwork in the school.

17 At the time Mrs. Jones was hired, I had already spent one full academic year in the field.

18 A placement test that takes thirty minutes or less and provides data that teachers can use to determine the initial placement of English Language Learners.

19 For those who worry about linguistic balkanization due to immigration from Spanish-speaking countries, Rumbaut, Massey, and Bean (2006) argue that there is nothing to fear because native language eventually dies out by the third generation.

20 Latino students who have successfully passed all state tests.

21 The Home Language Survey was sent out every year only to Latino parents to assess the primary language that the parent used at home. No such survey was distributed to African American parents whose children were automatically labeled as EOs.

22 This was met in different ways by Latina teachers. Some enjoyed working with low-level Latino students. Others, however were surprised when they were assigned to a higher-scoring Latino class because these were usually reserved for monolingual English-speaking teachers.

23 In *The Wrong Kind of Different*, Randolph (2013) compares multiracial schools with Black schools. She finds that teachers described multiracial schools as progressive, harmonious, and tolerant, while Black schools were reminders of America's past. Black schools represented segregation, disadvantage, and underachievement. While Hispanics receive ethnic credits in the classroom, Black students suffer from racial penalties.

24 Valenzuela (1999) documents the patterns of Mexican immigrant achievement and U.S.-born underachievement in an inner-city high school in Houston.

25 Unlike Goodwill Elementary, Compton Elementary did not have a formal GATE program.

26 I should note that Goodwill Elementary used the term *EL* to classify their English Learners, but I will use *ELL* in the remainder of the chapter to keep the terms similar.

27 Although I was in the teachers' lounge at Compton Elementary, I have no ethnographic accounts of Latina teachers' interactions with non-Latino-origin teachers in the lounge because they never ate in there. Most teachers opted to eat in their rooms by themselves, and Latina teachers described the space as a "dumping ground," meaning for storage.

28 Many of these parents had older children who had already completed the primary grades. Additionally, extended relatives and friends also asked other mothers about their childrens' teachers in the earlier grades.

29 The other Latino teacher taught a fifth-grade class.

30 Goodwill Elementary formally hired one Spanish-language translator, one Vietnamese translator, and one Chinese translator who spoke Cantonese and Mandarin.

31 State mandate requires school districts send a letter informing all parents of their option to send their children to another school.

32 Latina teachers were referring to Kumon Learning Centers that had sprouted in the area. Sociologist Cynthia Feliciano argues that the U.S. immigration process selects immigrant groups along particular lines, such as for their labor or high technology skills. Many Asian immigrant groups are selected for their high technology skills and have some form of schooling in their countries of origin.

33 Latina/o and Asian American students at Goodwill Elementary attended classrooms balanced by gender, race, and achievement level. With the exception of the GATE classes on campus, the school integrated all students in classrooms regardless of their academic achievement level or language profiency. Here, most EO students were second- and third-generation Latino-origin students whose parents noted on the Home Language Survey passed out at the beginning of the school year that the primary language spoken at home was English. Asian American students who were considered EO were largely children who had attained fluency and met state benchmarks. They received this designation only after successfully passing a series of state tests for ELLs indicating that they were now English proficient. Although Latino-origin children were more likely to be EOs in this region

because it was the primary language spoken at home, Latino children overall scored lower than their Asian American counterparts.

34 Small plastic bags filled with cheese and crackers and granola bars for a field trip.

35 Gilda Ochoa argues, for example, that Asians were academically, but not always socially, accepted in Latino/Asian high schools.

CONCLUSION AND EPILOGUE

1 The 1930s ushered in a new era of Mexican migration to the United States that dealt with the expulsion of Mexican families who were blamed for the country's economic ills at the time. This resulted in the deportation and repatriation of thousands of Mexican families and their children, many of whom were U.S. citizens. Union Station in Los Angeles was used to send Mexican families back to a country to which many of them no longer had cultural ties.

2 The Immigration Reform and Control Act of 1986, signed into office by President Ronald Reagan, gave undocumented immigrants the ability to apply for amnesty.

3 In *Hopeful Girls, Troubled Boys*, Nancy López argues that Dominican boys and girls develop different outlooks over educational attainment, where girls envision it as a route to independence, freedom, and mobility. Boys, on the other hand, worried about their prospects of succeeding in the higher echelons of the educational hierarchy.

4 Asians are a heterogeneous group and are also divided along class and educational lines.

5 Motoko Rich. 2015. "Teacher Shortages Spur a Nationwide Hiring Scramble (Credentials Optional)." *New York Times*, August 9.

6 Currently, 8.7 million U.S. children younger than eight years old have at least one foreign-born parent, a doubling from 4.3 million in 1990. Children younger than eight years old, approximately 24 percent, have immigrant parents (Fortuny, Hernandez, and Chaudry 2008).

APPENDIX B

Portions of this Methodological Appendix are related to a previous published article: Glenda M. Flores (2016), "Discovering a Hidden Privilege: Ethnography in Multiracial Organizations as an Outsider Within," *Ethnography* 17: 190–212.

1 Used to refer to the U.S.-born children of immigrants who are granted automatic citizenship.

2 The IRB informed me that I did not need district approval because I was selecting one school within each district. Toward the end of my fieldwork the principal in Rosemead informed me that to ensure the anonymity of my respondents I had to fill out district paperwork, which I successfully completed. I followed all protocol required. I have changed the names of the schools and teachers to ensure complete anonymity.

3 Principals did not require that I get fingerprinted again or do another TB test given my long history with the S.A.U.S.D. even though I said I would.

4 At the time I began my study I was twenty-six-years-old.

5 Mrs. Franco's close cousin, with whom I had previously chaperoned on a class field trip, set up a group blind date.

6 A Mexican expression applied to an older, unmarried woman meaning that it would be difficult for her to get married and start a family.

BIBLIOGRAPHY

Abbott, Andrew. 1988. *The System of Professions: An Essay on the Expert Division of Labor*. Chicago: University of Chicago Press.

Abrego, Leisy. 2006. "'I Can't Go to College Because I Don't Have Papers': Incorporation Patterns of Latino Undocumented Youth," *Latino Studies* 4: 212–231.

Acker, Joan. 1990. "Hierarchies, Jobs, Bodies: A Theory of Gendered Organizations." *Gender and Society* 4: 139–158.

———. 2006. "Inequality Regimes: Gender, Class and Race in Organizations." *Gender and Society* 20: 441–464.

Alba, Richard. 2005. "Bilingualism Persists, But English Still Dominates." The Migration Information Source. Retrieved on October 13, 2016, from http://www.migrationpolicy.org.

Alba, Richard, and Victor Nee. 1997. "Rethinking Assimilation Theory for a New Era of Immigration." *Center for Migration Studies* 31: 826–865.

Almaguer, Tomas. 1994. *Racial Fault Lines: The Historical Origins of White Supremacy in California*. Berkeley and Los Angeles: University of California Press.

Álvarez, Robert R. 1986. "The Lemon Grove Incident: The Nation's First Successful Desegregation Court Case." *San Diego Historical Society Quarterly* 32: 116–135.

———. 1994. "Changing Patterns of Family and Ideology among Latino Cultures in the United States." In *Handbook of Hispanic Culture in the United States: Anthropology*, ed. Thomas Weaver, 147–167. Houston, TX: Arte Publico Press.

Arce, Josephine. 2004. "Latino Bilingual Teachers: The Struggle to Sustain an Emancipatory Pedagogy in Public Schools." *International Journal of Qualitative Studies in Education* 12: 227–246.

Banks, James. 1993. "Multicultural Education: Characteristics and Goals." In *Multicultural Education: Issues and Perspectives*, ed. J. Banks and C. Banks. Boston: Allyn and Bacon.

Barrera, Mario. 1979. *Race and Class in the Southwest: A Theory of Racial Inequality*. South Bend, IN: University of Notre Dame Press.

———. 2008. "Are Latinos a Racialized Minority?" *Sociological Perspectives* 51: 305–324.

Beasley, Maya. 2011. *Opting Out: Losing the Potential of America's Young Black Elite*. Chicago: University of Chicago Press.

Bell, Joyce. 2014. *The Black Power Movement and American Social Work*. New York: Columbia University Press.

Belur, Jyoti. 2014. "Status, Gender and Geography: Power Negotiations in Police Research." *Qualitative Research* 14: 184–200.

Bernstein, Basil. 1971. *Class, Codes and Control: Theoretical Studies Towards a Sociology of Language*. New York: Routledge.

———. 1973. *Class, Codes and Control: Applied Studies Toward a Sociology of Language*. New York: Routledge.

Bonilla-Silva, Eduardo. 2003. *Racism Without Racists: Color-Blind Racism and the Persistence of Racial Inequality in America*. Lanham, MD: Rowman & Littlefield.

———. 2004. "From Bi-racial to Tri-racial: Towards a New System of Racial Stratification in the U.S.A." *Ethnic and Racial Studies* 27: 931–950.

Bourdieu, Pierre. 1977. "Cultural Reproduction and Social Reproduction." In *Power and Ideology in Education*, ed. Jerome Karabel and A. H. Halsey, 487–511. New York: Oxford University Press.

Bourdieu, Pierre, and J. C. Passeron. 1977. *Reproduction in Education, Society and Culture*. Thousand Oaks, CA: Sage Publications.

Brilliant, Mark. 2010. *The Color of America Has Changed: How Racial Diversity Shaped Civil Rights Reform in California, 1941–1978*. New York: Oxford University Press.

Browne, Irene, and Joya Misra. 2003. "The Intersection of Gender and Race in the Labor Market." *Annual Review of Sociology* 29: 487–513.

Calderon, Jose. 1995. "Multi-Ethnic Coalition Building in a Diverse School District." *Critical Sociology* 21: 101–111.

California Department of Education. 2012. "Certificated Staff by Ethnicity for 2009–2010: State Summary, Number of Staff by Ethnicity." Retrieved June 1, 2013, from http://dq.cde.ca.gov.

———. 2013. "Certificated Staff by Ethnicity for 2009–2011: State Summary, Number of Staff by Ethnicity." Retrieved February 9, 2014, from http://dq.cde.ca.gov.

———. 2015. "Certificated Staff by Ethnicity for 2009–2010: State Summary, Number of Staff by Ethnicity." Retrieved September 1, 2015, from http://dq.cde.ca.gov.

Camarillo, Albert. 1970. "Chicano Urban History: A Study of Compton's Barrio, 1936–1970." *Aztlan* 2: 79–106.

———. 2005. "Black and Brown in Compton: Demographic Change, Suburban Decline, and Intergroup Relations in a South Central Los Angeles Community, 1950 to 2000." In *Not Just Black and White: Historical and Contemporary Perspectives on Immigration, Race, and Ethnicity in the United States*, ed. Nancy Foner and George M. Fredrickson. New York: Russell Sage Foundation.

Carter, Prudence. 2003. "'Black' Cultural Capital, Status Positioning, and Schooling Conflicts for Low-Income African American Youth." *Social Problems* 50: 136–155.

Cassell, Joan. 2000. *The Woman in the Surgeon's Body*. Cambridge, MA: Harvard University Press.

Castagno, Angelina E. 2014. *Educated in Whiteness: Good Intentions and Diversity in Schools*. Minneapolis: University of Minnesota Press.

Catanzarite, Lisa. 2000. "Brown-Collar Jobs: Occupational Segregation and Earnings of Recent Immigrant-Latinos." *Sociological Perspectives* 43: 45–75.

Catanzarite, Lisa, and Lindsey Trimble. 2008. "Latinos in the United States Labor Market." In *Latinas/os in the United States: Changing the Face of America*, ed. Havidan Rodriguez, Rogelio Saenz, and Cecilia Menjivar, 149–167. Chicago: University of Chicago Press.

Chávez, Ernie. 2002. *¡Mi Raza Primero¡ (My People First!): Nationalism, Identity, and Insurgency in the Chicano Movement in Los Angeles, 1966–1978*. Berkeley and Los Angeles: University of California Press.

Chávez, Leo. 2008. *The Latino Threat: Constructing Immigrants, Citizens, and the Nation*. Stanford, CA: Stanford University Press.

Chávez, Maria. 2011. *Everyday Injustice: Latino Professionals and Racism*. Lanham, MD: Rowman & Littlefield.

Cheng, Wendy. 2014. *The Changs Next Door to the Díazes: Remapping Race in Suburban California*. Minneapolis: University of Minnesota Press.

Chong, Nilda. 2002. *The Latino Patient: A Cultural Guide for Health Care Providers*. Yarmouth, ME: Intercultural Press.

Christopher, Frank. 1985. "The Lemon Grove Incident." Documentary film. San Diego, CA: KPBS Television.

Civil, Marta. 2008. "Language and Mathematics: Immigrant Parents' Participation in School." *Center for the Mathematics Education of Latinos/as* 32: 329–336.

———. 2009. "Mathematics Education, Language, and Culture: Ponderings from a Different Geographic Context." *Center for the Mathematics Education of Latinos/as* 1: 131–136.

Clark-Ibanez, Marisol. 2015. *Undocumented Latino Youth: Navigating Their Worlds*. Boulder, CO: Lynne Rienner Publishers.

Collins, Patricia Hill. 1986. "Learning from the Outsider Within." *Social Problems* 33: 14–32.

———. 2000. *Black Feminist Thought: Knowledge, Consciousness, and the Politics of Empowerment*. New York and London: Routledge.

Conchas, Gilberto. 2006. *The Color of Success: Race and High-Achieving Urban Youth*. New York: Teachers College Press.

Current Population Survey. 2007. "Top 10 Occupations/Professions Latinas Enter." Bureau of Labor Statistics.

DeGenova, Nicholas. 2006. "Introduction: Latino and Asian Racial Formations at the Frontiers of U.S. Nationalism." In *Racial Transformations: Latinos and Asians Remaking the United States*, ed. N. DeGenova, 1–20. Durham and London: Duke University Press.

Delgado-Gaitan, C. 1992. "Consejos: The Power of Cultural Narrative." *Anthropology and Education Quarterly* 25: 298–316.

Delpit, Lisa. 2006. *Other People's Children: Cultural Conflict in the Classroom*. New York: The New Press.

———. 2012. *"Multiplication Is for White People": Raising Expectations for Other People's Children*. New York: The New Press.

Dhingra, Pawan. 2007. *Managing Multicultural Lives: Asian American Professionals and the Challenge of Multiple Identities*. Stanford, CA: Stanford University Press.

Dodson, Lisa. 2009. *The Moral Underground: How Ordinary Americans Subvert an Unfair Economy*. New York and London: The New Press.

Dominguez, Silvia. 2010. *Social Mobility, Public Housing and Immigrant Networks*. New York: New York University Press.

Ed-Data. 2009. "Fiscal, Demographic and Performance Data on K–12 Schools. Retrieved on March 26, 2014, from http://www.ed-data.k12.ca.us.

———. 2012. "Fiscal, Demographic and Performance Data on K–12 Schools." Retrieved on March 18, 2013, from http://www.ed-data.k12.ca.us.

Emerson, Robert M., Rachel I. Fretz, and Linda L. Shaw. 1995. *Writing Ethnographic Fieldnotes*. Chicago: University of Chicago Press.

Epstein, Cynthia F. 1993. *Women in Law*. Champaign: University of Illinois Press.

Espiritu, Yen Le. 1992. *Asian American Panethnicity: Bridging Institutions and Identities*. Philadelphia: Temple University Press.

———. 1997. *Asian American Women and Men: Labor, Laws, and Love*. Thousand Oaks, CA: Sage Publications.

Estrada, Emir. 2013. "Changing Household Dynamics: Children's American Generational Resources in Street Vending Markets." *Childhood* 20: 51–65.

Etzioni, Amitai. 1969. *The Semi-Professions and Their Organization*. New York: The Free Press.

Fabienke, David. 2007. "Perceptions of Minority Residents on Coalition Building in South Los Angeles." Los Angeles: Tomas Rivera Policy Institute.

Fairclough, Adam. 2007. *A Class of Their Own: Black Teachers in the Segregated South*. Cambridge, MA: Harvard University Press.

Falicov, Celia, J. 2002. *Latino Families in Therapy: A Guide to Multicultural Practice*. New York: The Guilford Press.

Feagin, Joe, and Melvin Sikes. 1995. *Living with Racism: The Black Middle Class Experience*. Boston: Beacon Press.

Feistritzer, Emily. "Profile of Teachers in the U.S." Retrieved September 5, 2006, from http://www.ncei.com.

Feliciano, Cynthia. 2005. *Unequal Origins: Immigrant Selection and the Education of the Second Generation*. El Paso, TX: LFB Scholarly Publishing LLC.

Ferguson, Ann Arnett. 2001. *Bad Boys: Public Schools in the Making of Black Masculinity*. Ann Arbor: University of Michigan Press.

Fine, Michelle. 1998. "Working the Hyphens: Reinventing Self and Other in Qualitative Research." In *The Landscape of Qualitative Research: Theories and Issues*, ed. Norman K. Denzin and Yvonna S. Lincoln, 70–82. Thousand Oaks, CA: Sage Publications.

Flores, Glenda Marisol. 2011a. "Racialized Tokens: Latina Teachers Negotiating, Surviving and Thriving in a White Woman's Profession." *Qualitative Sociology* 34: 313–335.

———. 2011b. "Latinos in the Hard Sciences: Increasing Latina/o Participation in Science, Technology, Engineering and Math (STEM) Related Fields." *Latino Studies* 9: 327–335.

———. 2015a. "Bicultural Myths, Rifts and Scripts: A Case Study of Latina Teachers' Cultural Pedagogy in Multiracial Schools." In *Inequality, Power and School Success: Case Studies on Racial Diversity and Opportunity in Education*, ed. G. Q. Conchas and M. Gottried. New York: Routledge.

———. 2015b. "Controlling Images of Space: Latina Teachers and Racial Positioning in Multiracial Schools." *City and Community* 14: 410–432.

———. 2016. "Discovering a Hidden Privilege: Ethnography in Multiracial Organizations as an Outsider Within." *Ethnography* 17: 190–212.

Flores, Glenda M., and Pierrette Hondagneu-Sotelo. 2014. "The Social Dynamics Channelling Latina College Graduates into the Teaching Profession." *Gender, Work and Organization* 21(6): 491–515.

Fong, Timothy. 1994. *The First Suburban Chinatown: The Remaking of Monterey Park, California*. Philadelphia: Temple University Press.

Fry, Richard, and Mark Hugo López. 2012. "Hispanic Student Enrollments Reach New Highs in 2011." Washington: Pew Research Hispanic Center.

Galindo, Rene. 1996. "Reframing the Past in the Present: Chicana Teacher Role Identity as Bridging Identity." *Education and Urban Society* 29: 85–102.

Gándara, Patricia. 1995. *Over the Ivy Walls: The Education Mobility of Low-Income Chicanos*. Albany: State University of New York Press.

———. 2009. *The Latino Education Crisis: The Consequences of Failed Social Policies*. Cambridge, MA: Harvard University Press.

Gans, Herbert. 1979. "Symbolic Ethnicity: The Future of Ethnic Groups and Cultures in America." *Ethnic and Racial Studies* 2: 1–20.

García, Mario T., and Sal Castro. 2011. *Blowout! Sal Castro and the Chicano Struggle for Educational Justice*. Chapel Hill: University of North Carolina Press.

García, Richard. 1991. *Rise of the Mexican-American Middle Class: San Antonio 1929–1941*. College Station: Texas A&M University Press.

García Bedolla, Lisa. 1999. *Fluid Borders: Latino Power, Identity and Politics in Los Angeles*. Berkeley and Los Angeles: University of California Press.

García-López, Gladys. 2008. "'Nunca te Toman en Cuenta' [They Never Take You into Account]: The Challenes of Inclusion and Strategies for Success of Chicana Attorneys." *Gender and Society* 22: 590–612.

Gilkes, Cheryl Townsend. 2010. "Going Up for the Oppressed: The Career Mobility of Black Women Community Workers." *Journal of Social Issues* 39: 115–139.

Gitomer, Drew. 2007. "Teacher Quality in a Changing Policy Landscape." Princeton, NJ: Educational Testing Service.

Goffman, Erving. 1959. *The Presentation of Self in Everyday Life*. New York: Random House.

Golash-Boza, Tanya. 2016. *Deported: Policing Immigrants, Disposable Labor and Global Capitalism*. New York: New York University Press.

Goldstein, Lisa S. 2008. "Kindergarten Teachers Making 'Street-Level' Education Policy in the Wake of No Child Left Behind." *Early Education and Development* 19: 448–478.

González, Gilbert. 1990. *Chicano Education in the Era of Segregation*. Philadelphia: Balch Institute Press.

———. 1997. "Culture, Language, and the Americanization of Mexican Children." In *Latinos and Education: A Critical Reader*, ed. A. Darder, R. Torres, and H. Gutierrez. New York and London: Routledge.

González, Norma, Luis C. Moll, and Cathy Amanti. 2005. *Funds of Knowledge Theorizing Practices in Households, Communities, and Classrooms*. New York: Routledge.

González, Roberto. 2015. *Lives in Limbo: Undocumented and Coming of Age in America*. Berkeley and Los Angeles: University of California Press.

González-López, Gloria. 2004. "Fathering Latina Sexualities: Mexican Men and the Virginity of Their Daughters." *Journal of Marriage and Family* 66: 1118–1130.

Gordon, June. 2002. *The Color of Teaching*. London: Routledge.

Granovetter, Mark. 1983. "The Strength of Weak Ties." *American Journal of Sociology* 78: 1360–1380.

Gottfried, Heidi. 2006. "Feminist Theories of Work." In *Social Theory at Work*, ed. Marek Korczynski, Randy Hodson, and Paul Edwards, 121–154. New York: Oxford University Press.

Grijalva, Cindy A., and Robert H. Coombs. 1997. "Latinas in Medicine: Stressors, Survival Skills, and Strengths." *Aztlan* 22: 67–88.

Gutierrez, David G. 1995. *Walls and Mirrors: Mexican Americans, Mexican Immigrants, and the Politics of Ethnicity*. Berkeley and Los Angeles: University of California Press.

Hakuta, Kenji. 1993. "Second-Language Acquisition, Bilingual Education, and Prospects for a Language-Rich Nation." In *Restructuring Learning: 1990 Summer Institute Papers and Recommendations by the Council of Chief State School Officers*, 123–131. Washington: Council of Chief State School Officers.

Hargreaves, Linda. 2009. "The Status and Prestige of Teachers and Teaching." In *International Handbook of Research on Teachers and Teaching*, ed. Saha Lawrence and Gary Dworkin, 217–229. New York: Springer.

Hart, Gary, and Susan K. Burr. 1996. "A State of Emergency . . . in a State of Emergency Teachers." Institute for Education Reform. Retrieved on May 15, 2010, from http://www.csus.edu/ier/emergency.html.

Hernández-Leon, Ruben, and Sarah Morando Lakhani. 2013. "Gender, Bilingualism, and the Early Occupational Careers of Second-Generation Mexicans in the South." *Social Forces*, 92: 59–80.

Higginbotham, Elizabeth. 2001. *Too Much to Ask: Black Women in the Era of Integration*. Chapel Hill: University of North Carolina Press.

Higginbotham, Elizabeth, and Lynn Weber. 1992. "Moving Up with Kin and Community: Upward Social Mobility for Black and White Women." *Gender and Society* 6: 416–440.

Higginbotham, Elizabeth, and Mary Romero. 1997. *Women and Work: Exploring Race, Ethnicity, and Class*. Thousand Oaks, CA: Sage Publications.

Hite, Linda. 2007. "Hispanic Women Managers and Professionals: Reflections on Life and Work." *Gender, Work and Organization* 14: 20–36.

Hochschild, Jennifer L. 1995. *Facing Up to the American Dream: Race, Class and the Soul of the Nation*. Princeton, NJ: Princeton University Press.

Hochschild, Arlie. 2003. *The Managed Heart: The Commercialization of Human Feeling*. Berkeley and Los Angeles: University of California Press.

Holmes, Seth. 2013. *Fresh Fruit, Broken Bodies: Migrant Farmworkers in the United States*. Berkeley and Los Angeles: University of California Press.

Holvino, Evangelina. 2008. "Intersections: The Simultaneity of Race, Gender and Class in Organization Studies." *Gender, Work and Organization* 17: 248–277.

Hondagneu-Sotelo, Pierrette. 1994. *Gendered Transitions: Mexican Experiences of Immigration*. Berkeley and Los Angeles: University of California Press.

———. 2001. *Domestica: Immigrant Women Cleaning and Caring in the Shadows of Affluence*. Berkely and Los Angeles: University of California Press.

hooks, bell. 1989. *Talking Back: Thinking Feminist, Thinking Black*. Boston: South End Press.

Hughes, Everett C. 1994. *On Work, Race, and the Sociological Imagination*. Chicago: University of Chicago Press.

Jacobs-Huey, Lanita. 2002. "The Natives Are Gazing and Talking Back: Reviewing the Problematics of Positionality, Voice, and Accountability among "Native" Anthropologists." *American Anthropologist* 104: 701–804.

Jiménez, Tomas R. 2004. "Negotiating Ethnic Boundaries: Multiethnic Mexican Americans and Ethnic Identity in the United States." *Ethnicities* 4(1): 75–97.

Jolly, Paul. 2005. "Medical School Tuition and Young Physicians' Indebtedness." *Health Affairs* 24: 527–535.

Jun, Helen H. 2006. "Black Orientalism: Nineteenth-Century Narratives of Race and U.S. Citizenship." *American Quarterly* 58.4 1047–1066.

Kanter, Rosabeth M. 1977. *Men and Women of the Corporation*. New York: Basic Books.

Keefe, Susan, and Amado Padilla. 1987. *Chicano Ethnicity*. Albuquerque: University of New Mexico Press.

Kelley, Robin D.G. 1996. *Race Rebels: Culture, Politics, and the Black Working Class*. New York: The Free Press.

Kim, Claire Jean. 1999. "The Racial Triangulation of Asian Americans." *Politics & Society* 27: 105–138.

Kozol, Jonathan. 1991. *Savage Inequalities: Children in America's Schools*. New York: Harper Perennial Publishers.

Kunjufu, Jawanza. 2002. *Black Students, Middle Class Teachers*. Sauk Village, IL: African American Images.

Kwon, Hyeyoung. 2015. "Intersectionality in Interactions: Language Brokers Doing American from an Outsider-Within Position." *Social Problems* 62: 623–641.

Ladson-Billings, Gloria J. 2005. "Is the Team All Right? Diversity and Teacher Education." *Journal of Teacher Education* 56: 229–234.

———. 2009. *The Dreamkeepers: Successful Teachers of African American Children*. San Francisco: Jossey-Bass.

Lareau, Annette. 2003. *Unequal Childhoods: Class, Race and Family Life*. Berkeley and Los Angeles: University of California Press.

Laz, Cheryl. 1998. "Act Your Age." *Sociological Forum* 13: 85–113.

Lee, Jennifer. 2006. *Civility in the City: Blacks, Jews, and Koreans in Urban America*. Cambridge, MA: Harvard University Press.

Lee, Jennifer, and Min Zhou. 2015. *The Asian American Achievement Paradox*. New York: Russell Sage Foundation.

Lewis, Amanda. 2003. *Race in the Schoolyard: Negotiating the Color Line in Classrooms and Communities*. New Brunswick, NJ: Rutgers University Press.

Lin, Nan. 1999. "Social Networks and Status Attainment." *Annual Review of Sociology* 25: 467–487.

Lin, Nan, Walter M. Ensel, and John C. Vaughn. 1981. "Social Resources and Strength of Ties: Structural Factors in Occupational Status Attainment." *American Sociological Review* 46: 393–405.

Lipsitz, George. 2006. *The Possessive Investment in Whiteness: How White People Profit from Identity Politics*. Philadelphia: Temple University Press.

Lipsky, Michael. 1980. *Street-level Bureaucracy: Dilemmas of the Individual in Public Services*. New York: Russell Sage Foundation.

Livers, Angela. 2006. "Black Women in Management." In *Gender, Race, and Ethnicity in the Workplace: Issues and Challenges for Today's Organizations*, ed. M. F. Karsten. New York: Praeger.

López, Nancy. 2002. *Hopeful Girls, Troubled Boys: Race and Gender Disparity in Urban Education*. New York: Routledge.

López-Sanders, Laura. 2009. "Trapped at the Bottom: Racialized and Gendered Labor Queues in New Immigrant Destinations." San Diego: The Center for Comparative Immigration Studies.

Lorber, Judith. 1984. *Women Physicians: Career, Status, and Power*. New York and London: Tavistock.

Lortie, Dan C. 2002. *Schoolteacher: A Sociological Study*. Chicago: University of Chicago Press.

Mariscal, Jorge. 2003. "Latinos on the Frontlines, Again." *Latino Studies* 1: 347–351.

Marrow, Helen B. 2009. "Immigrant Bureaucratic Incorporation: The Dual Roles of Professional Missions and Government Policies. *American Sociological Review* 74: 756–776.

———. 2011. *New Destination Dreaming: Immigration, Race, and Legal Status in the Rural American South*. Stanford, CA: Stanford University Press.

Maynard-Moody, Steven W., and Michael Craig Musheno. 2003. *Cops, Teachers, Counselors: Stories from the Front Lines of Public Service*. Ann Arbor: University of Michigan Press.

McClain, Paula D., et al. 2006. "Racial Distancing in a Southern City: Latino Immigrants' Views of Black Americans." *Journal of Politics* 68: 571–584.

McIntosh, Peggy. 1988. "White Privilege: Unpacking the Invisible Knapsack." Retrieved April 18, 2013, from http://ted.coe.wayne.edu.

Menjivar, Cecilia. 2000. *Fragmented Ties: Salvadoran Immigrant Networks in America*. Berkeley and Los Angeles: University of California Press.

Merton, Robert K. 1972. "Insiders and Outsiders: A Chapter in the Sociology of Knowledge." *American Journal of Sociology* 78: 9–48.

Mills, C. Wright. 1959. *The Sociological Imagination*. New York: Oxford University Press.

Mindiola, Tatcho, Yoland Flores Niemann, and Nestor Rodriguez. 2002. *Black–Brown Relations and Stereotypes*. Austin: University of Texas Press.

Moll, Luis C., Cathy Amanti, Deborah Neff, and Norma González. 1992. "Funds of Knowledge for Teaching: Using a Qualitative Approach to Connect Homes and Classrooms." *Qualitative Issues in Educational Research* 31: 132–141.

Montecinos, Carmen. 1996. "Multicultural Teacher Education for a Culturally Diverse Teaching Force." In *Practicing What We Teach: Confronting Diversity in Teacher Education*, ed. Renne J. Martin. Albany: State University of New York Press.

Monzo, Lilia. 2014. "Ethnography in Charting Paths Toward Personal and Social Liberation: Using My Latina Cultural Intuition." *International Journal of Qualitative Studies in Education* (DOI:10.1080/09518398.2014.891771).

Moore, Joan. 1970. *The Mexican Americans*. Englewood Cliffs, NJ: Prentice-Hall.

Moore, Joan, and Harry Pachón. 1985. *Hispanics in the United States*. Englewood Cliffs, NJ: Prentice-Hall.

Morando, Sarah J. 2013. "Paths to Mobility: The Mexican Second Generation at Work in a New Destination." *Sociological Quarterly* 54: 367–398.

Mosqueda, Eduardo. 2010. "Compounding Inequalities: English Proficiency and Tracking and Their Relation to Mathematics Performance among Latina/o Secondary School Youth." *Journal of Urban Mathematics Education* 3: 57–81.

Moulthrop, Daniel, Ninive Clements Calegari, and Dave Eggers. 2005. *Teachers Have It Easy: The Big Sacrifices and Small Salaries of America's Teachers*. New York: The New Press.

Muñoz, Laura K. 2001. "Separate But Equal? A Case Study of Romo v. Laird and Mexican American Education." *Magazine of History*.

———. 2006. *Desert Dreams: Mexican American Education in Arizona, 1870–1930*. PhD Dissertation. Arizona State University.

Muro, Jazmin. 2015. *Seeking Difference: Latino–White Relations in a Dual Immersion School*. PhD Dissertation. Los Angeles: University of Southern California.

Murti, Lata. 2012. "Who Benefits from the White Coat? Gender Differences in Occupational Citizenship among Asian-Indian Doctors. *Ethnic and Racial Studies* 35(12): 2035–2053.

Myers, Dowell. 2007. *Immigrants and Boomers: Forging a New Social Contract for the Future of America*. New York: Russell Sage Foundation.

Narayan, Kirin. 1993. "How Native Is a 'native' Anthropologist?" *American Anthropologist* 95(3): 671–686.

Nieto, Sonia. 1999. *The Light in Their Eyes: Creating Multicultural Learning Communities*. New York: Teachers College Press.

———. 2005. *Why We Teach*. New York: Teachers College Press.

Oakes, Jeannie. 2005. *Keeping Track: How Schools Structure Inequality.* New Haven, CT: Yale University Press.

O'Brien, Eileen. 2008. *The Racial Middle: Latinos and Asian-Americans Living beyond the Racial Divide.* New York: New York University Press.

Oboler, Suzanne. 1995. *Ethnic Labels, Latino Lives: Identity and the Politics of (Re) presentation in the United States.* Minneapolis: University of Minnesota Press.

Ochoa, Gilda. 2004. *Becoming Neighbors: In a Mexican American Community.* Austin: University of Texas Press.

———. 2007. *Learning from Latino Teachers.* San Francisco: Jossey-Bass.

———. 2014. *Academic Profiling: Latinos, Asian Americans, and the Achievement Gap.* Minneapolis: University of Minnesota Press.

Orellana, Marjorie Faultstich. 2009. *Translating Childhoods: Immigrant Youth, Language, and Culture.* New Brunswick, NJ: Rutgers University Press.

Orfield, Gary, Genevieve Siegel-Hawley, and John Kucsera. 2011. "Divided We Fail: Segregated and Unequal Schools in the Southland." The Civil Rights Project: Los Angeles.

Padavic, Irene, and Barbara Reskin. 2002. *Women and Men at Work,* 2nd ed. Thousand Oaks, CA: Pine Forge Press.

Park, Edward J.W., and John S.W. Park. 1999. "A New American Dilemma? Asian Americans and Latinos in Race Theorizing." *Journal of Asian American Studies* 2: 289–309.

Passel, Jeffrey S., and D'Vera Cohn. 2008. "U.S. Population Projections: 2005–2050." Pew Research Center, Social and Demographic Trends. Retrieved on September 13, 2008, from http://pewhispanic.org.

Patillo-McCoy, Mary. 1999. *Black Picket Fences: Privilege and Peril among the Black Middle Class.* Chicago: University of Chicago Press.

Peterson, Brooks. 2004. *Cultural Intelligence: A Guide to Working with People from Other Cultures.* London: Nicholas Brealey Publishing.

Picca, Leslie, and Joe Feagin. 2007. *Two-Faced Racism: White in the Backstage and Frontstage.* London: Routledge.

Pollock, Mica. 2005. *Colormute: Race Talk Dilemmas in an American School.* Princeton, NJ: Princeton University Press.

Portes, Alejandro, and Min Zhou. 1993. "The New Second Generation: Segmented Assimilation and Its Variants." *Annals of the Academy of Political and Social Science,* 530: 74–96.

Portes, Alejandro, and Ruben Rumbaut. 2001. *Legacies: The Story of the Immigrant Second Generation.* Berkeley: University of California Press.

———. 2006. *Immigrant American: A Portrait.* Berkeley and Los Angeles: University of California Press.

Posey-Maddox, Linn. 2014. *When Middle-Class Parents Choose Urban Schools: Class, Race and the Challenge of Equity in Public Education.* Chicago: University of Chicago Press.

Ramírez, Hernan. 2011. "Masculinity in the Workplace: The Case of Mexican Immigrant Gardners. *Men and Masculinities* 14: 97–116.

Ramírez, Hernan, and Pierrette Hondagneu-Sotelo. 2009. "Mexican Immigrant Gardeners: Entrepreneurs or Exploited Workers?" *Social Problems* 56: 70–88.

Randolph, Antonia. 2013. *The Wrong Kind of Different: Challenging the Meaning of Diversity in American Classrooms*. New York and London: Teachers College Press.

Reskin, Barbara, and Patricia A. Roos. 1990. *Job Queues, Gender Queues: Explaining Women's Inroads into Male Occupations*. Philadelphia: Temple University Press.

Resmovits, Joy. 2011. "Latino Teachers Needed for Classroom Role Models." *Huffington Post*, August 13.

Rios, Victor. 2011. *Punished: Policing the Lives of Black and Latino Boys*. New York: New York University Press.

Rochmes, Daniel A., and G. A. Elmer Griffin. 2006. "The Cactus That Must Not be Mistaken for a Pillow: White Racial Formation among Latinos." *Souls* 8: 77–91.

Rodríguez, Clara E. 2000. *Changing Race: Latinos, the Census, and the History of Ethnicity in the United States*. New York and London: New York University Press.

Rodríguez, Luis. 1993. *Always Running: La Vida Loca, Gang Days in L.A.* New York: Touchstone Books.

Romero, Mary, Pierrette Hondagneu-Sotelo, and Vilma Ortiz. 1992. *Challenging Fronteras: Structuring Latina and Latino Lives in the U.S.* New York: Routledge.

Rosales, Rocío. 2014. "Stagnant Immigrant Social Networks and Cycles of Exploitation." *Ethnic and Racial Studies* 37: 2564–2579.

Rosas, Ana Elizabeth. 2011. "Breaking the Silence: Mexican Children and Women's Confrontation of Bracero Family Separation, 1942–1964." *Gender & History* 23: 382–400.

Ruiz, Vicki. 1997. *From Out of the Shadows: Mexican Women in Twentieth-Century America*. Oxford: Oxford University Press.

———. 2004. "Tapestries of Resistance: Episodes of School Segregation and Desegregation in the Western United States." In *From the Grassroots to the Supreme Court: Brown v. Board of Education and American Democracy*, ed. Peter F. Lau, 44–67. Durham and London: Duke University Press.

Ryan, Kevin, and James Cooper. 2010. *Those Who Can, Teach*. Boston: Wadsworth Publishing.

Saito, Leland. 1997. *Race and Politics: Asian Americans, Latinos, and Whites in a Los Angeles Suburb*. Champaign: University of Illinois Press.

Sanchez, George J. 1995. *Becoming Mexican American: Ethnicity, Culture and Identity in Chicano Los Angeles, 1900–1945*. Oxford: Oxford University Press.

———. 2007. "Latinos, the American South, and the Future of U.S. Race Relations." *Southern Spaces*. Emory Libraries and Information Technology.

Sánchez, George I. 1997. "History, Culture and Education." In *Latinos and Education: A Critical Reader*, ed. Antonia Darder, Rodolfo D. Torres, and Henry Gutierrez, 117–134. New York and London: Routledge.

Santa Ana, Otto. 2002. *Brown Tide Rising: Metaphors of Latinos in Contemporary American Public Discourse*. Austin: University of Texas Press.

Segura, Denise. 1989. "Chicana and Mexican Immigrant Women at Work: The Impact of Class, Race, and Gender on Occupational Mobility," *Gender and Society* 3: 37–52.

——. 1992a. "Walking on Eggshells: Chicanas in the Labor Force." In *Hispanics in the Workplace*, ed. Stephen B. Knouse, Paul Rosenfeld, and Amy Culbertson, 173–193. Newbury Park, CA: Sage.

——. 1992b. "Chicanas in White Collar Jobs: 'You Have to Prove Yourself More.'" *Sociological Perspectives* 35: 163–182.

Sewell, William H. 1992. "A Theory of Structure: Duality, Agency, and Transformation." *American Journal of Sociology*. 98(1): 1–29.

Sherman, Rachel. 2007. *Class Acts: Service and Inequality in Luxury Hotels*. Berkeley and Los Angeles: University of California Press.

Sides, Josh. 2005. "Straight into Compton: American Dreams, Urban Nightmares, and the Metamorphosis of a Black Suburb." In *Los Angeles and the Future of Urban Cultures*, ed. Raul Homero Villa and George J. Sanchez, 85–108. Baltimore and London: The Johns Hopkins University Press.

——. 2006. *L.A. City Limits: African American Los Angeles from the Great Depression to the Present*. Berkeley and Los Angeles: University of California Press.

Simmel, Georg. 1921. "The Sociological Significance of the 'Stranger.'" In *Introduction to the Science of Sociology*, ed. R. E. Park and E. W. Burgess, 322–327. Chicago: University of Chicago Press.

Simón, Laura. 1997. "Fear and Learning at Hoover Elementary." Ho-Ho-Kus, NJ: Transit Media.

Skrentny, John D. 2014. *After Civil Rights: Racial Realism in the New American Workplace*. Princeton, NJ: Princeton University Press.

Sleeter, Christine E. 2001. "Preparing Teachers for Culturally Diverse Schools: Research and the Overwhelming Presence of Whiteness." *Journal of Teacher Education* 52: 94–106.

Sleeter, Christine E., and Carl A. Grant. 2009. *Making Choices for Multicultural Education: Five Approaches to Race, Class and Gender*, 6th ed. Hoboken, NJ: Wiley.

Smith, Robert C. 2005. *Mexican New York: Transnational Live of New Immigrants*. Berkeley and Los Angeles: University of California Press.

Sokoloff, Natalie. 1992. *Black Women and White Women in the Professions: Occupational Segregation by Race and Gender, 1960–1980*. New York: Routledge.

Stanton-Salazar, Ricardo. 2001. "A Social Capital Framework for the Study of Institutional Agents and Their Role in the Empowerment of Low-Status Students and Youth." *Youth and Society* 43: 1066–1109.

Stepick, Alex, and Carol Dutton Stepick. 2009. "Diverse Contexts of Reception and Feelings of Belonging." *Forum: Qualitative Social Research* 10(3): Art. 15.

Stone, Pamela. 2007. *Opting Out? Why Women Really Quit Careers and Head Home*. Berkeley and Los Angeles: University of California Press.

Straus, Emily. 2009. "Unequal Pieces of a Shrinking Pie: The Struggle between African Americans and Latinos over Education, Employment, and Empowerment in Compton, California." *History of Education Quarterly* 49: 507–529.

———. 2014. *Death of a Suburban Dream: Race and Schools in Compton, California.* Philadelphia: University of Pennsylvania Press.

Strauss, Anselm L. 1987. *Qualitative Analysis for Social Scientists.* Cambridge: Cambridge University Press.

Strum, Philippa. 2010. *Mendez v. Westminster: School Desegregation and Mexican-American Rights.* Lawrence: University Press of Kansas.

Stuesse, Angela. 2016. *Scratching out a Living: Latinos, Race, and Work in the Deep South.* Berkeley and Los Angeles: University of California Press.

Su, Zhixin. 1996. "Why Teach: Profiles and Entry Perspectives of Minority Students as Becoming Teachers." *Journal of Research and Development in Education* 29: 117–133.

Suárez, Elizabeth. 2002. *A Calling of the Heart: A Comparative Study of Meanings and Motivations of Chicana and Mexican American Teachers.* PhD Dissertation. Department of Education, Claremont Graduate University.

Suárez-Orozco, Carola, and Marcelo Suárez-Orozco. 2001. *Children of Immigration.* Cambridge, MA: Harvard University Press.

Subedi, Binaya, and Jeong-eun Rhee. 2008. "Negotiating Collaboration Across Differences." *Qualitative Inquiry* 14(6): 1070–1092.

Taningco, Maria T., Bessie Matthew, and Harry Pachon. 2008. "STEM Professions: Opportunities and Challenges for Latinos in Science, Technology, Engineering and Mathematics." Los Angeles: Tomas Rivera Policy Institute.

Telles, Edward E., and Vilma Ortiz. 2008. *Generations of Exclusions: Racial Assimilation and Mexican Americans.* Berkeley and Los Angeles: University of California Press.

Thomas, David C., and Kerr C. Inkson. 2009. *Cultural Intelligence: Living and Working Globally.* Oakland, CA: Berrett-Koehler Publishers.

Tomaskovic-Devey, Donald. 1993. *Gender and Race Inequality at Work: The Sources and Consequences of Job Segregation.* Ithaca, NY: ILR Press.

Tuan, Mia. 1999. *Forever Foreigners or Honorary Whites? The Asian Ethnic Experience Today.* New Brunswick, NJ: Rutgers University Press.

Turvo, Nelson N. 2012. "A 'Balikbayan' in the Field: Scaling and (Re)producing Insider's Identity in a Philippine Fishing Community." *Qualitative Research* 12(6): 666–685.

Urrieta, Luis. 2010. *Working from Within: Chicana and Chicano Activist Educators in Whitestream Schools.* Tucson: University of Arizona Press.

U.S. Bureau of Labor Statistics. 2010. "Employed Persons by Detailed Occupation and Sex, 2007 Annual Averages." In *Women in the Labor Force: A Databook.* Retrieved on July 31, 2010, from http://www.bls.gov.

U.S. Department of Education. 2011. "Our Future, Our Teachers: The Obama Administration's Plan for Teacher Education Reform and Improvement." Washington, D.C.

Vaca, Nicolas C. 2004. *The Presumed Alliance: The Unspoken Conflict between Latinos and Blacks and What it Means for America.* New York: HarperCollins.

Valdes, Guadalupe. 1996. *Con Respeto: Bridging the Distances between Culturally Diverse Families and Schools: An Ethnographic Portrait.* New York: Teachers College Press.

Valenzuela, Abel. 1999. "Gender Roles and Settlement Activities among Children and Their Immigrant Families." *American Behavioral Scientist* 42: 720–42.

Valenzuela, Angela. 1999. *Subtractive Schooling: U.S. Mexican Youth and the Politics of Caring.* Albany: State University of New York Press.

Vallejo, Jody Agius. 2009. "Latina Spaces: Middle-class Ethnic Capital and Professional Associations in the Latino Community." *City and Community* 8(2): 129–154.

———. 2012. *Barrios to Burbs: The Making of the Mexican Origin Middle Class.* Palo Alto, CA: Stanford University Press.

Vallejo, Jody Agius, and Jennifer Lee. 2009. "Brown Picket Fences: The Immigrant Narrative and Patterns of Giving Back among the Mexican Origin Middle-Class in Los Angeles." *Ethnicities* 9: 5–23.

Vargas, Joao Costa H. 2006. *Catching Hell in the City of Angels: Life and Meanings of Blackness in South Central Los Angeles.* Minneapolis and London: University of Minnesota Press.

Velez, William Yslas. 2000. "The Invisible Minorities in Mathematics." *Mathematics and Education Reform Forum* 12: 3–7.

Villenas, Sofia. 1996. "The Colonizer/Colonized Chicana Ethnographer: Identity, Marginalization and Co-optation in the Field." *Harvard Educational Review* 66(4): 711–731.

Vomvoridi-Ivanović, E. 2012. "Using Culture as a Resource in Mathematics: The Case of Four Mexican American Prospective Teachers in a Bilingual After-School Program." *Journal of Mathematics Teacher Education* 15: 53–66.

Wagle, Tina, and David T. Cantaffa. 2008. "Working Our Hyphens: Exploring Identity Relations in Qualitative Research. *Qualitative Inquiry* 14: 135–159.

Waldinger, Roger, and Michael Lichter I. 2013. *How the Other Half Works: Immigration and the Social Organization of Labor.* Berkeley and Los Angeles: University of California Press.

Walsh, Janet. 2012. "Not Worth the Sacrifice? Women's Aspirations and Career Progress in Law Firms." *Gender, Work and Organization* 19: 508–531.

Washburn, David E. 1996. *Multicultural Education in the United States.* Philadelphia: Inquiry International.

Waters, Mary. 1999. *Black Identities: West Indian Immigrant Dreams and American Realities.* Cambridge, MA: Harvard University Press.

Wax, Rosalie. 1979. "Gender and Age in Fieldwork and Fieldwork Education: No Good Thing Is Done by Any Man Alone." *Social Problems* 26(5): 509–522.

Wei, Li. 1997. "Ethnoburb versus Chinatown: Two Types of Urban Ethnic Communities in Los Angeles." http://cybergeo.revues.org.

———. 2009. *Ethnoburb: The New Ethnic Community in Urban America.* Honolulu: University of Hawai'i Press.

Williams, Christine. 1992. "The Glass Escalator: Hidden Advantages for Men in the 'Female' Professions." *Social Problems* 39 (3): 253–267.

———. 2006. *Inside Toyland: Working, Shopping, and Social Inequality*. Berkeley and Los Angeles: University of California Press.

Wilson, William J. 1987. *The Truly Disadvantaged: The Inner City, the Underclass, and Public Policy*. Chicago: University of Chicago Press.

Wingfield, Adia H. 2009. "Racializing the Glass Escalator: Reconsidering Men's Experiences with Women's Work." *Gender and Society* 23(1): 5–26.

Wollenberg, Charles. 1978. *All Deliberate Speed: Segregation and Exclusion in California Schools, 1855–1975*. Berkeley and Los Angeles: University of California Press.

Youngclaus, James, and Julie A. Fresne. 2012. "Physician Education Debt and the Cost to Attend Medical School." Washington: Association of Medical Colleges.

Zamora, Sylvia. 2016. "Racial Remittances: The Effect of Migration on Racial Ideologies in Mexico and the United States. *Sociology of Race and Ethnicity* (DOI: 10.1177/2332649215621925).

Zarate, Estela, and Harry Pachón. 2006. "Perceptions of College Financial Aid among California Latino Youth." Los Angeles: Tomas Rivera Policy Institute.

Zavella, Patricia. 1987. *Women's Work and Chicano Families: Cannery Workers of the Santa Clara Valley*. Ithaca, NY: Cornell University Press.

Zhou, Min. 2009. *Contemporary Chinese America: Immigration, Ethnicity, and Community Transformation*. Philadelphia: Temple University Press.

Zhou, Min, and Jennifer Lee. 2008. "Becoming Ethnic or Becoming American? Reflecting on the Divergent Pathways to Social Mobility and Assimilation among the New Second Generation." *Du Bois Review* 4(1): 189–205.

Zinn, Maxine B. 1979. "Field Research in Minority Communities: Ethical, Methodological and Political Observations by an Insider." *Social Problems* 27(2): 209–219.

———. 2001."Insider Field Research in Minority Communities." In *Contemporary Field Research: Perspectives and Formulations*, ed. R. M. Emerson, 159–166. Long Grove, IL: Waveland Press.

INDEX

AAVE. *See* African American Vernacular English

abundance mentality, 116

Academic Performance Index (API), 160, 231n1

Academic Profiling (Ochoa), 124

academic tracking: academic fate determined by, 232n15; impact of, 3; as standardized, 164

Acker, Joan, 162

affirmative action programs, 12

African Americans, 14; Compton as space of, 112, 125; as ELL students, 197; as EOs, 163, 224n39; Latina teachers distancing from, 195; Latina teachers racism towards, 104; Latinos tensions with, 22, 72, 113, 161; media representations of, 103; as minority group, 97; negative characterization of, 171; as racial missionaries, 76; racism towards, 97

African American Vernacular English (AAVE), 174

age: ethnographic studies influenced by, 208–9; Latina teachers, controlling images and, 210

agency: as collectively informed, 193; definition of, 59; as free will and choice, 3; Latinos assisted by, 61; social structure constraining, 2

Almaguer, Tomas, 21

Always Running La Vida Loca: Gang Days in L.A. (Rodríguez), 101

amabilidad (kindness), 133, 155

Amanti, Cathy, 131–32

Americanization: to Latinization from, 5; practice of, 16, 194; script of, 9; state policies rewarding, 95; tolerance replacing, 131

Annual Yearly Progress (AVP), 181

API. *See* Academic Performance Index

Asians: cultural capital lacking in, 191; Latinos outperformed by, 183; as minority group, 28, 32; racialization of, 180; U.S. populations of, 101

assimilation: students pressured into, 8; of white culture, 15

The Autobiography of Malcolm X, 127

AVP. *See* Annual Yearly Progress

Baby Boomers, 12, 196

Back to School Night, 163; interactions at, 112, 211; strategies explained at, 116

Barrera, Mario, 232n9

Bernstein, Basil, 139

bilingual education, 1–2; conflicts over, 118; credentials for, 42; as dire, 41; immigration influencing, 40; lack of, 84, 135; parents confusion of, 222n7; programs for, 6, 40, 222n6; racism in, 227n12; state opinions on, 84

Bilingual Education Act, 40–41

Black History Month, 21, 130, 229n7

Blacks. *See* African Americans

Bourdieu, Pierre, 44, 128

Bracero Program, 43

Brilliant, Mark, 18

valorization, 32, 98; of Asians, 23, 124, 194; as relative, 114, 126

Vomvoridi-Ivanović, E., 150

Wagle, Tina, 205

Watts riot, 99

Wax, Rosalie, 214

Wei, Li, 102

white culture, 15

white dominance, 114

Williams, Christine, 37

Wingfield, Adia, 37

working class: backgrounds of, 14, 29, 53, 58, 76, 94, 145; constraints of, 36, 61;

families as, 60, 62, 101; growing up as, 8, 128; hardships of, 95; interactions with, 154; jobs of, 46; language among, 136; opportunities for, 60; as position, 203; social class of, 44; support for, 72; valuable experience of, 32

workplace inequality, 161

yard duty supervisors, 5, 46, 62

Zarate, Estella, 60

Zavella, Patricia, 13

Zhou, Min, 185

Zinn, Maxine Baca, 204, 209

ABOUT THE AUTHOR

Glenda M. Flores is Assistant Professor of Chicano/Latino Studies and Sociology (by courtesy) at the University of California, Irvine. She was born and raised in Santa Ana, California.